JOURNEY

INTO

AFRICA

THE LIFE AND DEATH OF KEITH JOHNSTON, *SCOTTISH CARTOGRAPHER AND EXPLORER* (1844–79)

James McCarthy

Whittles Publishing

Published by
Whittles Publishing Limited,
Roseleigh House,
Latheronwheel,
Caithness, KW5 6DW,
Scotland, UK
www.whittlespublishing.com

Typeset by
Samantha Barden

ISBN 1-904445-01-2

Printed by
J.W. Arrowsmith Ltd., Bristol

Contents

Foreword

——

Africa – 'Fatal Africa' in H. M. Stanley's words – fascinated the nineteenth-century geographical imagination as perhaps no other topic. Why? Geographers' interests centred upon the continent's great rivers, mapping the interior and understanding the diversity of peoples and natural resources. For churchmen, Africa was a huge mission field, a largely unknown space occupied by the ungodly. For commercial entrepreneurs and for imperial adventurers such as Stanley, Africa meant opportunity, and opportunity meant money. For European governments, Africa was part of an empire whose boundaries and contents demanded – like one's imperial neighbours – constant surveillance. For the publics of metropolitan Europe, reading books and newspapers or hearing the lectures of returned explorers and missionaries served to intensify interest in the 'Dark Continent'.

If, then, Africa meant Christianity, Civilisation and Commerce, so it also meant Geography, Science and Exploration. Indeed, these themes went hand in hand: missionaries provided new information about lands and peoples, traders facilitated geographical expeditions, and the natives figured in everything – as guides, objects of study, souls for redemption. In the fascinating figure of Keith Johnston, here brought memorably to life in deed and word, the combined themes of geographical enquiry, map-making and spiritual involvement with Africa found rich individual expression.

Keith Johnston hardly had time to make an impact on Africa. He died from dysentery aged 34 in June 1879, his involvement with the Royal Geographical Society's 1878–1880 Expedition to the Central Lakes of Africa, and with geographical enquiry as a whole, cut cruelly short. Yet, even unfinished, this and his earlier work was outstanding. Not least, his own morals and sympathetic attitude toward Africa and the Africans distinguished Johnston in the eyes of contemporaries. 'Of all the victims insatiable Africa has claimed in the cause of Science and Civilisation' (noted a President of the Royal Geographical Society), 'this is one of the noblest, for Keith Johnston was a young man of exceptionally high attainments'.

James McCarthy tells Johnston's story with sympathy and insight. In one sense, Keith Johnston might be seen as part of that longer-run 'tradition' of Scots Africanists: James Bruce, Mungo Park, Hugh Clapperton, John Kirk, Joseph Thomson and, most notably, David Livingstone, the last three of whom figure in this account. But, as McCarthy shows, Johnston's life and work is also to be explained with reference to his Edinburgh background and to the intellectual and practical training he received from his father, Alexander Keith Johnston, the leading Scottish cartographer. For both father and son, map-making was a vital means of representing and advancing geographical knowledge. Exploration helped inscribe boundaries. But geography and cartography also helped transcend boundaries – between intellectual geographers in different countries and between the different peoples at work in the vastness of Africa.

McCarthy's book is a story of geographical discovery and achievement twice over. It is the story of Johnston's own fascination with Africa, and with the details – the heat, the flies, the cumbersome equipment and awkward colleagues – of how Africa came to be geographically known. Yet we owe this rich narrative to the author's own energies in transcribing Keith Johnston's long-lost diary and for his related researches. Johnston's work commands our attention for what it reveals of the nature of geography and exploration in nineteenth-century Africa. McCarthy's book demands it for bringing Johnston and his endeavours so clearly into the light.

Charles W. J. Withers
Professor of Historical Geography
University of Edinburgh

Acknowledgements

———

One of the pleasures of writing a narrative such as this is the sheer variety of contacts with interested people which emerge, several of whom have given most generously of their time and talents. I am indebted to the late Professor Terry Coppock of Edinburgh University who, in his capacity as chairman of the grants panel of the Carnegie Trust for the Universities of Scotland, provided valuable advice on my successful application to that body for travel funding, for which I am most grateful to the Trust.

Professor Roy C. Bridges, Emeritus Professor of History at Aberdeen University, gave very helpful and scholarly guidance throughout, but especially on the background to East African exploration and the history of the Royal Geographical Society. Professor Charles Withers of the Department of Geography at Edinburgh University has particularly directed me to relevant sources relating to early-nineteenth-century Scottish personalities, among others. Professor Forbes Munro, formerly of Glasgow University, guided me expertly on the context of Sir William Mackinnon's activities in East Africa. All made valuable comments on drafts. Professor Jeffrey C. Stone of the Department of Geography at Aberdeen University provided useful papers on African cartography. Dr J. A. Hellen, formerly of Newcastle University Department of Geography, kindly provided papers relating to German cartographers, as did David Smith on W. & A. K. Johnston. For the translation of several of these papers from the German, I am indebted to the late Ms Annie Aschtul. I appreciated the helpful comments of Professor Charles McKean of the Department of History at Dundee University and those of Professor T. C. Smout, Her Majesty's Historiographer in Scotland, especially regarding chapters 2 and 3.

I have been pleased to make use of the archives and special collections of a number of institutions including, the University of St Andrews, aided by Dr Norman Reid, the manuscripts available in the Alexander Turnbull Library in Wellington, New Zealand, the National Archives of Tanzania in Dar-es-Salaam and the Zanzibar Archives. The Royal Society of Edinburgh kindly granted access to its reference library, as did the Royal College of Physicians of Scotland, while Edinburgh University Library did likewise.

I have received consistently attentive service from the staff of the National Library of Scotland, while those of the National Maps Library, especially its Director Diana Webster, have been especially helpful in locating cartographic material and allowing me convenient access to Keith Johnston's expedition diary: Miss Margaret

Wilkes, former Director of that library has responded very knowledgeably to my requests for advice on early map-makers. I am grateful to David Munro, Director of the Royal Scottish Geographical Society (RSGS), not least for bringing Keith Johnston's expedition diary, which was donated to the RSGS. by Mrs F. J. Henderson, to my attention. I have appreciated the information and maps provided by the Maps Curator at the Royal Geographical Society, Francis Herbert, and to the Society for access to its archives.

The story of Keith Johnston would have remained largely unwritten were it not for the genealogical expertise of Tony Reid, who led me to Mrs Elspeth Green MM, and I am particularly indebted to her for so kindly making family papers available to me, notably Grace Johnson's *Recollections of the Keith Johnstons*, from which I quote extensively. Other descendants of the Johnstons who have kindly provided information include Ian Jameson and Heather Redfearn. I also owe a debt to John C. Bartholomew, previously of that renowned map-making firm, for indicating in the Bartholomew archive the correspondence between Mrs Kirk of Zanzibar and the Johnston family. Both John Capon and the late Bernard Gilchrist, formerly of the Tanganyika Game Department and Forest Department respectively, have generously provided historical material and illustrations, while I am grateful to those in present-day Tanzania who have eased my travel and research there, especially Dr Rolf Baldus and Dr Ludwig Siege of the Selous Conservation Programme, John Corse, Managing Director of Nomad Safaris (Tz) Ltd, and the staff of the Sand Rivers Safari Camp.

Perhaps more than anyone, I have leant heavily on the expertise of Mike Shand of the University of Glasgow Department of Geography and Topographic Science, particularly for his knowledge of Tanzania cartography. His continuing interest in this project from the beginning, and his companionship during travels in Tanzania, have been a great encouragement; I am especially grateful for his map illustrations for this publication and for his expertise in scanning and organising many other illustrations in digital format.

Finally, my special thanks to my wife (who must sometimes have thought that the ghost of Keith Johnston had moved in with us) for her forbearance and support.

1

Searching for Keith Johnston

———

In the premises of James Kirkwood and Son, situated on the second story of the tall six-storey tenement building, no one leaving their work for the day noticed the pot of linseed oil, used for inking the copperplates, slowly heating on the stove.[1] It was a clear windless evening on 15 November 1824, and the smoke from the burning oil issuing from under the door went unseen for some time in the Old Assembly Close in the heart of Edinburgh's Old Town, amidst a warren of close-packed high tenements and commercial premises which made up the grossly overcrowded High Street. The door led to one of the most highly regarded copperplate engravers in a street renowned for publishers, engravers and printers. The firm of James Kirkwood was notable not only for engraving, but also for map-making – it had, for example, produced in 1817 the first plan and elevation of the New Town of Edinburgh and a few years later a world atlas of quality. Within minutes, the engraver's premises with its wooden floors and beams had become a raging inferno which brought awe-struck crowds into the street. The fire had started about 10.00 pm, and by 11.00 pm the whole building was enveloped in flames.

A contemporary observer noted 'the three front tenements were yielding to destruction...and the sparks sent forth by the flames rose high in the air, like embers shot from the crater of a volcano...showers of burning flakes fell upon the densely assembled crowd and many of the chimneys in the neighbourhood were set on fire by these embers. The spectacle was awfully sublime.'[2] Little did the reporters of the *Edinburgh Evening Courant* who had gathered to record the conflagration know that their own premises would be completely devoured in what came to be known, as it spread throughout the Old Town, as 'The Great Fire of Edinburgh'. Between 300 and 400 families would be burnt out of their homes and at one time the fire threatened the whole of the historic centre of the capital of Scotland, with considerable loss of life and injury.[3] Long sermons were subsequently preached from the pulpits of this severely religious town, ascribing the calamity to the displeasure of the Almighty who had visited His wrath upon the sinful city.[4] (By a singular coincidence, at the time of writing in December 2002, the second 'Great Fire of Edinburgh' devastated part of the Old Town only a matter of yards from the conflagration of 1824, destroying some buildings which had survived the original fire.)

On the evening of that fateful day, two brothers, William and Alexander Keith Johnston, had left the premises of Messrs Kirkwood, where Alexander worked as a diligent apprentice, learning the meticulous art of copper engraving and printing, including the making of maps and the construction of geographic globes, while his brother apparently held a more responsible position in the firm.

Neither William nor Alexander would have known of the disaster which had overtaken their employer until the news reached them as they trudged from the suburbs to their daily six o'clock start at Kirkwoods, when the Old Town was still burning. The intriguing – and awful – question was, were either of them responsible for leaving that pot of linseed oil on a lit stove in the premises of James Kirkwood, resulting in a fire which had not only extinguished their livelihoods and that of many others, but devastated the ancient capital? Whatever the answer, Alexander had almost reached the end of his apprenticeship, and William, as the elder brother, had some experience. Given his subsequent career, it is likely also that he had both the confidence and commercial acumen to help to make the decision to start up an independent business, with Alexander as a partner – later they were to take into further partnership their younger brother, Thomas. It could be said that one of the foremost cartographic publishing houses in Britain, which survived for over 150 years, was born out of 'The Great Fire of Edinburgh'.

The business, started by William at the age of 23 on Christmas Day 1825 as a steel plate and copperplate printer, was successful from its inception, probably due to the contrasting but complementary personalities and aptitudes of the two brothers, Alexander having joined in May 1826. In time, William would become first a *baillie* or town councillor and then Lord Provost of Edinburgh, much involved in politics and public works. At Kirkhill, a fine country mansion on the south side of the city, he lived in some style, entertaining on a lavish scale, often to secure the compliance of potential opponents in his political schemes. Obviously an extrovert, of handsome and dignified appearance, most definitely 'a man of the world', he enjoyed success and provided a striking contrast to his brother Alexander, who was as gentle as William was forceful. We shall look at Alexander's character and personality in some depth, not only as the father of the main subject of this story, but because never can the adage 'like father, like son' have been more aptly applied than to these two individuals. What is more, Keith's education, training, values and career choice were hugely influenced by his father.

Early in 2000, I knew nothing of this when I was invited by the Royal Scottish Geographical Society (RSGS) to transcribe the last unpublished expedition diary of Alexander's son, Keith Johnston, who initially followed in his father's footsteps as a cartographer in Edinburgh. The purpose of this East African expedition was to explore a feasible route for a road, mainly for the purposes of developing natural resources and trade between the coast and the interior. I blew the dust off a worn, calf-covered Lett's foolscap diary and began to try to decipher the hand-written manuscript entries from January 1879 to 12 June of that year. It was hard work. Instead of the expected Victorian copperplate, the script was small and in places almost illegible, the ink having spread into the paper from humidity and time. There were numerous unexplained abbreviations, some use of Swahili words, and the spelling of place names was idiosyncratic. With the aid of a large magnifying glass and considerable patience over several months, the story of the 1878–80 Royal Geographical Society's Expedition to the Central Lakes of Africa was revealed – or at least the first six months of it. For by June 1879, within weeks of setting out from Zanzibar, Keith Johnston, at the age of 34, was dead. He had died of dysentery at a small village named Behobeho.

I checked its location. The village lay not far from the Rufiji River within the northern sector of the present Selous Game Reserve, and was distinctly marked on German maps around the turn of the century. Covering an area slightly larger than Switzerland, the Selous was also a largely inaccessible forest reserve, flooded for much of the year. In 1961 as a newly minted assistant conservator of forests in what was then Tanganyika,[5] I was responsible for forest protection over a district of approximately 100,000 square kilometres, but with the specific task of the forest exploration of the Kilombero Valley, now lying within the northern sector of the Selous. There was a proposal for a trans-Tanganyika railway which would run through this valley, allowing the exploitation and transport of the area's resources, including its timber – not a far cry, albeit under very different circumstances, from the object of the Royal Geographical Society (RGS) expedition some 80 years earlier.

Keith Johnston was born and raised in my adopted city of Edinburgh; I began to wonder if there were any other connections. I discovered that, following Keith Johnston's death, his young deputy, Joseph Thomson, on a later expedition was the first to name the Aberdare Mountains in Kenya where I had spent some 12 months with the King's African Rifles during the Mau Mau campaign in the early 1950s. (In yet another coincidence, my interest in Scottish explorers in Africa started not with Keith Johnston, but with Thomson.) Further back, my geography lessons at school were informed by the wall maps of the world – with so much of the world still coloured pink representing the then extent of the British Empire – published by the well-known firm of W. & A. K. Johnston, started by Keith Johnston's uncle William in the early nineteenth century.

The key stimulus to writing the story of Keith Johnston and his times was, however, quite unexpected. I had the bare bones of his career from the sparse record of his life gleaned from such sources as the Dictionary of National Biography and the Proceedings of the RGS, but nothing of the man himself – his background, character, motivation. From a published request for any information on Keith Johnston, a professional genealogist, Tony Reid, kindly offered to search for any descendants. To cut a long story short, our combined efforts revealed the daughter of the original donor of the diary, Mrs Elspeth Green, a great-niece of Keith Johnston, who lived a few minutes' walk from my home in Edinburgh. (At a similar distance in the opposite direction, Merchiston Castle previously housed the school which Keith Johnston attended.) She casually mentioned that she had some family papers 'probably of no particular interest' on the Johnston family. These were in fact the unpublished *Recollections of the Keith Johnstons* written around 1911, and running to two substantial bound volumes of neatly typewritten memoirs and letters of the explorer's younger sister Grace Johnston.[6]

Although only a fraction of these *Recollections* relate to her brother, together with other sources, they provided sufficient material to convince me that there was a story worth telling – not only about Johnston's last journey, but also about the circumstances in which this was set. The expedition took place in the context of Victorian exploration, more especially in East and Central Africa, and the links to the RGS at a time when the increasing international interest in this part of the world was challenging both Britain's primacy there and indeed that of the Society. It is also the story of how, during this period, educated upper-middle-class Scots became fully integrated into the great enterprise of the British Empire.

Given that Keith Johnston's expedition diary reveals almost nothing about his personal thoughts or feelings, or even about his reactions to experiences, the memoir by his sister is especially valuable in throwing some light on his character and personality. Further reading led back to the history of the developing subject of geography, in which Keith Johnston and his father were deeply involved, and the crucial influence which the latter was to have on his son's career: the fact that they shared the same name –Alexander Keith Johnston – is symbolic of the parallels in both their personalities and professional interests. These were so close that the story has inevitably become that of father and son (to reduce confusion between them I have used 'Alexander' for the former and 'Keith' for the latter throughout, and similarly forenames have been used for other members of the Johnston family). It might reasonably be asked why a biography ostensibly concerning the junior Keith Johnston should dedicate so much space to his father. The fact is that it is almost impossible to understand Keith's life and career without this background of paternal influence.

Apart from the main sources mentioned above, there was one unexpected find in the massive archive of that other great Edinburgh map-making firm, Bartholomew. The surviving member of the family firm, John Bartholomew, pointed me to some correspondence after her son's death between Keith's mother and Mrs Kirk, the wife of the Consul General in Zanzibar, which throws light on the serious incompatibilities between Keith and Thomson. The more I investigated this, especially in the light of Grace's comments in her *Recollections*, the more it became obvious that to a large extent this difference was symptomatic of the Victorian social mores of the time and of the class distinctions which permeated the notoriously establishment institution of the RGS. In yet another of the coincidences which surface in this story, it was the brash Henry Morton Stanley whose methods and style most upset the more conservative members of that august body, whom Keith, to his dismay, encountered in Zanzibar at the start of his expedition. It is ironic that, on the establishment of the Scottish counterpart of RGS, the Royal Scottish Geographical Society, in 1884, whose inception was stimulated by David Livingstone's daughter, Mrs Livingstone Bruce, the inaugural address should be given by the same H. M. Stanley.

Throughout the story of the Johnstons, the controversial figures of both Livingstone and Stanley keep cropping up, not simply as explorers, but also as emblematic icons of their times, symbolising the public's need for popular heroes in this age of Empire: the only modern parallel would be the space explorers of the latter half of the twentieth century. If the question is raised of why both Alexander and Keith were so intimately involved with Africa, then this association with Livingstone, who was both a family friend and a professional colleague, is significant. The whole question of the source of the Nile, which so obsessed Victorians, revolved around field exploration and the crucial accuracy of the available maps, in which the Johnstons were pre-eminent; their skill and standards were acknowledged on several occasions by Livingstone himself. Alexander was a staunch churchman in the Scottish tradition, who would have been, like so many at this time, inspired by the whole ethos behind Livingstone's missionary endeavour. This adds yet another dimension to his professional cartographic interests in this part of the world, while the example of so many other fellow Scots[7] explorers and missionaries in Africa would have been another stimulus for the involvement of the Johnstons. Both Keith and Thomson were undoubtedly moved by the example of Livingstone, whose exploits and achievements run like a connecting thread not only through their lives – both Johnston and Thomson at very different ages expressed a desire to join the Livingstone rescue expedition – but through the whole story of mid-Victorian exploration of Africa.

It has to be said that finding information, especially on Keith Johnston Jnr, has been akin to an archaeological dig, in which a great deal of extraneous material has had to be sifted through to find a small shard of pottery and, even at the end of the process, only an approximate shape of the vase is revealed. There is no biography of either of the Johnstons and few sources of other material apart from their obituaries, the expedition diary, and Grace's *Recollections*. In these, Grace states that 'her letters to Keith were among the large correspondence found after his death – scarcely a line from his own kindred had he failed to preserve': none of this original correspondence has been found.

Keith Johnston's story so far is an unwritten one – his cartographic career has been largely overshadowed by the much longer one of his father, while his relatively short time as an explorer has been quite overtaken by that of his colleague Thomson, who gained fame from his successful completion of the 1878–80 RGS expedition and subsequent African journeys, not least because of the gripping published narratives of his travels. Writers on Thomson, not unreasonably, focus attention on his sole leadership of the famous crossing of Masailand in 1883–4, and sideline his first expedition, initially under Keith's command. But it is this expedition which started him on his many African journeys, providing him with the necessary reputation to be given subsequent commissions. (Thomson's life has been well covered by Professor R.I. Rotberg[8] who noted that, at the time of writing in 1971, neither Thomson's nor Johnston's diaries had been found.) While Thomson's achievements are celebrated by a memorial in his native village of Penpont in Dumfriesshire, where a museum in his memory is being developed in the cottage where he was born, there is no memorial to Keith Johnston, other than the inscription on his family grave in Grange Cemetery in Edinburgh. As is related in the final chapter, an attempt to locate his African gravesite in 2001 proved abortive.

The 1878 expedition, at the end of the 'classic' African exploration period and just before the so-called 'Scramble for Africa', embodied Livingstone's belief in promoting communications to further civilisation, and Christian endeavour through trade and commerce. The more spectacular explorations, focussed on the sources of the Nile and the discovery of the great Central Lakes system, had caught the popular imagination, allied to the moral purpose and altruism associated with Livingstone's objectives. That phase had ended, and yet only the barest outline of East Africa's geography was known, with much in-filling yet to be done over large swathes of country. Africa was still the last great 'unknown' at least in the popular imagination – the 'Dark Continent' suggesting both mystery and impenetrability. It was certainly one of the greatest challenges to explorers and geographers. Travel in this region was still hazardous and problematic: from the sheer logistics of mounting an expedition, which involved large numbers of men for porterage and defence, to the ever-present threat of lethal diseases.

What is of interest to me is that, even as late as the 1960s, the physical conditions of journeys 'in the bush' and away from main roads were not markedly different from those described a century earlier, with the important exception of the availability of effective prophylactics, especially against malaria. For such unroaded and wilderness areas as the Selous, the maps available in the mid-twentieth century still showed large blanks, only partly compensated for by incomplete aerial photographs of very variable quality. While nineteenth-century expeditions in East Africa utilised as far as possible often well-trodden trade and slaving routes, forest exploration a hundred years later necessitated getting off the beaten track. At the same time, this survey work did not require the large number of porters to carry trade goods over lengthy journeys – the great burden of earlier expeditions through territories where such toll was exacted by tribal chiefs, great and small. The justification for including in this account the logistics of the RGS expedition in some detail, apart from being the first and last such venture mounted by the Society's African Exploration Fund, is that it was acknowledged as being probably the best organised of any expedition to the interior of Africa, supported by specific information, for example, on the tribal origins of the porters.

Among African explorers, Keith Johnston was distinguished by being both a trained cartographer and professional geographer of considerable repute, despite his relative youth. The history of geography, and indeed of terrestrial exploration is of course intimately intertwined with map-making, of which the Johnstons were renowned exponents. While the map-makers provided the cartographic framework for systematic exploration, in turn the explorers produced the results of their work in the form of survey material for further refinement of maps and scientific observations to complete the loop. The making of maps based on prescribed survey techniques was a stated objective of the RGS. This society, perhaps more than any other scientific institution in the latter half of the nineteenth century, was at the hub of a series of social, scientific, and political circles – a nexus which embraced many complementary interests, not excluding commercial ones, such as engravers, publishers, cartographers, explorers, philanthropists, missionaries, and frequently the military. The linkages between these were sometimes overt, but often, if not covert, then certainly filtered through institutions and groupings which ostensibly promoted the more altruistic objectives of British policy in science and Empire.

The story of the Johnstons starts in the city of Edinburgh in the first half of the nineteenth century, still in the afterglow of the Scottish Enlightenment with its flowering of intellectual and cultural life – a context which provided Alexander and his elder brother William with both stimulus and commercial opportunity against the background of increasing integration of Scotland into the British state. Some space is therefore dedicated to describing the circumstances of both Scotland and its capital at this time, with William occupying the position of Lord Provost of the city from 1848 to 1851, when he was knighted. Scots played a disproportionate part in the imperial enterprise in every capacity, especially in Africa, and there is no doubt that the Johnstons utilized to the full their association with Scottish explorers, scientists, missionaries and others. Inevitably the demands of an expanding British Empire also required maps to serve scientific, commercial and military purposes.

This was also the period when geography was developing as a science, amidst the controversies about the purposes of exploration: whether this was primarily to describe new and interesting regions, or to conduct more systematic and comprehensive scientific surveys. Much of this centred on the key institution of the RGS. All of the various influences mentioned above combined to lend to Keith's last journey a certain inevitability: the restless cartographer, stimulated not only by Livingstone, and other Scottish missionary endeavours and commercial enterprise in Africa, but also by the close association with the RGS at the height of Empire building. All of these, together with his father's deep involvement with scientific geography and their mutual interest in African cartography, provided a logical springboard for Keith's final exploration.

Finding the appropriate balance between the human story of the Johnstons, including the family background and the more academic interest provided by the context of historical geography and the development of cartography in the nineteenth century has posed a challenge. Either of these aspects could have been written separately but, for better or for worse, an attempt has been made to integrate these into a coherent narrative, even if strict chronology has occasionally been put to one side. The inclusion of so much material on Alexander's life and cartographic achievements may be questioned under a title which might imply that this is largely the story of an expedition, initially led by his son. However, the bigger picture of the triumph and tragedy of Empire, the way in which scientists and geographers became caught up in the social, political and military establishment, and the way they were used to give credibility to imperial ambitions, cannot be fully understood without an insight into this earlier background.

The other question which might be raised justifiably is why it is considered worthwhile to write the story of a largely unknown Scottish cartographer whose very short life hardly allowed for the accumulation of any significant achievements. Perhaps the fact that nowadays he is so unknown could be a justification in itself. However, between them, Alexander and Keith made important and innovative contributions, not only to a wide range of cartographic issues but, perhaps more significantly, to the development of scientific geography in the nineteenth century, integrating many aspects of physical geography and promoting education in this field. Both extended the frontiers of traditional geography to embrace geology and other earth sciences, climatology and meteorology, biogeography, and many aspects of social geography. We now take these for granted, but in their time they were highly original. Importantly, these topics were not treated simply by the Johnstons as additions to the field, but as integral elements of this broad discipline.

Their lives shed a little more light on how great institutions of the time, such as the RGS, influenced both exploration and the development of Empire, in particular the study and mapping of Africa in which both were deeply involved. Keith's story is important in revealing how, under the aegis of this society, an African expedition was instigated and developed at a crucial time in the exploration of the continent. The RGS record of this is probably more comprehensive than for any other exploration, while Johnston's own organisation of the expedition is acknowledged as being the most detailed in the annals of East African exploration.

The Johnstons themselves were also very much part of a scientific and cultural establishment of savants whose world, although international, was also an exclusive one. This is shown by their initial attitudes towards Joseph Thomson, and their disparagement of Stanley throughout his life. Specifically, the Johnston story says much about middle-class professional life in the Edinburgh of the time, exemplifying the style and mores of an establishment family at the height of the Victorian period. However, Keith's relationship with Thomson also adds something to our understanding of this renowned African explorer, and the general attitudes of the time to those who were not from the middle-class professional stable. An appreciation of the full dimensions of Keith's last journey requires an understanding of the social and professional world in which Alexander, and subsequently his son Keith, moved. *Journey into Africa* is both a metaphor for two strongly intertwined lives, leading to the undoubtedly tragic end of Keith Johnston, and of course the story of his last expedition.[9]

NOTES

1 Schenck (1999), 64.
2 *The Scotsman*, 17 Nov. 1824.
3 *Edinburgh Evening Courant*, 29 Nov. 1824.
4 Gilbert (1901), 60–1.
5 The name Tanganyika has been used for Tanzania before its independence in 1962, and thereafter the modern name Tanzania.
6 Grace Johnston was the only unmarried daughter of Alexander Keith Johnston senior and helped her father in his geographical and cartographic work; she was clearly very close to her brother Keith. Most of her unpublished *Recollections* are edited extracts from correspondence with other members of the family. (Because of inconsistent chapter and page numbering in these *Recollections*, no further note references are given to the many quoted extracts from this work.) She died in 1929.
7 For a concise summary of the Scots involvement in Africa, see Calder (1996), 79–108. See also Johnston, G. (1875), 1.
8 Rotberg (1971).
9 The remainder of the expedition, following Keith's death, is described in Thomson's published narrative *To the Central African Lakes and Back: The Narrative of the Royal Geographical Society's East Central African Expedition, 1878–80.*

PART I

A FATHER'S FOOTSTEPS

2

Auld Reekie:
Edinburgh in the Nineteenth Century

———

In 1830, when Alexander Johnston was 26, he undertook a walking tour of the Highlands, when he saw something of the condition of the land and its people. Here were the last remnants in Scotland of a peasant agrarian society, impoverished through population expansion, and scarcity of cultivable land, with primitive housing and a monotonous diet.[1] The clearances and resulting mass migrations meant that, by the middle of the 1830s, there were no fewer than 22,000 Highlanders in Glasgow alone, while many had left to go overseas.[2] The Gaelic culture and language was withering, despite the romantic picture of Highland life depicted in the novels of Sir Walter Scott and the subsequent glamorisation of this by Queen Victoria, with its espousal of 'tartanry' and the hunt.[3]

In the Lowlands and the more fertile parts of the Highlands, the Agricultural Revolution of the latter part of the eighteenth century and the early part of the nineteenth century had stimulated extensive agricultural improvements. These in turn created a demand for more accurate topographic maps, both to assist, for example, boundary demarcation and effective drainage systems based on contoured plans, and to provide a framework for geological field survey. Field survey was especially important for soil assessment and was taken up vigorously with the Ordnance Survey by the Highland and Agricultural Society and others, including Alexander, through his connections with this and the influential scientific societies of the time.[4]

In the urban areas, there was a huge expansion of population notably in the central belt, with Glasgow's population increasing by 5,000 each year in mid century.[5] Overall the population of Scotland had doubled between 1774 and 1841,[6] but by 1850 some 32 per cent of the population lived in towns,[7] double the number at the beginning of the century, as a result of the immigration from rural areas and from Ireland.[8] The unprecedented urban population expansion created a crisis in the provision of both employment and services, and the 1830s and 1840s saw great distress in the cities – at one point almost a quarter of the population of Paisley was living on charity.

As a result of these conditions, and in the absence of any effective sanitation and public health measures, a great fear was the spread of waterborne diseases and epidemics such as typhoid and cholera. (As Lord Provost of Edinburgh, William had to contend with two outbreaks of cholera during this time.) The most serious outbreak of the disease occurred in 1832, which claimed up to 10,000 lives in Scotland, with nearly 2,000 cases in Edinburgh,[9] many of these in the grossly overcrowded Old Town. Here there was civil disobedience against preventative and control measures, with rumours that bodies were destined for the dissecting tables of the university – a fear greatly exacerbated by the ghoulish activities of the grave robbers, notably the notorious Burke and Hare. In 1820 William had spent every night for a month in a watchtower in Buccleuch Churchyard with a loaded pistol guarding the grave of his brother John, who had died of typhoid. In 1828 he had attended a meeting of the High Constables of Edinburgh to provide against any disturbances of the peace during Burke's trial; after Burke's execution, 24,000 people went to see his body on the dissecting table.

The condition of the city, particularly in the Old Town, was one of marked contrasts. In Edinburgh, there had been a concentration of long-established industries and national institutions paralleled by a similar concentration of professions – notably legal, medical and ecclesiastical – which undoubtedly gave to the capital a sense of being the centre of the country, supported by its financial houses.[10] In the field of publishing and printing, in which the Johnstons were involved, Edinburgh rivalled London, stimulated by scientific and cultural activity of this northern metropolis, not least its academic institutions. In the same year as William joined the town council, both *Chamber's Journal* and the *Edinburgh Magazine* began publishing, and four years later the Philosophical Society of Edinburgh, established to further the arts and sciences, was founded. There was also a civilised social life with grand events in the fashionable Assembly Rooms and Music Hall. In his capacity of Lord Provost, William received Queen Victoria and Prince Albert when the Prince Consort laid the foundation stone of the National Gallery, heralding another milestone in the artistic life of the capital. The council complimented the provost on his organisation of this visit 'whereby all accidents had been avoided and the peace of the City most effectively preserved'. As a result of his exertions, William was invited to sit for a full-length portrait – hurriedly changed from the half-length one suggested by the original more frugal proposer – to be painted by Sir John Watson Gordon commissioned by the Royal Scottish Academy for permanent display in their new gallery.[11]

The other side of this coin was the sheer squalor and poverty of the Old Town, right in the heart of the capital, well dubbed 'Auld Reekie' from the smoke and soot of the innumerable coal fires which blackened its fine buildings. The overcrowding, which bred disease and contributed to early mortality, was as bad as anything in Europe at the time, as foreign observers noted. The respectable populace going about their business were assaulted by the brawling and thieving of bands of uncontrolled youths, and the inordinate number of drinking dens encouraged violent drunkenness. There were 622 cases of prosecution against professional beggars dealt with in 1813[12] and prostitutes were commonplace even in the most popular thoroughfares.[13] Before 1820 this degree of social degradation, combined with the propensity of Edinburgh to assemble riotous mobs whenever there seemed to be a cause, created a measure of alarm among the middle classes, who sometimes feared for both their property[14] and their persons – as much from the threat of contagious disease as anything.

Those who could afford to, such as the Johnstons, moved to the extending suburbs but, in time, the middle classes realised that the answer lay in effective provision of modern services, notably in sanitation, hospital facilities, and education.[15] Yet, in Edinburgh, it was not until 1865 that a comprehensive report was made on the sanitary condition of the city, which Alexander would have been very aware of, since his firm was responsible for drawing up the necessary plans. His brother William, as a newly elected town councillor in 1832 (the same year in which the city had gone bankrupt as a result of financial mismanagement resulting in a debt of £400,000) would have been in the thick of these urban challenges.[16] During his time as Lord Provost, William was noted for his concern for financial reform and improvements, particularly to the overcrowded closes of the Old Town and the provision of lodging houses for the working classes.[17] Not all of the proposals met with universal approval: the eminent judge Lord Cockburn addressed a letter to William in his capacity as Lord Provost *On the best ways of spoiling the beauty of Edinburgh*, railing against the suggested use of Calton Hill as a place of public execution, the recently constructed marshalling yards for the railway and, not least, the 'insane' proposal to build houses on the south side of Princes Street, which fortunately was never carried out.[18]

Another response to the social deprivation, apart from direct alleviation of physical want, was to develop education and moral inducements from the 1820s onwards, largely based on the religious ethics of the time. There was a good deal of organised philanthropy, with societies being established for everything from the control of begging to the distribution of Bibles, from church extension to the encouragement of savings banks, and temperance groups. There was no lack of good works in the douce capital, nor concern for the wider world, for example in the huge meetings in the mid-1820s to debate West Indian slavery. Much later, Alexander was to become a £5 subscriber to Thomas Chalmers's campaign to provide a church school in the desperately wretched West Port area of the Old Town,[19] which Alexander, in a letter of 1846, described as 'your noble enterprise', the smallness of the amount being justified by 'urgent claims in another department of the church'.[20] The famous divine Chalmers was the Professor of Theology at Edinburgh, noted for his oratory, and the leader of the great church Disruption of 1843. From the form of Alexander's address, they must have been on intimate terms.

Until the early 1840s, much education and a great deal of the social provision in Scotland was parish-based, centred on the local church, in the absence of any other effective decentralised civic authority. The Presbyterian Church, supported by the establishment of the day, retained considerable authority over the people. However, the developing radicalism of the early part of the nineteenth century, combined with the mass movement of population into urban areas, had eroded that authority, and there was considerable dissent, not least against the alliance of the Church with the 'moderate' establishment. Among the working classes, there was great evangelical fervour, founded on a conservative and puritan Presbyterianism, which was shared to a large extent by the middle classes, including Alexander's family, in cities such as Edinburgh.[21] The question of patronage in the appointment of ministers of the Church brought the factionism of the previous years to a head in the traumatic Disruption of 1843, which effectively ended the parish state and the previous monopoly of power by the established Church. In our secular times, it is quite difficult to imagine the popular passions which were aroused in the mid-nineteenth century by some of the arcane theological discussions and when a lecture by Thomas Chalmers would be a standing-room only event.[22]

From 1827 onwards, substantial improvements to the city were mooted,[23] including access to the Old Town, and the laying out of green spaces such as the Meadows (overlooked by Alexander's house at Lauriston Lane). All of these improvements, and sanitary improvements, involved the survey and mapping skills of the firm of W. & A. K. Johnston. Clearly it did no harm to the company to have William close to the centre of municipal decision-making. During his period as Lord Provost, William was much involved in such improvements and the opening up of parks to the public, seen as a contribution to the health and welfare of the citizens who lived in overcrowded town precincts.[24] Likewise the creation of a system of town wards represented by local councillors following the Burgh Reform Act required the delineation of these constituencies, a task which was given – no doubt profitably – to the same firm. An interesting sidelight on the feelings created by the original bill was the stoning of the Lord Provost Allan (who was also the Chief Magistrate), an opponent of the bill. He almost lost his life when the town mob threatened to throw him from the North Bridge,[25] but he was rescued by the High Constables of Edinburgh, including William who was then Moderator of this early police force.[26]

Parallel to the new sense of a Scottish identity at this time, albeit often based on a romantic rural mythology, there was also paradoxically a developing sense of 'Britishness' among Scots. This was closely linked to the influence of Britain in the world through military conquest, colonisation and trade, with Glasgow being generally considered the premier industrial city of Empire. As with many other professional Scots, Alexander became deeply involved with such archetypal British institutions as the RGS and the British Association for the Advancement of Science, while retaining a powerful sense of his own Scottish culture and roots. Like so many of his day, he was familiar with the works of both Burns and Scott, perhaps the most influential writers in terms of defining – if in totally different ways – the popular image of the Scots and Scottish history. In the words of Lynch, 'bourgeois respectability linked arms with the British state'.[27] Increasingly through the century, Scottish talent, encouraged by the improvements in communications (the first railway link to England was completed in 1848), was being drawn from 'North Britain' to London, as exemplified by the young Keith Johnston at an early stage in his career.[28]

Both the Agricultural and Industrial Revolutions stimulated great social, economic and scientific changes which were contemporaneous with the development of modern geography, and in particular the development of thematic maps, i.e. the spatial correlation of different phenomena. A very obvious example is the development of geological maps – in which Alexander had a considerable interest – not only for mapping different soil distributions for agricultural improvement, but also for locating important mineral deposits for industry. The first ten-year populations censuses taken at the beginning of the nineteenth century provided the basis for thematic maps comparing, for example, concentrations of disease and crime, which became a particular concern with the growth of industrial conurbations.[29]

Another of Alexander's interests was in meteorology and climatology which, together with soil survey, provided the basis of thematic maps for agriculture. Indeed, the first half of the nineteenth century was probably the most important period in the development of such thematic maps, to which Alexander made a very significant contribution.[30] The improvement in communications – the building of ports, canals and railways in particular – directly involved the Johnstons, who prepared plans for some of the early industrial railways. In the 1840s the firm of W. & A. K. Johnston published maps relating to all new developments, including for example a nautical map of the Forth Estuary for the guidance of shipping. The rapid expansion of the towns required housing and street maps – the entrance to the Edinburgh Room of the Scottish Library is graced by a large-scale plan of the capital by W. & A. K. Johnston showing all developments up to 1851, the first to be compiled by a full ground survey of the city.

The much-vaunted Scottish education went through its own crises in the first part of the nineteenth century, contemporaneous with urban expansion. The venerable town High School, which had educated Sir Walter Scott and Henry Cockburn among many other luminaries, and which was attended by the Johnston brothers, was described as 'tumultuous' by 1815, with only its rector and four masters to control and teach over 800 pupils.[31] Through dire poverty and the need for children to help to support their indigent families, many town children in Edinburgh and elsewhere received little or no schooling, although Scotland had achieved a reputation for being one of the most literate societies in Europe. Universities took in students as young as 14–15, but large classes in some subjects resulted in low standards.[32] However, among the more mature students, Scotland was noted for its intellectual independence, much of this generated by the vigorous evidence-based debates in university societies, as in the classes themselves. While the classical emphasis declined, the philosophical tradition permeated the increasingly popular natural sciences, in which Alexander had a special interest, and there was increasing use of laboratories, museums and field work.

*The High Street of the Old Town of Edinburgh near the premises of James Kirkwood
in the mid-nineteenth century (Source: Cavaye Collection of Thomas Begbie
prints/City Arts Centre, City of Edinburgh Museums and Gallaries)*

By the mid-nineteenth century there was a trend in schools away from the classics into science (especially physics and chemistry), mathematics and modern languages, of which Alexander's son, Keith, was the beneficiary when he attended the more progressive Edinburgh Institute of Mathematics and Languages in the late 1850s. There was clearly an iteration between the schools and the universities in this trend, and indeed between the theoretical advances developed in the universities and their practical application in the great scientific discoveries and collaboration between academics of the nineteenth century. An outstanding example of this was that of Alexander's colleague James Forbes, the precocious Professor of Natural Philosophy at Edinburgh University, who gave encouragement to James Clerk Maxwell whose revolutionary studies in electricity and magnetism in the 1870s led to so many modern practical applications.

Until the Universities (Scotland) Act of 1861, town councils not only had considerable control over universities through their preponderant representation on the university committee, but the Lord Provost was also the Rector, while the Principal of the University was regarded largely as an agent of the town council. Council control of the curriculum and conditions of graduation, for example, were subjects of considerable tension between the university senate and the town council. With Alexander becoming increasingly involved in university affairs and with William as Lord Provost from 1848 it is not difficult to imagine that there may have been considerable differences between the scholarly cartographer and the wily politician on this topic. Nevertheless, what these new middle-class professionals would have shared was a societal ethos which one observer described as keeping 'the bourgeois emphasis on family training and religious observance, the obligation of acceptable work, professional standards of responsibility and the enjoyment of sober intellectual culture'.[33] Nothing could have described the Johnston ménage more accurately.

In their life and work, both Alexander and William developed important links with a number of areas of Scottish life in the first two thirds of the nineteenth century, at a time of quite dramatic economic, political and social change. Several of these connections derived from Alexander's business, for example, in the survey and mapping requirements of new industrial and commercial enterprises. Some were closely connected to Alexander's scientific and educational interests, while others were associated with his strong church connections and the great religious schisms of the day. The Johnston brothers lived through the latter part of the Scottish Enlightenment, the post-Enlightenment period and the mid-Victorian era, with all that this meant in terms of great changes in the life of the people of Scotland. Alexander, in particular, made his own quite unique contribution to the development of Empire in its most expansionist phase by providing maps not only for the exploration of Africa, but also for emigrants to such far corners of the globe as Queensland in Australia; he published a map of the tea-producing lands of Bengal and some of the earliest maps of New Zealand, for example in the Scheme of the Colony of the Free

Church in Otago in 1845. But this world-wide span of interest was to have the inauspicious start described above in the narrow wynds of Edinburgh's venerable Royal Mile.

NOTES

1 Smout (1986), 11–12.
2 Lynch (1991), 371.
3 Ibid., 355.
4 Boud (1986), 15.
5 Lynch (1991), 392.
6 Smout (1986), 8.
7 Saunders (1950), 79, 89.
8 Ibid., 187.
9 Ibid., 182,189.
10 Ibid., 81–2.
11 Edinburgh City Council Minutes (1850–51), 305.
12 Gilbert, W. M. (1901), 56.
13 Saunders (1950), 93.
14 Smout (1986), 9.
15 Saunders (1950), 89–90.
16 Ibid., 94.
17 Whitson (1932), 120.
18 Cockburn (1874), Appendix. Henry Thomas Cockburn, a judge at the Edinburgh Court of Session from 1834, and previously the Solicitor-General for Scotland, was particularly noted for his *Memorials of His Time* (1856), which gave an entertaining picture of Edinburgh in the first half of the nineteenth century. He conducted a well-publicised trial of the firm of W. & A. K. Johnston for allegedly allowing Sunday working.
19 Thomas Chalmers, a theologian, was noted for his powerful preaching, and became Professor of Moral Philosophy at St Andrews University. He is best known for leading the Disruption in the Scottish Church, to found the Free Church of Scotland. He promoted geography for the moral improvement of society, a subject developed in detail in *Geography, Science and National Identity* (C. W. J. Withers, 2001, 168–72).
20 New College Edinburgh MS Special Collections. CHA.4.335.36, Johnston to Chalmers, 22 January 1846.
21 Smout (1969), 484.
22 Gilbert, W. M. (1901), 89.
23 Saunders (1950), 85–9.
24 Whitson (1932), 120.
25 Gilbert, W. M. (1901), 94.
26 *Edinburgh Evening Dispatch*, 3 March, 1904.
27 Lynch (1991), 358.
28 Ibid., 357.
29 Delano-Smith & Kain (1999), 228–40.
30 Robinson (1982), 67, 100–1, 197.
31 Stevens (1849), 92.
32 Saunders (1950), 307 *et seq.*

3

Alexander Keith Johnston:
'A Painstaking and Untiring Diligence'

———

Early interests

In the early nineteenth century, Edinburgh was a renowned centre of learning, with its famed and rapidly expanding university and the headquarters of the national Church. It had become second only to London in its concentration of publishing and printing houses to service these centres of learning and its literary, scientific and philosophical societies in the aftermath of the Scottish Enlightenment. On a global scale, following the Napoleonic Wars, British naval hydrographers made considerable advances in the mapping of continental coasts and, in the first part of the nineteenth century, Australia and Africa were being opened up, stimulating mapping of these vast areas. British India and the coasts of the USA and Canada were relatively well mapped, but much of the rest of the world was without maps until almost the end of the century. However, only in Europe were precise methods of topographic survey and mapping developed to any extent.

In Britain, the Agricultural Revolution was creating a demand, not only for more sophisticated estate and field boundary mapping, but also for more specialist needs such as geological and soils mapping. Industrial development and municipal expansion required more detailed and accurate maps for road and railway construction and urban services. In the early part of the century, mapping was carried out by independent map-makers, who for example produced many of the first county maps, often at a scale of one inch to a mile, and in this way most of the settled lowland parts of Britain were covered reasonably comprehensively by the time that Alexander and William set up their business. However, the quality of this mapping was very variable: topographic detail was often absent, and the maps suffered from repeated copying from earlier versions, perpetuating previous errors. It was the Napoleonic Wars and the threat of invasion which prompted the establishment of the Ordnance Survey, who adopted the one inch scale as their standard. Their accurate triangulation of the whole country, started in 1798 and largely completed by 1853, coupled with the expansion of the sources of information, such as the new population censuses, brought about the greatest improvement in the quality standards of the commercial cartographers. By 1840, the Ordnance Survey had completed the outline survey of the whole country at six inches to one mile.

In Edinburgh, with a concentration of fine engravers, the skill of copperplate engraving was raised to a high art, as exemplified by such fine exponents as Kirkwoods and Lizars. A number of such engravers had produced maps from the late seventeenth century onwards: Daniel Lizar had published a small map of Scotland in 1782 for his guidebook, while Kirkwood had produced a *Travelling Map of Scotland* at 11 inches to one mile in 1804 and became well known for his several plans of Edinburgh from 1819.[1] Although copperplate engraving could produce maps of very high quality, it was very laborious and time-consuming, involving the drawing of maps in reverse, and it was not until the advent of lithographic printing (invented in 1796, but not adopted in Britain until the middle of the next century) using stone blocks that maps could be produced relatively quickly and on a mass scale, while chromolithography enabled maps to be produced in several colours consistently without the need for the old – and very variable – hand tinting. The numbers employed in the printing business in Scotland were huge: in 1860, it was reckoned that 10,000 people were engaged in this activity, half of these in Edinburgh, which supported no fewer than 30 printing firms.[2]

Earlier map-makers such as John Adair, who attempted large-scale mapping on their own without the financial underpinning of an engraving enterprise, had found the combined costs of survey, cartography and printing prohibitive. A good example was John Thomson, who attempted a large *Atlas of Scotland* involving some 58 maps on a county basis at scales of 1–2 miles to one inch – a task which eventually bankrupted him by 1830. His unsuccessful efforts to complete this work involved William as draughtsman. The plates of the *Atlas* were eventually acquired by W. and A. K. Johnston, who re-issued this map in 1855 in cooperation with William Blackwood and Sons,[3] but with all the names of the original surveyors and engravers removed and replaced by Johnston's name.[4] If this did not bring them credit for probity, it would have enhanced their cartographic reputation.

William and Alexander, both in their early twenties, were two of the five sons of Andrew Johnston and Isobel Keith. Andrew was a solicitor, but also a joint proprietor of the long-established Esk Paper Mills; the Keith family had been connected with paper-making over many generations, and may have introduced this industry to Scotland, which was renowned for the quality of its paper production. The sons therefore came from a relatively affluent middle-class family, and in due course would have been expected to set up their own businesses. By the standards of the time, they were well-educated, both having worn the blue coats and yellow waistcoats of the venerable town school, the Royal High School of Edinburgh, where Sir Walter Scott had been a schoolboy. Alexander, a gentle boy, recalled on his first day watching in trepidation, as his schoolmaster laid out on his desk no fewer than seven pairs of *tawse* or leather thongs in order of size, expressing the wish that he would not have to use these instruments of punishment. Alexander should not have been concerned, since he came to the town school at a high point in its history of over 300 years under the rectorship of a remarkable educator, James Pillans.

Andrew Johnston – Keith's paternal grandfather
(Source: W. & A. K. Johnston Archive, Trustees of the National Library of Scotland)

Isabel Keith Johnston – Keith's paternal grandmother
(Source: W. & A. K. Johnston Archive, Trustees of the National Library of Scotland)

Very courageously, Pillans confronted the tradition of corporal punishment and its frequent abuse in Scottish schools and succeeded in reducing its use to the most serious behavioural offences, although in his initial period to restore order in the school he had wielded the *tawse* as effectively as anyone.[5] He believed that excessive physical punishment made heroes out of miscreants and did not encourage either learning or respect for masters. One former pupil describes some of the distinguishing features of the school in Alexander's time as being the variety of social classes 'for I used to sit between a youth of ducal family and the son of a poor cobbler'. Another was the fact that, in comparison to comparable English schools, the boys would go home to female company in the form of mothers and sisters and had ready access to the town.[6] Alexander would also have benefited from mixing with the many nationalities among its pupils, attracted by the growing overseas reputation of the school under Pillans.

Alexander would have spent six years at this school, the last two of these at the feet of the rector who took the two top classes. He was particularly fortunate in having as a mentor not only one of the most progressive and respected educators in the country, but one who had a special interest in the teaching of physical geography and cartography, which under his tutelage became a very popular subject, stimulating boys who had previously shown no aptitude for other subjects to gain distinction.[7] Eschewing traditional teaching of ancient geography based on the study of the classics and the perusal of place names and political boundaries on existing detailed engraved maps, Pillans used a blackboard: he is generally credited for being the first to introduce coloured chalks into teaching practices to draw different physical features focussing on river systems as the basis of human development and communication.[8] He encouraged his pupils to draw their own maps, the best of which were displayed in the classroom, eventually leading to finely produced ink versions. Such was the popularity of these classes that pupils gave up their free time to continue study and map-making.

While geography had normally been taught as the basis of classical history ('the eye of history'), Pillans was convinced that the study of geography should start with an understanding of the main natural features of a region, such as a river basin, with an emphasis on broad outlines in the first instance, using printed maps for reference only, and linking both ancient and modern geography. It is not difficult to imagine that Alexander would have been greatly stimulated by this approach, given his subsequent abiding professional interest in physical geography, and that he might well have been one of Pillans's star pupils in the execution of his first maps. Pillans continued his interest in geography and wrote a number of papers on the subject, including his *Elements of Physical and Classical Geography* (1844). During his tenure as Professor of Humanities at Edinburgh University, he was instrumental in securing a bursary for a poor student, James Young Simpson, who was to feature later in Alexander's life and was to revolutionise surgery with his discovery of the anaesthetic properties of chloroform.[9]

As a boy, Alexander was notoriously studious: apparently, he gained a prize for spelling – at the age of four! At the same age it was recorded that he was able to join in the reading of the chapter from Scripture which closed each day's work. A gentle child, he was marked out by his thoughtful earnestness. He was apparently a less robust child than his brothers, tending not to join in their more rumbustious games. A fellow pupil at the High School, by the name of Tait, who subsequently became Archbishop of Canterbury, records that he had 'a vision of him as I came home at night tired with a long afternoon's sport, and kicking the football before me, bent at a large old-fashioned desk covered with books and hard at work by candle-light. Nothing would induce him to relax till he had accomplished his set task'.

From an early age he showed an interest in geography and acquired numerous books; later in life, his library became the centrepiece of his home – it was said that he had in it every scientific publication of note in Europe. (After his death, nearly 500 volumes, many rare and valuable, were sold at public auction, for the astonishingly low price of £170.) Working long hours as an apprentice, he nevertheless found time to learn languages in the evenings, believing throughout his life that translations could not match reading in the original language – a belief shared by his son Keith. With the example of two elder brothers who had entered the world of medicine, Alexander began to attend lectures in that field at Edinburgh University, but apparently the sight of operations so distressed his sensitive soul that he gave up this intention, and instead entered James Kirkwood's establishment.

As a young man, despite his studiousness, he was also very fond of physical exercise: he enjoyed boxing and playing football, while he was so keen on fencing that he would walk the considerable distance from his house in South Newington to St James's Square in the city centre to arrive punctually at 6.00 am for his fencing class, even in the depths of winter. As an infant, he had learned to ride a pony at his grandparents' house south of Edinburgh and rode for the rest of his life. On work days, he and William would rise at five or six in the morning to race over the hills on their ponies, and at weekends they would ride deep into the Border country to explore the castles and keeps of that mythical land, Alexander stopping every so often to make one of his many sketches. His daughter Grace recalls that before breakfast he would ride daily for one or two hours around the base of Arthur's Seat, that astonishing ancient volcanic crag near his Edinburgh home – the family joke, alluding to his geographical obsessions was: 'There goes Globe on Atlas!' A boyhood riding companion, the Rev. James Fairbairn, recalls his geographic acumen, even on horseback, when following fox hounds: 'I was struck even then by the remarkable power that he had of calculating distances and directions. There he was with card and pencil in hand, sketching the bearings of the country, so that, by dint of skilful strategic movements, he and I were sometimes more nearly in at the death than many a roughrider better mounted than we.'[10]

27

To counterbalance this physical activity, he was – hardly surprisingly for a cartographer – a very competent artist. His surviving sketch of Loch Fyne (now in the possession of a relative) shows great skill and feeling for the West Highland landscape. Grace, in her *Recollections*, comments: 'Father himself was a clever amateur artist, and liked to see his children express themselves in this way...when we were small children, it was a fascinating occupation to watch him cut out little paper models of ponies, dogs, cows, etc. with a pair of Mother's embroidery scissors...in all ways he was clever with his hands, so he could take a lock or a clock to pieces with the best of skilled workmen, and make good any defect.'

Alexander's more energetic activities would have stood him in good stead when in 1830, with a cousin and an English friend, he undertook an arduous walking tour in the Highlands. In preparation for this, he and his friends would undertake such feats as walking 18 miles before breakfast. This trip was full of incident, including being assailed by superstitious locals who claimed that ill-luck and bad weather had befallen them when Alexander and his companions attempted some amateur archaeological digs in search of the seat of a Pictish kingdom. It also says something about Alexander that, towards the end of any particularly exhausting day, he would attempt to revive their flagging spirits by raising interesting subjects for discussion. However, there were two important results from this trip, during which Alexander had been making detailed observations. He became convinced that he could improve on existing maps, which he found inadequate, resulting in 1830 in his very first publication, *A Travellers Guide Book* with original maps, which was used extensively by later visitors.[11] Perhaps more significantly, the experience was a turning point in Alexander's life, setting him on a career path that would make him arguably the most distinguished cartographer of his time.

In 1832 William's political career started in earnest when he joined the town council and became Moderator of High Constables – steps which would eventually lead him to the Lord Provost's chair and knighthood.[12] But it was almost certainly Alexander's technical skills which resulted in the firm, less than 10 years after its establishment, becoming appointed in 1834 as engravers to King William IV. This was followed by Alexander's elevation six years later as Geographer to the Queen in Scotland.[13] In 1839 the company had moved its premises to the prestigious St Andrews Square on the edge of the New Town, where William characteristically became chairman of a committee of the square's wealthy proprietors which set about its improvement, paving footpaths, erecting railings and removing unwanted shrubbery, but retaining the central garden which, like its counterpart in Charlotte Square at the west end of George Street, provides a green contrast to the stately stone buildings around.

In the same year that William joined the town council, Alexander became involved in educational work which had considerable influence in its day. Before the 1830s, scientific education had been held to be the province of the middle to upper social classes and those with formal access to universities and other centres of learning. Edinburgh at this time was renowned for the number of its men of learning, who often had to migrate to England and abroad to earn a living. Many of these men established centres of educational excellence wherever they went, including for example the poet Thomas Campbell, who founded the University College of London, with its distinctly Scottish educational character. At the same time, the prevailing nineteenth-century ethos of self-help, combined with the Scottish veneration for education, convinced a group of Edinburgh citizens of what were described as the 'mercantile classes' – shopkeepers, merchants, clerks and artisans – that they should have access to a scientific education through a lecture series strictly under their own control.[14]

Thus the Edinburgh Philosophical Association (EPA) was born, recruiting its lecturers from the universities and other centres of learning, and paying for these through course and individual lecture tickets on subjects from botany and physiology to astronomy, but with a strong focus on natural science. Membership was to be open to all those engaged in 'active industry' of one sort or another or to *bona fide* students, including women, who up to this time had few opportunities for scientific education and, most daring of all, they were to be allowed to take the classes in physiology. Membership would exclude 'literary or scientific characters…for this be it observed is the grand novelty, which will form a sort of epoch in the history of Edinburgh, and confer upon it a real name, instead of one borrowed from the fame of a few men of genius, whom it has occasionally produced.'[15]

Henry Cockburn described it as a popular unendowed college showing defiant independence from established cultural institutions The lectures were to be delivered at 8.30 pm for the convenience of those working during the day. It was enormously successful, and with, for example, geology courses costing 7 shillings and sixpence or chemistry courses 10 shillings and sixpence, sold 4,500 tickets in its first year. Alexander was elected to its first governing council at the relatively early age of 28, when he was described as an 'engraver' and would therefore be classed as an artisan. (Later he would sit on the councils of distinguished scientific societies which would be heavily laden with established *savants*.) He had a lifelong interest in education, both for his own family and others, and in the Scottish tradition; for example, he tried to reduce the price of many geographical works to bring them within the reach of poorer students and institutions.

An important society was the British Association for the Advancement of Science, established in 1831 which in its aims referred to 'the cultivation of science in different parts of the British Empire' and had many eminent Scots within its membership, including Alexander. (At its meeting of 1871 Alexander was to be the President of its Geographical Section.) Edinburgh supported a disproportionate number of such learned associations, many of which could be called 'scientific' (although that term together with 'scientists' was not formally used till 1834) including the Royal Society of Edinburgh, the Royal Scottish Society of Arts, the Geological Society of Edinburgh, the Scottish Meteorological Society, and the Royal Botanical Society, among others. The results of their work was publicised in such periodicals as the *Edinburgh Review*, the *North British Review*, and *Blackwood's Magazine*.[16]

All the indications are that Alexander was not a businessman and, at least initially, that aspect of the company almost certainly fell to the shrewder William. Alexander was prepared to forego profit in pursuit of quality and scholarly integrity – some of the early atlases were the result of years of unremitting and financially unrewarding labour, pioneering a new (at least in Britain) form of geographical representation. Alexander was a scientist – in the literal sense of that word – to his finger-tips, dedicated to his field, but far from exclusive in his interests. Nor were these interests parochial – in 1835, in company with a future brother in law, he took the first of many trips abroad, visiting Holland, Belgium, Rhineland and France. Although subsequently his foreign travels would be focussed on his professional concerns, he took the time to broaden his knowledge of the culture of the countries he was visiting, often learning something of the languages involved, and reporting back in detail to his family on the places he had visited, in letters that are both amusing and informative, complete with fine sketches of the places he had visited, but also betraying his deep love of home and family. On a later continental trip he ends one letter to his wife with the words: 'I shall hasten from Vienna to Munich, where I hope your letter will be awaiting me, and then every step of my progress will be towards all that are dear to me on earth – to you – and our darlings...ps. I have looked in vain in this country for such pretty children as ours!'

From Berlin he writes 'here I am almost the only Englishman in the town...I have many things to tell you...and must hasten for the post. The Posthaus is more than a mile distant, but I shall post the letters myself, for I would not disappoint you when I know you are expecting to hear.' His love of family was noted by a friend on the occasion of Alexander's first visit to his brother Archibald's grave in Lisbon, remarking that even after the lapse of time since he had known his brother in boyhood, 'it was as if for a brother but lately lost that he mourned as he bent over his tomb. What showed itself thus in one instance was true of all his domestic ties, in all of which there was a rare, a gentle and most winning tenderness.' If today in a more cynical age this might be considered somewhat sentimental, it is entirely in keeping with the estimates of many of Alexander's friends and relatives.

On his return from his continental journey in 1842, when he met many distinguished scientists and geographers, he wrote to the RGS, intimating his proposed *Physical Atlas,* but took the opportunity to castigate the 'great ignorance which prevails even among the educated classes of this country on the subject of geography' which obliges him to produce the work at his own expense. Some 25 years later, he was still making the same complaint:

It appears that we are far behind in many things...when we hear of our Prime Minister giving away the Island of Java because he could not find its place on the map, and would rather lose it than confess his ignorance – of another, who, after enforcing the necessity of defending Annapolis, coolly turned round and asked – 'But where *is* Annapolis?' ...of a Governor of Australia memorialising the home authorities for increased means of communication with Tasmania, and of the wise rejoinder of the London official: 'Why not build a bridge?'

He also relates the proposal of the London authorities, in response to a request for a new boat to carry defence supplies up the Forth: 'if a new boat must be had the old one need not be lost, for if not sea worthy, it will at least serve to carry ammunition and stores from the port of Leith to Edinburgh Castle'.

Cartographic achievements

In a professional life dedicated to cartography, what were Alexander's outstanding achievements? Of the enormous number of maps, globes, and other geographical publications which he produced, several are especially worthy of note because they pioneered new developments in this field. His first original work was his *National Atlas of Historical, Commercial and Political Geography* published in 1843 and 1854, with important contributions by Heinrich Berghaus and Dr Gustav Kombst. It was regarded as a significant advance in cartography. In his *Atlas of Physical Geography* (1852) with its strong focus on land forms, he was innovative in his delineation of mountain ranges with higher altitudes by a corresponding thickness of line.[17] In the *Physical Atlas* (1848) Alexander pioneered the technique of burnishing roughened copperplate to show, for example, intensity of rainfall.[18] Even more ambitious was his indication in the same atlas of the distribution of individual species of animals and birds by shading on hand-coloured copperplate engraving.[19] He introduced tonal progressions to illustrate changes in density and was innovative in providing separate indexes for individual maps.

But it was his *Physical Atlas of Natural Phenomena*, which appeared in three editions from 1848 to 1856, in both engraved and lithographed versions, that made his name as a truly scientific map-maker. Dedicated to the renowned Baron von Humboldt, it was the first such atlas to be published in Britain. It was hugely ambitious in scope and was a forerunner of the popular thematic atlases of the twentieth century: his 'natural phenomena' included for the first time geology, meteorology, hydrology and natural history, the 32 hand-coloured world maps being accompanied by detailed explanatory notes. These run to 96 folio pages, some by the most distinguished experts in their field, such as Sir Roderick Impey Murchison[20] on geology, Professor Edward Forbes[21] on marine life, Colonel Sabine[22] on weather, but many were compiled by Alexander himself,[23] while the work is embellished by fine engravings of plants and animals.

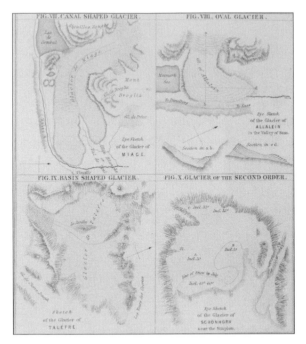

*Vignette of alpine glaciers from the **Physical Atlas of National Phenomena**
by Alexander Keith Johnston (Source: Trustees of the National Library of Scotland)*

*Vignette of reptiles of the world from the **Physical Atlas of National Phenomena**
by Alexander Keith Johnston (Source: Trustees of the National Library of Scotland)*

He pioneered the use of colour tones (he was accredited with the first use of the colour blue for all water – probably erroneously, although given his experience of colour map-drawing under James Pillans as a schoolboy, this is not unlikely) while W. and A. K. Johnston were the first to introduce colour printing in Britain around 1835.[24] His technique of shading was highly innovative for the time, and the consistency of treatment of the topics to produce a coherent whole represented a considerable advance on any previous attempts to produce thematic maps.[25] While thematic maps had been developing considerably in Britain for individual subjects, such as geology and the representation of medical statistics, Alexander developed this on a global scale through this world atlas. He was undoubtedly the leading exponent of this approach, condensing vast amounts of information in a visual form.

Logo of W. & A. K. Johnston
(Source: Post Office Directory)

However, Grace, who was considerably involved in assisting Alexander in his work, makes the point in commenting on the *Physical Atlas*: '…nobody had heard anything of this new science, and nobody cared much to learn. Everybody who saw the curious maps so strangely interlined and coloured, declared that their issue would be a complete failure. Cautious publishers declined to risk the outlay that was necessarily involved on so large an undertaking.'

Although it gained Alexander international recognition – there are recorded requests from Edward Sabine for 50 copies for distribution abroad[26] and from Baron Plana on behalf of the Royal Academy of Sciences in Turin,[27] for example – it was more a labour of love than a profitable venture. It had taken 10 years of intensive work but, at 20 guineas a copy, it sold only 2,500 copies and barely broke even. Presumably Alexander was able to indulge in this and other pioneering projects (such as his later educational atlases which sold at a price that students could afford) by the profitability of the other routine engraving and mapping which the firm undertook. That said, despite their initial unprofitability, it was these prestige works which enhanced the reputation of the firm and, in time, brought in very lucrative commissions.

Another prestigious work was Alexander's construction of the very first physical globe of the world, incorporating much of the information contained in his physical atlas; the globe gained the Gold Medal at the Great Exhibition at Crystal Palace in 1851. This was a labour of immense technical complexity, bringing together all of the current information on world geology, hydrology and physical features, on a huge 30 inch globe, set on a pedestal of intricately carved wood, representing the four corners of the Earth. The recently restored 31 inch diameter globe, in all its magnificence, can be seen in a pride of place at the headquarters of the RGS in London, having survived some rough treatment in the nursery of a London relative. In 2001 a much more modest pair of W. and A. K. Johnston globes of 1907 sold for £29,000. (In 1896, his nephew Thomas Ruddiman Johnston made an abortive proposal to have constructed for public display a globe 84 feet in diameter!)

Alexander's *Dictionary of Geography, Descriptive, Physical, Statistical and Historical* (1850) went through no fewer than 10 editions of 1,000 each in the period 1850–77. His maps to accompany Sir Archibald Alison's monumental *History of Europe* (1848), focussing on the French Revolutionary and Napoleonic Wars, were described by the author as 'superior to anything of the kind that has yet been published in Great Britain, but more perfect than anything on a similar scale that has yet appeared on the Continent'.

Royal favour was bestowed on Alexander's 1855 *Royal Atlas of Modern Geography* only on condition that the Prince Consort, before he would allow the Royal dedication that Alexander desired, was able to inspect every sheet as it was produced – the Prince Consort made it plain that he did not believe that any English version could compare with the German cartographic masters: 'he had never known a good map of Germany done by an Englishman'. So each sheet as it was produced was sent to Buckingham Palace for inspection; apparently the Prince 'offered much advice and many criticisms' on the map of Germany in particular. There is a delightful vignette of the Prince on his hands and knees with Alexander at Balmoral Castle poring over a sheet while, out of the corner of his eye, Alexander espies through the window the Prince of Wales having a quiet smoke with the stable grooms.

On his death, praise was lavished on Prince Albert for his interest in science and meteorology by the members of the Scottish Meteorological Society when Alexander was moved to recollect that 'he had received warm encouragement from his Royal Highness in connection with a publication which he was then commencing, and during three years the Prince continued to communicate with him through his Secretary, giving him information and hints of the utmost value…'.[28] Alexander, despite his modesty, was clearly not above a little judicious name-dropping. Another commercial prize was the sole contract to prepare the maps for the Ordnance Survey in Scotland in 1865, some fourteen years after the Royal Society of Edinburgh had published a closely argued paper[29] by Alexander highly critical of the Survey's neglect of Scotland:

we learn that the survey of Scotland was begun in 1809, but its progress appeared to have been considered of so little importance in comparison with the survey of other portions of the kingdom, that, whenever it was found convenient, the whole of the men and instruments employed were unceremoniously removed to England or Ireland...

While Alexander's motives in raising this concern would no doubt have been genuine, he would not be unaware that such neglect inevitably reduced cartographic commissions to his firm. However, he was strongly supported by others: as early as 1835, Sir Roderick Murchison, the eminent geologist and long-standing friend of Alexander's, had prepared a strongly worded memorial on this issue for the Edinburgh meeting that year of the British Association for the Advancement of Science which the association adopted and forwarded to the Chancellor of the Exchequer. Supported by the early nineteenth-century society, the Wernerian Natural History Society, Alexander claimed, in a formal memorial to the Treasury, that the poor standard of maps in Scotland pre-empted accurate geological survey. (In 1834 Murchison had described Scotland as standing 'almost alone in Europe as a Kingdom without a map' and that his country was 'in a disgraceful condition in respect to geography'.)[30]

Alexander was co-opted to a committee of the influential Highland Agricultural Society, which had campaigned vigorously for the resumption of the national survey over several years, to press its case with government, and was deeply involved in advising the Society on the appropriate scale of mapping for this work. The eventual success of this campaign, against considerable London opposition, was yet another example of the effectiveness of influential bodies in Scotland, in this case representing both scientific and agricultural interests reinforcing each other's case. (The Highland Agricultural Society was dominated by wealthy landowners and had within its ranks no fewer than 48 members of Parliament.)[31] In this Alexander provided an important technical credibility which probably matched that of the Ordnance Survey.[32]

The German influence

Alexander developed a very strong connection with the renowned German geographers and cartographers of the time and this association was carried on enthusiastically by his son Keith. The Germans were pre-eminent in the field of physical geography, although it was in Paris that the first northern geographic society was founded in 1821 and where Baron Alexander von Humboldt was based for much of his life. Humboldt, forever – to his annoyance – associated with the South Atlantic current named after him, was an aristocratic and wealthy Prussian, who had achieved world-wide fame following his pioneering travels in South America between 1799 and 1804, the results of which occupied him for the following 20 years. Among his greatest achievements was the establishment of many latitudes and longitudes on that continent, and he was one of the first to use the new chronometer for observations of longitude on land, and barometric pressure for fixing heights. He can justifiably be considered as the founder of modern geography, including its focus on the relationship between different subjects such as natural history and geography, and was a significant early influence on Charles Darwin, among many other natural scientists.

Like his friend and rival Carl Ritter,[33] Humboldt pioneered the methodology of the collection and correlation through graphic display of precise physical data of all kinds – a sort of visual language of geography, which was to have immediate resonance with Alexander when they met, and which was to provide the inspiration for much of his life's work. Humboldt was the main stimulus for Alexander's *Physical Atlas* published in 1848, which followed on that of Berghaus, and it has been claimed that Humboldt probably contributed the data for more thematic maps than any other individual.[34]

Alexander had studied German intensively under the ethnographer Dr Gustav Kombst – in the 1830s Kombst published documents regarding traitorous activities among the German nobility and then escaped to Paris, living there as a Swiss citizen.[35] He remained there until he was forced to leave for Edinburgh in September 1836 where he lived for about 10 years in the New Town. It was Gustav Kombst who initiated a connection between the firm of W. & A. K. Johnston and the geographic houses of Germany, an association that was to become a turning point in Alexander's career. It was Kombst too who contributed the very original ethnographic map of Europe to Alexander's first thematic atlas.

One of Humboldt's early disciples was Heinrich Berghaus,[36] who founded the Geographic Art School in Potsdam. In 1842, Alexander made his first visit to Germany specifically to discuss with Berghaus a British version of Berghaus's innovative *Physical Atlas*, which resulted in 1843 in Alexander and Berghaus announcing the proposed *Atlas of Natural and Physical Science*. Among Berghaus's apprentice pupils were Heinrich Lange and Augustus Henry Petermann – at one time a cartographer working for Humboldt – both of whom came to work for W. & A. K. Johnston in Edinburgh in 1843 and 1844, the year of Keith's birth, where they became great friends of Alexander and his family.

Alexander employed the two cartographers as apprentices, and they added a number of maps to the ones of those available from Berghaus; the first edition of the *Physical Atlas* in 1843 included the name of Berghaus. In 1848 Humboldt strongly recommended that the English version be used as a reference guide for Berghaus's own atlas (published in 1852) because it contained much new information relating to the geography of plants and animals, to wind directions, sea currents and magnetic field maps, for example. He was very complimentary about the so-called 'English' version, telling Berghaus: 'You cannot begin your physical work without having the English edition of the Atlas to hand. It contains much which is excellent and absolutely new.' For Johnston's second edition Alexander asked experts to improve or renew the Berghaus maps (he had purchased the copyright of some of these) and they provided detailed descriptions to accompany each of the maps. In effect only five of the original Berghaus maps stayed unchanged and Berghaus's name was dropped from the Atlas, which resulted in some public criticism in the German press.[37] Initially, Alexander could find no publisher willing to take the risk on these huge productions, which he had therefore to publish from his own resources, with the first edition costing 10 guineas, rising to 20 guineas for the third edition.

In compiling this giant work, starting with his basic engraving and cartographic skills, Alexander would have had to become familiar in some detail with the subjects covered by the various plates, even where the material was not provided initially by himself, in order to ensure that the graphical representation accurately reflected the data. He would have had to cross-examine the experts in geology, hydrography and climatology, etc., and to do this required a fair knowledge of these subjects. In time, he would through his studies himself become an acknowledged expert in some of these topics, and publish learned papers on them.

In 1845, Alexander had visited Humboldt in Paris, when the great man was in his 76th year and would have empathised strongly with his holistic views of the world of geography ('not a mere encyclopaedia for separate sciences') encompassing as it did not only physical features, but also their relationship to human enterprise and culture. Humboldt had a very high opinion of Alexander's *Physical Atlas* and, following this visit, he presented Alexander with a finely engraved and signed portrait of himself. If not the first, Humboldt was certainly an early biogeographer in all but name, developing a vision of the interrelated nature of the universe, with a special focus on plants: he was made an Honorary Fellow of the Botanical Society of Edinburgh in 1832.[38] His explicit linkage of vegetation and fauna with geology, which Edward Forbes developed to explain the enigma of disjunct populations of plants, greatly stimulated Murchison, who saw this as supporting his claims for integrating geological sciences with geography and natural history – it was this vision which also made Charles Darwin a devotee of Humboldt.

Both Alexander and Humboldt were dedicated to science, similar in their rather unworldly attitudes towards material things, but committed to gaining a broader public understanding of their chosen subject. It was the same year in which Humboldt published *Cosmos*, described as a 'sketch for a physical description of the world', a vastly ambitious work in five volumes which saw nature as a whole and man as a part of nature: a very modern idea, but here including the arts, linking poetry and painting to ecology – a 'physics of the world'.

Petermann worked in London from 1845 to 1854, became a Fellow of the RGS and was for a time the Society's secretary on Alexander's recommendation ('one of the young men of the School of Potsdam, whom I will gladly recommend...'). This collaboration between Germany and Britain was undoubtedly important in raising the standard of cartography in Britain and was largely established by Alexander's initiatives, following his first visit in 1842.[39] Alexander encouraged Petermann to produce his own *Atlas of Physical Geography* in 1850 and other thematic works which earned Petermann the title of 'Physical Geographer and Engraver on Stone in Ordinary to the Queen'.

An interesting connection with Petermann is through the latter's interest in the demography of disease in Britain. In 1852 he had produced a map of the British Isles showing, by means of variable shading, the areas affected by cholera in the 1831–2 epidemic. He was able to demonstrate from population maps which he had compiled using a similar technique that the worst affected areas were those with the highest population densities and that the progress of the disease was correlated with temperature rise, and therefore the season.[40] It happens that one of the worst affected areas was the central belt of Scotland, particularly Edinburgh, especially in the grossly overcrowded Old Town.

This form of conversion of statistics into graphical form and subsequent visual correlation in relation to geography (later to be known as medical geography), which the Germans pioneered, was groundbreaking. Great interest was therefore shown in Alexander's plates of the distribution of health and disease across the world in the second edition (1856) of his *Physical Atlas,* one of the earliest cartographic representations of this topic, which is likely to have been stimulated by Petermann when he worked with Alexander in Edinburgh. Alexander's early medical studies at the University of Edinburgh led him to spend a considerable amount of time on this project, which earned him his election as Corresponding Member of the Epidemiological Society of London. The president of that body remarked that 'no scholar out of the domain of medicine has ever before contributed so valuable a document to medical literature – a paper so rich in research'. Here again Alexander had demonstrated how sheer application to a topic outwith his own profession could produce important results.

As a young man Petermann had accompanied Alexander on a tour of the Highlands and it was from this that their friendly relationship was much later to turn sour. It seems that Alexander had made some physiographic sketch of the Grampian Mountains which long afterwards Petermann published without Alexander's permission, with the result that, in 1854, he was fiercely denounced – most uncharacteristically – by Alexander in strong language:

> I have much reason to condemn Petermann's unprincipled conduct, and could have exposed him as a mere pretender years ago…and agreed with my friend Mr Pentland that he would soon be found out in London and brought down to his proper level. My only wonder is that he deceived you all for so long…he should have been trumpeted up as an authority in geography…I found that there was no truth or accuracy in anything he did…failing in his attempts to sell my pictures…he appears to have made use of them…stolen wholesale from my National Atlas Map[41]

This diatribe against his colleague was not entirely justified, as Petermann, even if he had been guilty of plagiarism, had many real geographical accomplishments to his name, including his contributions to Johnston's *Physical Atlas*.[42]

Despite this, Keith stated that this marred Petermann's association with his father only 'for a short time'.[43] Throughout her life, Alexander's wife, Margaret Gray, maintained a particularly fond relationship with Petermann's daughter, Nellie, continuing this after both Alexander's and Petermann's deaths. There can be little doubt that both Petermann and his colleague Heinrich Lange were treated most hospitably by the Johnstons, which was reciprocated when Keith later stayed in Germany. Grace recalls that the young Germans made the Johnston family very happy by introducing a Christmas tree, perhaps the first ever seen in Edinburgh.

The membership of the RGS, which features so largely in the lives of both Alexander and his son, was headed by a number of peers, but included many army and navy officers, diplomatists and practical men, such as geographers, surveyors, hydrographers, engineers and doctors described by Bridges as the 'service class', which was to provide the link with later imperialism.[44,45] Somewhat lower in the pecking order were representatives of related interests such as papermakers, engravers, printers, publishers, cartographers, all of whom might have had a commercial interest in becoming fellows and promoting their interests through the equivalent of an 'old boy' network. It was in effect a rather prestigious and highly influential club, deriving from the days of the aristocratic grand tour, claiming to be strictly scientific in its pursuit of knowledge. It was also highly competitive and there was no doubt considerable 'back-scratching' (or back-stabbing) involved.

A scientific churchman

Alexander was described as 'deeply religious' and his convictions remained throughout his life. Notwithstanding his scientific integrity – and being contemporaneous with Darwin, whose writings would have been quite familiar to him – he was able to say in his last speech on being awarded the Victoria Medal in 1871: 'Every step in the progress of physical geography appeared to me like a new revelation of the power, wisdom, and goodness of God in creation as revealed in the wonderful adaptation of plants, animals, and men to the several spheres they were destined to occupy on our beautiful globe'[46] This was the last speech he made, and it is interesting in combining an appreciation of what would now be termed ecology with a deeply spiritual approach to science, which for him was entirely holistic.

He faithfully attended St George's Church in central Edinburgh; one of the reasons for his move from March Hall, then on the outskirts of the city, to the New Town, was to be more accessible to his church. It was led by the charismatic and scholarly minister Robert Smith Candlish, one of the leading proponents of that great schism in Scottish religious life, the Disruption of 1843. This traumatic event, when ministers and their congregations rebelled against the proposal to remove the right of church members to call their own ministers, resulted in over 500 ministers leaving the established Church of Scotland to form the Free Church of Scotland, with the prospect of losing their livelihoods, churches, and homes – arguably the most important public issue of the nineteenth century in Scotland. Alexander, who had been a supporter of the Disruption movement from its inception, was present at Edinburgh's Tanfield Hall on the historic and emotional occasion when the dissenting ministers arrived there to form the new Free Church of Scotland after processing solemnly through the streets of Edinburgh from St George's and St Andrews Church in George Street.

Alexander must have been similarly moved in following Dr Candlish when he led his supporters to found a new church at the west end of the city, St George's Free Church. (However, after a long association with the Free Church, William left it in 1882, when there were further schisms.)

In a three-month visit to the Holy Land with the Rev. Dr Hanna in 1863 (Alexander was the honorary secretary of the Palestine Exploration Scheme), Alexander's knowledge of the Bible was put to good use in identifying and interpreting many Biblical localities,[47] which are described in considerable detail in letters to his family. One of these is written from the top of the Great Pyramid of Ghizeh, characteristically providing a comprehensive geographical and anthropological description of all that could be seen from this ancient vantage point, with relevant scriptural references.

At this time also, certainly among the establishment and the 'respectable classes' of Edinburgh, Sunday observance would have been strict. At the time of divine service, a great stillness would fall over the city like a pall, and many everyday activities were severely curtailed. The Church complained of Sabbath breakers; one minister chastised the board of the Edinburgh and Glasgow Railway who proposed running Sunday trains in 1842 that they were 'infidels, scoffers, men of unholy lives, the enemy of the righteous, moral suicides, sinners against light, traitors to their country, robbers, and murderers'. Not long afterwards, Alexander's firm of W. and A. K. Johnston were tried by jury for allowing men to work on a Sunday, quite coincidentally on plans for the Glasgow and Greenock Railway. Given Alexander's position in the Church, this was not a case he could afford to lose, but fortunately the case, taken by the renowned Lord Cockburn, was dismissed.[48]

Alexander's religious convictions and his professional interests came together in his friendship with the missionary and explorer David Livingstone, who was apparently a family friend. Alexander gave a lecture (of which there is no record) to the Greenock Philosophical Society in 1868 on 'Geographical Discovery and Research during the 19th Century with Special Reference to Africa' in which, according to his daughter Grace, 'his allusions to his old friend Livingstone were, as usual, full of feeling'. This would have been the development of a paper which appeared in the

North British Review five years earlier[49] where Alexander opens by exhorting all travellers to observe the methods of Humboldt and Carl Ritter. In this he displayed his knowledge of European travel literature and provided a masterly summary on the then known topography of Africa before focussing on African exploration, more especially the journeys of Speke, Grant and Livingstone around the perennial question of the source of the White Nile. It was Alexander who prepared the map published in 1863 by William Blackwood to accompany Speke's *Journal of the Discovery of the Sources of the Nile* – an extant copy of this important map has extensive later annotations by Livingstone himself.

In her *Recollections*, Grace records Livingstone visiting the Johnston's house at March Hall in company with Sir Roderick Murchison, the then President of the RGS. In a letter she comments: 'They are both at this moment on the library floor preparatory to being assisted to the top of a bookcase for a change of air. Indeed I think we should help the doctor to mount the heating apparatus to acclimatise him after Africa.'

Apparently it was the painter and photographer D.O. Hill (jokingly referred to by the family as 'do ill'), who had sent Livingstone, no doubt in his own carriage from his house nearby on this occasion, saying he 'wanted to take off his head!', presumably for his wife to sculpt as a bust. David Octavius Hill had gained fame with Robert Adamson for their early calotypes, now acknowledged as probably the finest of the time. He was so moved by the sight of the solemn procession of the dissenting ministers through the city at the time of the great Disruption that he resolved to make a giant portrayal in oils of those involved, a project that took 20 years, and included both Alexander and his brother William. It was Hill's wife Amelia who sculpted the powerful figure of Livingstone, still standing at the east end of Edinburgh's Princes Street Gardens. (Before Keith's departure to Paraguay, Amelia entertained Grace 'by showing us her pets, the latest addition...being two bright green toads brought from a friend from Paris. A large spider was procured and we witnessed one of the toads dining off it – rather horrid! If you can bring home alive *anything* that crawls or creeps, Mrs Hill will be enchanted.')

The portrait (possibly by Hill) of Alexander, aged about 60, shows him seated by his maps and globes. It is a powerful portrait of a rather forbidding figure with a high forehead and slightly grim expression which belies the description of his having always a 'sweet disposition', but may simply have been due to the length of time he had to remain motionless for these early photographs. (A photograph of his son Keith in his early thirties shows a similar somewhat serious expression.) Keith's interest in photography is likely to have been encouraged by Hill, who was also a pioneer in lithography, being the first in Scotland to draw on stone. He used this technique for a series on Perthshire landscapes, and it was a process which Alexander's firm quickly adopted for all their map printing, and which revolutionised the mass printing of maps and illustrations.

*Alexander Keith Johnston aged about 60 (Source: **An Edinburgh Centenary: 100 Years of Map-making: W. & A. K. Johnston**, photographer unknown)*

The Rev. Robert Candlish was another lifelong friend, who must have been a tower of strength on the early deaths of several of Alexander's children, and who survived to preach at Alexander's funeral service. Another was Sir George Harvey (after whom one of Alexander's nephews was named), noted for his landscape pictures and scenes from Scottish rural life. Baron Lyon Playfair of St Andrews, who held the chair of chemistry at Edinburgh University and was chemist to the Geological Survey (among his very many public appointments), would have assisted Alexander in his interpretation of geology for his first *Physical Atlas*. The author of the classic work on the Old Red Sandstone of Scotland and editor of the evangelical newspaper *The Witness*, Hugh Miller (understandably miscalled by one of the children as 'Huge' Miller), was a frequent visitor to the Johnston home. Alexander had many contacts in Edinburgh University, such as Sir Alexander Grant of Bombay, the Indian educationalist, whom he actively supported in his successful bid for the post of Principal against James Douglas Simpson of chloroform fame.[50]

The explorer Sir Julius Haast, who explored the Southern Alps in New Zealand, was sufficiently close to Alexander to name a mountain range after him in that country,[51] in the manner of imperial explorers of the time, rather cavalierly ignoring the existing Maori names. He also did this for other renowned European geographers, including Johnston's colleagues and friends Augustus Petermann and Sir Roderick Murchison. (W. & A. K. Johnston published over 30 maps of New Zealand between 1844 and 1890.) Correspondence in the National Library of New Zealand in Wellington indicates that towards the end of 1863 Alexander had received a map of the District of Canterbury from Haast, and Alexander compliments him not only on producing a very creditable map, but also for being the first to explore the 'great Southern Alps', while commending Haast on his writing on the physical geographical problems of the Southern Hemisphere. Alexander also asks to be remembered to a Dr Hector, to whom he sends a copy of a map of New Zealand. (I uncovered this link quite coincidentally on a trip near Christchurch on South Island to view the rare Hector's Dolphins, named after the scientist who had conducted the first autopsy on the species.)

Hector was a distinguished professor of natural history at Edinburgh University before his departure to New Zealand. At the age of 23, on Sir Roderick Murchison's recommendation, he had been appointed surgeon and geologist to an expedition to find a route through the Rocky Mountains – Kicking Horse Pass is named after an almost lethal incident involving Hector's horse – and subsequently he was awarded the Gold Medal of the RGS. It is yet another example of Alexander's world-wide scientific contacts, often started by an association at Edinburgh University, in this case possibly through their links with the Wernerian Robert Jameson,[52] which was continued because of the mutual advantage involved: Alexander received scientists' maps from around the globe, the new material being incorporated in his atlases, etc. while in turn they saw their attributed work represented accurately by one of the finest map-makers of his day. A good example is indicated in a letter to Haast on 5 August 1864,[53] when he apologises for the delays in his replies to Haast due to the need to complete his *Geographical Dictionary*, which apparently left him quite exhausted, before his departure on a well-earned holiday with his family in Switzerland. He offers to provide Haast with a copy of his *Dictionary* (in which some 50,000–60,000 geographical locations are described) and indicates that he has put Haast's name to his most recent explorations in the South Island in a map of New Zealand to be presented in London shortly.

The only substantial surviving professional correspondence is with the precocious James David Forbes, who became a Fellow of the Royal Society of Edinburgh at 21 – the earliest permissible age – and Professor of Natural Philosophy at Edinburgh University at 23, subsequently becoming Principal of St Salvator's College at the University of St Andrews in 1859. Forbes commissioned Alexander to draw maps for his *Travels through the Alps and Savoy* where he had been invited by the famous Swiss geomorphologist Louis Agassiz (who was later to give his name to a scheduled geological monument in Edinburgh where he proclaimed that he recognised the action of ice in the scratches on a glacial boulder). Forbes was the first to make the important observation that a glacier moves faster than the ice below it and more rapidly in the centre than at its sides. He was one of several eminent scientists to make a significant contribution to the section on glaciology in Alexander's *Physical Atlas* – for the use of his extensive notes and map, Alexander offered him 20 guineas and a copy of the final atlas. Their relationship was not without turbulence, as Forbes on several occasions complained in the strongest terms about the delays in forwarding proofs of maps and notes, and, surprisingly, on the poor quality of several of the maps produced by W. & A. K. Johnston, as well as their cost.[54] Forbes was the brother of Sir John Stewart Forbes of Pitsligo and Fettercairn, who had been instrumental, with Alexander, in founding the Scottish Meteorological Society in 1855, while James Forbes himself wrote papers on Scottish climate.

Alexander became deeply involved with Forbes in the campaign to establish the first-ever Chair of Geology at Edinburgh University. The machinations of this are revealed in the correspondence between Alexander and Forbes, with the latter at one point offering to write to the Duke of Argyll, the president of the British Association for the Advancement of Science, and to approach the Chancellor of the Exchequer on his forthcoming visit to Edinburgh 'in one of his softer moments'. For his part, Alexander rails at Professor Simpson, for his 'blabbing' about the possibility of Sir Roderick Murchison, the wealthy geologist, funding such a Chair which if it came to his notice 'would have an injurious effect'. On the same subject, Alexander is equally dismayed at Dr Lyon Playfair's suggestion that he (Alexander) should ask Murchison direct about this, 'since he could easily afford it'. In the event, Murchison donated £6,000 and exercised his patron's privilege in nominating Archibald Geikie (later Sir Archibald Geikie) as the first professor, notwithstanding the objection of the

Government, who were also contributing from the public purse, and felt it inappropriate that a private individual should have this privilege.

In an obituary, the President of the Royal Society of Edinburgh, Sir Robert Christison[55] credits Alexander with formulating the idea of a Chair of Geology '…and at the instance of Mr Johnston, and through the weight which his genuine love of science commanded with many men of influence, Sir Roderick was induced to alter his intentions, from a *post-obit* foundation, to an immediate gift of the Chair'. It was the first professorship of geology in any Scottish university.[56] (Murchison had in fact already provided for this chair in his will.[57]) At one point, when Alexander was 41, he obviously felt in need of formal education in physics, as he obtained from Forbes a ticket for his classes in natural philosophy in 1845. His interest in natural philosophy – what is now more commonly referred to as 'physics' – is reflected in the firm's production of educational wall charts in this subject, covering such topics as astronomy, human anatomy, steam engines and boilers, etc., but would also have been extremely useful in his developing studies of meteorology and oceanography.

Unlike his brother William, who cultivated influential personages for political purposes, to the extent of offering lavish hospitality to potential opponents at his grand country house outside Edinburgh, the totally honest and unworldly Alexander would have drawn to himself those men of science and intellect who appreciated his scholarship, cultural interests and integrity. What is interesting is that this largely self-taught man, who had started in the trade of an engraver and was not a university graduate, should have, through his own efforts, become a very respected figure in the scientific and academic world, and a colleague and friend of some of the most eminent men of his time. When he received the honorary degree of LL D in 1865, with the Chair occupied by his old friend, Sir David Brewster, the Principal and Vice-Chancellor of the University, among the long list of academic list of officials present, not one if any would be unknown to Alexander. Nor were these friends confined to scientists, but included, for example, the highly respected Ambassador to Rome, Joseph Pentland, after whom one of Alexander's daughters was named.[58]

Alexander had a lifelong interest in meteorology, making daily observations from recording instruments in his garden, becoming a founder member and Honorary Secretary to the first Meteorological Society of Scotland,[59] in which he played a prominent part up to his death. The council and membership of the Society was an eminent one, including many of the foremost scientists of the day such as Sir Roderick Murchison and Professor James Forbes, and not a few of the landed gentry, such as the president, the Marquis of Tweeddale, concerned to promote meteorology in the interests of both public health (Alexander was a member of a special Medico-Climatological Committee under its chairman, the Commissioner for Lunacy, Arthur Mitchell) and agriculture. Here Alexander would have met the Duke of Argyll and Thomas Stevenson of the 'lighthouse' family, both of whom accompanied Alexander on a tour of the lighthouses of Scotland in 1851 with Lord de Mauley. An interesting sidelight on the parsimony of government support for such practical scientific societies was that the Scottish Meteorological Society was allowed the use of two cramped attic rooms in the General Post Office of Edinburgh for which they paid £30 per annum on condition of supplying meteorological statistics to the Government for the use of the Registrar-General.[60]

In the course of the Holy Land visit in 1863, Alexander established three meteorological recording stations in Jerusalem, Damascus and Cyprus, recruiting resident British observers and supplying them with the necessary instrumentation on behalf of the Society.[61] In 1870 he presented a learned paper to the Royal Society of Edinburgh on the temperature of the Gulf Stream in the North Atlantic, which was subsequently reprinted in the first volume of *Nature*[62] following an earlier paper on the same topic. Both of these made a significant contribution to an understanding not only of the variation in the Scottish climate but also of hydrography and climatology generally in the North Atlantic.

Family life and later years

Alexander's interests were not solely scientific – both he and his wife, Margaret Gray, whom he married in 1837, had a broad interest in literature and a considerable knowledge and love of Scottish poetry, ballads, and song – they were thoroughly familiar with the works of Scott, Burns, and others. Grace records that on their honeymoon, in the evenings, Alexander read the latest chapters of *The Pickwick Papers* – which at that time was being issued in impatiently awaited parts – to his new wife! She was noted for her fine features, with large dark blue eyes, and well arched eyebrows, considered a mark of beauty at the time.

Margaret Gray had a quite distinguished pedigree, her family being derived from the Nimmos who claimed a genealogy to before Queen Elizabeth's reign, and had connections with Sir Walter Scott, the Scott-Moncrieffs, and W. E. Gladstone. She shared many of Alexander's cultural interests: she had learned Italian with her own father, from whom she inherited a great love of literature and music, having a fine voice; and these accomplishments were no doubt encouraged by the rather superior Miss Playfair's School at St Andrews which she attended. At a time when British geography and cartography was relatively insular, much of Alexander's work involved delving into the untranslated writings of eminent foreign geographers and explorers and, at least in the first years of married life, Margaret helped her husband with such enthusiasm that they became so absorbed in their researches 'the dawn often surprised them deep in books'.

Grace refers to her mother being practical rather than mystical, but the imaginative side of her nature showed itself in her intense love of colour, of scenery and of music, although she had no toleration for what she was apt to call 'fine writing'. Because of the pre-eminence of German scientists and geographers at that time, both Alexander and Margaret studied German in depth under Dr Kombst. The learning of foreign languages was a constant theme in this household – when Alexander's brother Archibald came back from Spain, both commenced learning Spanish together.

Margaret Gray, Alexander's wife (Source: W. & A.K. Johnston Archive, Trustees of the National Library of Scotland)

Margaret shared with her husband a love of nature and was a clever gardener and enthusiastic botanist, searching out rarer mosses and ferns on trips to the Highlands, and alpine plants on her occasional visits to Europe. More unusually, she was interested in zoology and would bring back from the rock pools of Arran and elsewhere various sea creatures for her salt-water aquarium (with sea water supplied at intervals from Portobello): her children remarked on her lack of concern for bruises as she scrambled over sea rocks and cliffs in search of 'beasts' (as she called them) and plants. Even in her seventies, she could be seen climbing over stone dykes to garner plants to decorate a holiday home, and making collections of wild flowers. She instructed her own children in the ecology of wild plants, their nomenclature and how to collect them. Although she frequently had to act as hostess for the many distinguished guests who came to their home, Margaret was not a socialite, much preferring country pursuits and life to the bustle of the city. She was a devoted family woman, noted for her fine embroidery and crewel work rather than fashion or socialising. Much later in her long life (she died in her mid-eighties) she lost much of her natural reserve. Herself very robust and healthy, she was impatient of other people's illnesses and certainly did not allow her children to malinger.

Between the years 1838 and 1854 she would not have had much time for socialising, for in this period, she bore no fewer than 11 children: the first of these, Marianna White, died before her second birthday, twin boys in 1848 did not survive, while her last two male children, John William and Frank Richardson, died in infancy within a year of one another of the scarlet fever which was raging through the country at this time. Of the remaining girls, all married except Grace. Keith, born in 1844, was the only son who survived infancy. Later in life he was to describe the family as 'unlucky' but of course, at this time, it was not at all uncommon to have multiple infant deaths in one family. What was perhaps unusual was the relatively early deaths of two of his father's brothers who had both entered the medical profession. In the year of Keith's birth, his uncle Archibald, at the time a naval surgeon died in Lisbon of typhoid contracted while he carried out a post-mortem dissection on a sailor who had himself died of the disease. He distinguished himself by faithfully recording the progress of his own demise virtually up to his certain death. His brother John died from the same cause while nursing an old school friend.

In 1871 Alexander received a letter from the President of the RGS, his old friend Sir Roderick Murchison, who at the time was seriously ill, advising Alexander that he had been awarded the Patron's or Victoria Gold Medal 'for his long-continued and successful services in advancing geography, as proved by numerous publications of maps, and especially for his merit in carrying out his scheme of physical atlases, by which the varied phenomena of physical geography are displayed by means of cartography'. He had also been named as President of the Geographical Section of the British Association's Edinburgh Meeting in August of that year, a meeting which he greatly looked forward to and which might be attended by Livingstone (if he returned) among other very distinguished personages. However, he himself was terminally ill at this stage – it was reputed that he suffered from a heart condition brought about by 'mental toil' – and he had to prepare his son Keith to accept the gold medal and to make an acceptance speech on his behalf. In the event, he was able to travel to receive the medal himself at the hall of the University of London on 22 May, which Keith says: 'even beyond our hopes and expectations, the presentation of the medal was a complete success. After Sunday's rest, Papa looked ever so much better and made quite a long and proper speech in returning thanks and the cheering which his name, and the various points of Sir Bartle Frere's address about him drew from the audience showed how well deserved the reward was considered to be.'[63]

He did not survive to the anticipated August meeting of the British Association – of which Keith was the Secretary – and there is a poignant record by Grace on the day of another daughter's wedding, before her departure with her new husband to take up residence in Madrid. 'I remember him drawing me down to him where he sat and saying: "*You'll* never leave me! I can't do without all my bairns. Promise you will stay with me!"'

At the end of his life, Alexander's obituaries, and the comments of his family, show a complete consistency in describing his character, which was remarkable for his application to work, unassuming modesty, delight in nature, deep scholarly interests, and love for his family, according to those who knew him best. A relative who had known him from early boyhood remarked that he 'could not remember one angry word that that ever fell from him; he was always the good and equal-tempered man of a most kindly nature'. On the basis of his thematic atlases alone, he would be ranked as a pioneer in geography and cartographic representation[64] but, in addition, he was responsible for many educational maps and booklets at a price students could afford, which provided a mainstay of the firm's revenues long after his death. Sir Roderick Murchison, President of the Royal Geographical Society, said of him: 'You have really introduced the study of physical geography to the youth of our country.'[65] Sir Robert Christison said:

> His extensive acquaintance with the upper ranks of what it has become the custom to call the 'citizen class' in Edinburgh enabled him often quietly to direct public opinion in the nice exercise of scientific, literary, and professional patronage, when sound direction was greatly needed.[66]

If Alexander had a fault, it might have been his single-mindedness in pursuit of cartographic interests, shutting himself up in his study for days at a time, asking not to be disturbed while he wrestled with complex geographical calculations. His old friend Dr Candlish alluded to this when he said of Alexander's scientific research 'which he prosecuted to the close of his days with such a minutely painstaking and untiring diligence as made him at the last almost a victim or a martyr in his self-forgetting and enthusiastic devotion to his loved work…' The president of the RGS described Alexander as 'scarcely ever diverging to take an active part in public affairs, or to engage in political matters. His life was thus one of quiet but incessant industry, as such offering little of personal incident.'[67] If this suggests either a paragon of virtue or a narrow-minded 'workaholic' this is belied by his many other interests. Spanning much of the nineteenth century, his career and associations provide a fascinating insight into upper-middle-class professional life in the Edinburgh of that period, during a time when Scotland was undergoing massive economic and social changes. Many of these were generated by the scientific and technological advances which W. & A. K. Johnston contributed to, and by the expanding British Empire in which Alexander's son Keith would play his own part.

NOTES

1   Moir, D. G. (1973), 124.
2   Smith (1985), 30.
3   William Blackwood (1776–1834), a publisher who in 1827 started the Tory *Blackwood's Magazine*, which had many famous contributors.
4   Moir, D. G. (1973), 132–3.
5   *Dictionary of National Biography* (1909), 1188–91.
6   Stevens (1849), 180.
7   Pillans (1852), 109–18.
8   Withers (2001), 178.
9   *Proc. R. Soc. Edin.* (1870–71), 247.
10 Anon., (1873).
11 A copy of this publication has not been found.
12 National Library of Scotland, Edinburgh, W. & A. K. Johnston Archive II.
13 Anon. (1922).
14 Shapin (1983), 157–78.
15 Simpson, J. (1836), Appendix IV.
16 Morrell (1973), 354.
17 Robinson (1982), 100–1.
18 Ibid., 197.
19 Ibid., 105–6.
20 Sir Roderick Impey Murchison (1792–1871): a distinguished geologist and one of the founders of the Royal Geographical Society of which he was president for 16 years. He was a friend of many eminent explorers, such as David Livingstone.
21 Professor Edward Forbes (1815–54): an eminent naturalist and geologist, notably in the field of paleontology and molluscs; he was appointed curator to the Geological Society and subsequently became Professor of Natural History at Edinburgh University.
22 Sir Edward Sabine (1788–1883): a renowned soldier, who also made important scientific contributions to ornithology and terrestrial magnetism. He held the post of general secretary to the British Association for twenty years.
23 Smith, D., personal communication.
24 Johnston, W. & A. K. (1875), 59.
25 Smith (1985), 432–45.
26 New College Library Edinburgh, Special Collections CM/SI.
27 Ibid.,CM/S95.
28 Scottish Meteorological Society, Council Minutes, 10 January 1862.
29 Johnston, A K, Snr (1851), 31–41.
30 Boud (1986), 5.
31 Ibid., 9.
32 Ibid., 15.
33 Karl Ritter (1779–1859): a pupil of Humboldt, he headed the Berlin Society for Geography and became Professor of Geography there in 1829. He helped to lay the foundations of modern scientific geography, emphasising the connection between people and environment.
34 Robinson (1982), 67.
35 Kelner (1963), 196–7.

36 Heinrich Berghaus (1797–1884): a founder member for the Berlin Society for geography, who was active in the distinguished cartographic house of Justus Perthes of Gotha. In 1839 he started the Geographical School of Arts in Potsdam where Augustus Petermann was a student.

37 Englemann (1977), 66–7.

38 Browne (1983), 41–8.

39 Linke, Hoffman and Hellen (1986), 75–80.

40 Gilbert, E. W. (1958), 172–83.

41 Herbert (1983), 71.

42 Smith (2000), 12–13.

43 RGS Archives, fo.25.

44 Bridges (1987a), 11.

45 Bridges (1973), 226–7.

46 *Proc. RGS* (1870–71), Address by Sir Bartle Frere 247–51.

47 Anon. (1873).

48 National Library of Scotland (NLS), W. & A. K. Johnston Archive II.

49 *North British Review* (1863), 357–78.

50 National Library of Scotland, Edinburgh, MS. 10740.

51 The author has been able to locate the Johnston Range (now Mount Cook) by that name only in one of W. & A. K. Johnston's atlases of the time.

52 Robert Jameson (1774–1854) occupied the chair of natural history at Edinburgh University for 50 years from 1804, and established the influential Wernerian Natural History Society.

53 National Library of New Zealand, Wellington, Haast Family Papers.

54 University of St Andrews Mss Collection: Papers of James David Forbes, Letterbox IV, No. 12.

55 *Proceedings of the Royal Society of Edinburgh* (1871–72), 536.

56 Geikie (1875), 341.

57 Morrell (1973), 376–8.

58 Joseph Barclay Pentland (1797–1873) was a traveller in South America where he made a number of new fossil finds at high altitude and subsequently wrote handbooks on Italy and Rome while British Ambassador there.

59 *Proc. RGS* (1871) 304–6.

60 Morrell (1973), 270.

61 Johnston, A.K. Snr (1870), 640.

62 Johnston, A.K. Snr (1851), 37–41.

63 Sir Bartle Frere (1815–84): a statesman and one-time governor of Bombay. He was appointed president of both the Asiatic Society and the Royal Geographical Society in 1872. He negotiated with the Sultan of Zanzibar for the suppression of the slave trade.

64 Shirley (2000), 31–5.

65 *Sunday at Home* (1872), 647–50.

66 *Proc. R. Soc. Edin.* (1871–72), 537.

67 *Proc. RGS* (1872), 305.

Part II

The Making of a Cartographer

4

'Johnston Secundus'

_____

A privileged start

Alexander's first son, also named Alexander Keith Johnston, was born in 1844 at 8 Lauriston Lane, within sight of that great fortress immediately to the north, Edinburgh Castle, while to the south lay the green Meadows which remain open space to this day. Keith's uncle William recorded in his diary[1] two years earlier the great distress caused by unemployment in these 'Hungry Forties' with many thousands of starving families, and how he as a magistrate became the chairman of a relief committee which raised over £1,000 per month from private donations during this time. The toddler Keith (described by Grace as 'a very pretty little fellow in a linen blouse and Leghorn hat with a long blue feather' which she obviously coveted) enjoyed the amenities of a large house and garden, with its vinery and various household pets in a salubrious part of the town. But the Royal Mile, only 10 minutes walk away, was a very different scene. The Third _Statistical Account of Scotland_ described the condition of the High Street in the Old Town of Edinburgh in the last half of the nineteenth century as 'not only of dirt, near-starvation and chronic poverty, but almost incredible overcrowding. Thus in 1865 there were 646 people to the acre in the Tron area of the High Street.'[2] One observer commented that, with the exception of some districts in Liverpool, it was thought that in no part of the world did there exist greater crowding of population. The Johnston family would not have been unaware of this environment, as one of the early offices of the firm of W. & A. K. Johnston was located only yards away from the Tron Kirk.

The city would have had distinct hierarchies, from some of the worst conditions anywhere in Britain in the Old Town to the ultra respectability, if not aristocratic living, in the New Town and with all shades of nuance in-between. Large houses were being built on the south side, so well described by David Daiches:[3]

> The villas and terraced house in the South Side expressed with considerable precision the class and social status of their inhabitants. The tenements of flats with their back greens, have a different social flavour from the houses with their neat front gardens. Immediately south of the Meadows, for example, one finds Livingstone Place (named after David Livingstone, who was made an honorary burgess of Edinburgh in 1857), where the flats are made for artisans, and the street immediately adjacent to it on the west, Millerfield Place, which was a full notch up on the social scale...

It was to this expanding south side, in the district of Newington, that Alexander moved his family in 1854, when Keith was 10 years old. (A photograph at about this time shows Keith in Highland costume, made fashionable by Queen Victoria's love affair with the country, sporting the long-hair sporran then favoured – his somewhat round unsmiling face suggests he is not too enthusiastic about the occasion.) The *Statistical and Topographical Gazetteer* of 1842 described the district as 'a little town of no common beauty…, a picture, in every part, of cheerful ease and refined taste'. Here Alexander built an imposing stone villa called March Hall, then in an outer suburb of the capital, with one of the finest outlooks of any city in the land, commanding an open view of the volcanic massif of Arthur's Seat. As an amateur geologist, Alexander would have known that this was one of the sites from which the great James Hutton, examining these rocks, developed his revolutionary and controversial work *A Theory of the Earth*[4] which fundamentally altered current notions of the world's age. From the house, on a clear day it is possible to see the white mass of the Bass Rock rising out of the Firth of Forth some 20 miles away and, from the upper storey, the range of the Pentland Hills to the south are clearly visible. The building still survives, with its distinctive tall gable ends and elaborately carved wooden bargeboards, albeit in a somewhat run-down state, as a local care home.

In building this residence on the fringes of the city, Alexander introduced such modern innovations as large bay windows of plate glass, and it was one of the first houses in the city to use gas for cooking. Within its 2 acres of grounds it boasted a fountain and winter garden; at one end of the terrace, a flight of steps led down to a miniature alpine garden, carefully and lovingly tended by Margaret. Here she grew many treasures, adding to them from her visits to Switzerland or Bavaria. Forays were also made by horse and coach into the Highlands to collect ferns and mosses, and the greenhouses were her pride and joy – on leaving in later years she was greatly distressed to hear that the new owner had removed these.

The gardener Johnston lived with his wife and large family in the lodge at the entrance to the house, jealously presiding over 'his' garden, apparently becoming quite tyrannical over the cutting of 'his' flowers. The 250 feet length of garden allowed not only for a bowling green and cricket lawn, but also the instruments used by Alexander to keep various meteorological and astronomical records. His family were pressed into service for this purpose – Grace recalls their lack of enthusiasm for this task on cold, snowy nights. In time, however, this would provide valuable training for Keith in mastering the skills of taking fixes on moon and stars. Donald, the coachman, lived in the stables, one of his important duties being to make all the transport arrangements for the family when they departed on holiday. An insight into their life-style is provided by the complaints of the young ladies that, when crinolines came into fashion, the coach taking them to church was insufficient to accommodate their voluminous skirts: Alexander's wife preferred to see all her daughters dressed alike.

The Johnston family around 1857, with Keith on left and Grace at back right
(Source: W. A. K. Johnston Archive, Trustees of the National Library of Scotland)

March Hall, the home of the Johnston family (Source: W. & A. K. Johnston Archive, Trustees of the National Library of Scotland)

The centrepiece of this rather grand house (which in 1875 was valued at the then considerable sum of £8,000) was Alexander's purpose-built library, with its beautifully carved wooden panels, which was claimed to contain an unrivalled collection of scientific works from all over Europe. This library adjoined the drawing room, and these two fine rooms could be easily converted into one for the staging of *tableaux vivants* which the many artist friends of the Johnstons liked to stage. All these rooms had finely executed ceilings, with pendant mouldings, 'delicately tinted and gilded' with individually designed gas brackets. The children would be encouraged to use the library for their own education, which was mainly in the hands of both resident and daily governesses in addition to private tutors, with a schoolroom on the upper storey dedicated to this purpose – all of their several houses in Edinburgh were similarly equipped. That schoolroom contained the overflow from the library in bookcases all round the walls, on top of which was ranged a variety of curious and rare stuffed animals, including a duck-billed platypus.

Keith's mother, as much as his father, insisted on a thorough education for all of their children, at a time when, for girls, this was not common, other than to provide them with the social graces. Everything was subordinated to education, to such an extent that the youngsters were so attended to by the servants to allow for extra lesson time that the girls were quite old before they learned to make, mend, or do their own hair; later both Grace and her mother were to lament, like so many of their class, the difficulty of finding responsible servants. When a German governess was appointed, Keith's mother took lessons with her and the other children in the schoolroom, apparently regularly fulfilling her language task every evening. In the same schoolroom, Alexander had fitted up a cupboard, with the shelves representing geological layers, using this as a teaching aid. On one occasion, illustrating how coal was formed, Alexander's lesson was interrupted by Grace from her favourite place under a table, timidly enquiring where the coal came from that burns in hell fire!

It perhaps says something about the care with which the tutors were chosen that Edward Sang, Keith's mathematics tutor, was not only a fellow of the Royal Society of Edinburgh, but also a one-time professor of civil engineering in Manchester. He was eminent in both astronomy and the calculation of logarithmic tables, and was awarded the degree of LL D from Edinburgh University.[5] The children had a governess in residence until their mid-teens, and continued their education with masters and classes long after the accepted formal school age, and were encouraged to find out things for themselves rather than be spoon-fed. Grace records:

> It was Father's invariable custom, when not too busy...to read to his wife and girls while they sewed or drew — mostly travel, essays, or biography — but was very willing to interpolate a good modern novel for our benefit...but he stipulated for a certain amount of solid reading e.g. *Don Quixote*. Modern science of course took a large place, alongside Sir Walter Scott, Burns, and Alan Ramsay ...there was never a winter during our Father's lifetime when we were not encouraged to add

to the education supposed to be completed. Even the invalid Berta in her sick room read many 'solid' books...

Later several of the young people would be sent to the continent to complete their studies (including Grace who recalls her tearful apprehension on departure from Scotland for the first time). This was a family which placed a very high premium on a sound education, part of which would undoubtedly have come from the procession of distinguished guests from many different parts of the world who received hospitality at March Hall, but part also from more humble visitors. An annual dance was given, which in one year brought two attractive South American students, who subsequently started up an Amateur Literary Society with Alexander as its president. One night each week, at his instigation, was also set aside as an 'open evening' for welcoming friendless students, for whom he had great sympathy. Grace tells how 'many Scotch lads who have since made for themselves honourable names, came to these informal gatherings, and some of them may still recall their budding efforts at "poetry" or "romance", or the impromptu dances where their unskilled feet were beguiled by Molly's music'. There was in fact considerable entertainment and social life, particularly during the Edinburgh 'season' at the beginning of the year, with a succession of dinners and dances when, almost on a daily basis, March Hall came to Charlotte Square and vice versa, the Square with its highly fashionable New Town houses providing the most up-market residences of the time.

Keith attended various local private schools, including Archibald Munro's in nearby Newington, and Grange House School situated in the mediaeval Grange House originally attached to the Collegiate Church of St Giles run by a Mr Walter Scott Dalgleish, who as a member of the Scottish Meteorological Society shared Alexander's interest in this subject. For a short time, between 1858 and 1860, Keith also attended Merchiston Castle School,[6] which still survives as a rather exclusive educational establishment now in the Colinton district in Edinburgh. At the time when Keith attended, however, it was housed in the romantic if stark, fortified stone keep of the original Merchiston Tower, renowned in the sixteenth century as the home of the founder of logarithms, John Napier, and later for its pear tree under which Mary Queen of Scots was reputed to have sat. At this time, the school, which also took in boarders, was heated by open fires and lit by gas – only a short time previously, the boys would have gone to their beds up the shadowy spiral staircases illuminated by candles in sconces on the walls, and were granted a hot foot wash (in lieu of baths) once weekly by the gardener who presided over a row of tubs and a boiler in his garden house. The smallest boys were looked after by a Mother Brunton who personally soaped and sponged them in turn on Saturday nights.[7]

The extra-curricular activities included gardening, football (rugby was to come later), cricket and shinty, while the school was known for its instruction in country and Highland dancing, dances being held regularly on Saturday evenings. Scientific excursions were taken to the surrounding hill country and to the nearby Union Canal, a busy waterway before the arrival of the trains. The football games must have been quite a sight, played in ordinary clothes, with no goal posts, no rules, and no limit to the number who could play, including the masters in their tall silk hats. The school had all the characteristics of the archetypal English public school, modelled on Dr Arnold's prototype at Rugby, with a very good record at games. Keith does not feature in the school sporting records, but he is known to have taken prizes in gymnastics and fencing, although this is likely to have been at a subsequent establishment. In Keith's time at Merchiston Castle, the headmaster was a Thomas Harvey, who was a brilliant classical scholar, but apparently not an educational leader. This may have been the reason why Keith removed to Melville School, or as it was known 'The Edinburgh Institution for Languages and Mathematics', a public day and boarding school for boys. There the earlier emphasis on the classics was relegated by its vigorous head, Dr Robert Ferguson, in favour of more practical subjects, incorporating modern German scientific thought.[8] Here Keith would have received a more scientific education linked closely to his father's interests, although there is no record of how long he attended this establishment. The marks made by earlier pupils can still be seen in the very fine white marble fireplace which graces a splendid Adams room, now part of the prestigious premises in Queen Street of the Royal College of Physicians in Scotland.

Keith was fortunate in being a day boy, able to enjoy not only all the comforts of home, but also its diversions. There were pets aplenty and a veritable platoon of dogs, a favourite of Keith's being a Dandie Dinmont, which against the house rules, he sometimes surreptitiously secreted under his bed. There were many varieties of pigeons and in the aviary, some of the first Australian parakeets to be brought into the country, eventually housing more than a hundred different species. Saturdays were special days when the youngsters had holidays and when they were often joined by cousins for games of cricket on the lawn, where a wide ball would land in the flowery meadows below Arthur's Seat. Many leisurely summer days passed in this way. On one well-remembered occasion, the children were asked the way by a group of well-groomed laughing horsemen who turned out to be the Prince of Wales and the Duke of Edinburgh, plus their entourage, riding out from nearby Holyrood Palace. Keith could have been said to have had an idyllic childhood, with a home which was virtually in the countryside, yet with all the interests of a vibrant capital city on his doorstep, while he was surrounded by adoring sisters – his nick-name of 'Sonnie' is suggestive of a deal of mothering from them.

He would no doubt have outgrown this when at the age of 19, he joined the First Midlothian Royal Garrison Volunteers as a lieutenant. His mother wrote: 'He is to get his uniform and sword on Saturday, and they ought to be very handsome from the price. Perhaps this will give him the companionship he needs.' This was at a time when the cost of the uniform was borne entirely by the officers themselves. The

Artillery were known to consider themselves a cut above other volunteers, caparisoned in dark blue tunics, adorned with five rows of black cord on the breast, black cord shoulder knots, collars of scarlet with silver embroidered grenades, while the blue trousers sported a broad scarlet stripe; the whole outfit was topped by a busby for formal occasions.[9]

Such an occasion would have been the Great Review of Volunteers in Holyrood Park in 1860 where an observer noted: 'Here, with their band at their head, come a regiment of riflemen trooping to rendezvous. There combining ease with economy, a dozen artillerymen rattled along in one cab, which seemed to a fanciful view an overcrowded nest of paraquets, so lively were the uniforms and so loquacious their wearers.' (Some years later, at a similar review Alexander was highly amused to see those, men and women alike, who had climbed higher up the grassy slopes of Arthur's Seat rolling downhill ignominiously on the dry slippery grass after a very hot summer.)

Keith was tall, well-proportioned and athletic and no doubt, with the beginnings of the luxuriant moustache which his later photographs show, would have cut a dashing figure in such an outfit, though there is no record of his military activities. Such volunteer units mushroomed from 1859 onwards in a patriotic response to the threat from Napoleon III of France, then at least verbally threatening Britain. The individual units were often drawn from particular professions or corporations, while the artillery specifically were expected to defend coastal towns and 'find time to learn how to work a great gun mounted in their immediate neighbourhood'. The remark of Keith's mother on companionship is not insignificant and is of a piece with another, when she refers to him bringing a friend to dinner but being 'as quiet as ever', reflecting at this early age a shy and quite withdrawn personality who did not make friends easily, a characteristic which would remain with him to the end of his short life.

The year when Keith reached his twenty-first birthday was eventful for his father. The revolutionary process of lithography, involving etching on stone, was adopted by his cartographic firm as standard for the colouring of all maps, he was awarded the degree of LL D by Edinburgh University, and W. and A. K. Johnston published the maps for the US edition of the *Encyclopaedia Britannica*. Clearly the star of the Johnstons was in the ascendant, and the family could afford some relaxation.

Holidays were often taken away from home: when Keith was only three years old, Alexander and his wife went on a continental touring holiday taking in Switzerland, Milan and Venice, leaving the young people in the capable charge of their nurse Lizzie and her sister, the under-nurse – yet another indication of an enviable life-style. More often, the whole family would decamp to the small attractive weaving towns along the Tweed, such as Peebles and Innerleithen, where there was access to both river and hill land, and where the air was considered beneficial to health compared with the ever-increasing murkiness of Edinburgh. These were described by Grace as 'summer migrations' involving stays of as long as two months, during which the head of the household would return to business in the city, as was common practice among professional people at the time. Such 'migrations' involved great preparations for weeks beforehand, with everything from books to silverware and linen being packed in a wagonette housed in the stables, to be sent off in advance with George the coachman, accompanied by such servants as were needed.

There were extended excursions into the Central Highlands round Pitlochry where the family had friends who would provide hospitality. Even further afield were their holidays on the Ulster coast and in North Wales where Keith reached the summits of both Cader Idris and Snowden by pony. After 1857, however, most of their holidays appear to have been spent on Arran, where they occupied a series of houses, several of them on a grand scale. Situated at the southern end of the Firth of Clyde, Arran has spectacular coastal and mountain scenery, the most westerly demonstration of the Highland Boundary Fault cleaving the island into two distinct parts – a typical northern mountainous highland district and a softer rolling lowland area to the south, providing a great variety of landscapes. It was here that they were visited by the painter Sir George Harvey, and Sir Archibald Geikie, Professor of Geology at Edinburgh University, engaged on one of his numerous field trips on an island renowned for its range of rock types. (After her father's death, Grace severely castigated Geikie in her memoirs for neglecting the family, given that he received much hospitality and many favours from Alexander.) By a curious coincidence, one of Geikie's protégés was the young Joseph Thomson, who was to accompany Keith on his last journey, while Geikie's interest in physical geography had been considerably influenced by the teaching of Alexander's headmaster, James Pillans.

The family's summer stays on Arran were enhanced by carriage drives round its dramatic coastal cliffs and beach picnics: 'with so many strong pairs of arms to row, we almost lived upon the sea...Keith at Holy Island taught us the stars and after much persuasion sang *Tom Bowling*' said Grace, referring to the occasion when, returning from London, Keith brought with him the son of the Moore family whose home provided congenial quarters in that city. On another occasion, a party of eight was got up to walk a very fatiguing 60 miles round the island in two and a half days. They would have ascended Goat Fell, the highest point, to view a particularly fine example of an ice-carved corrie, littered with the great boulders plucked from crags by the glaciers. Alexander's wife Margaret found this jewel of an island a happy hunting ground for her collection of ferns and mosses which thrived in the damp shady woods round Brodick Castle. An absorbing topic of conversation in the evenings during their stay in 1870 was the progress of the Franco-Prussian War, when characteristically the family followed the campaign with pins plotted on to a map – Alexander had friends in both countries, and was particularly anxious for their welfare. One such was a Dr Manskopf who was said to have lost an arm and a leg in the conflict, but Alexander was relieved to hear from Henry Lange that he was hale and hearty and had never been involved!

A geographic apprenticeship

Keith did not always holiday with the family, and after one period of intense work when he apparently fell ill (and had, according to his mother, inflamed eyes due to too much proof-reading) he took himself off for a boating and camping trip up the River Tay to get away from a very sedentary occupation. On another occasion he went off to the Highlands 'to …sniff the heather breezes in a walk of I don't know what extent, from Blair Atholl to Braemar'. The route is in fact a well-known long walk of about 35 miles along the very scenic Glen Tilt, with its grand waterfalls and dramatic views over the Grampians. At this time, Keith had been busy writing an article on 'The Annual Range of Temperature over the Globe' to be read before the Royal Society of Edinburgh – his sister Molly said '…the poor boy is still very busy at his diagrams, working till far on in the morning' for his paper on the following Monday. Clearly Keith had inherited his father's industriousness and application.

The paper itself is a remarkable compilation of all the known temperature records from every extant recording station in the world, showing for the first time the significance of temperature ranges, i.e. the maximum and minimum temperatures of the warmest and coldest months (rather than simply mean annual temperatures). Keith established a formula for calculating the temperature from the mean annual temperature and its range, and he was also able to show that, in temperate regions, west coasts have 15 degrees less range than east coasts, and that this difference may rise to as much as 40 degrees, while high mountains have a very limited range compared with lowlands – a work much ahead of its time.[10]

In 1871 Keith had been involved in preparing maps for Admiral Irminger, the Danish naval hydrographer,[11] who had discovered that there were alternating cold and warm bands of water in the northern seas and that these were accompanied by a warm current flowing from southern to northern latitudes – a continuation of the Atlantic Drift which was subsequently confirmed by the famous *Challenger* expedition.[12] From his father's work on the Gulf Stream, Keith would have been very familiar with the arguments, particularly as Alexander had studied Admiral Irminger's observations closely for his own papers on the subject. What neither Keith nor his father would have known was that they were making early contributions, in their studies of both terrestrial and oceanic temperatures and movements, going well beyond conventional cartography, and forming the basis for current concerns about global warming and its consequences.

Keith was raised in the expectation that he would follow in his father's footsteps and was trained accordingly from a relatively early age, although there is no record of formal instruction in cartography, nor of any contractual employment with the firm. In 1866, for example, he accompanied his father on a visit to Wigtown on the instructions of the Court of Session to help to resolve a very complex issue over disputed shore rights in relation to fishing which would set an important precedent.

Indeed the whole family, including Alexander's wife, were involved in the business of cartography, being used to assist in Alexander's many publications. In a sunny upper room at March Hall the family at one point was occupied for over a year in carefully calculating the latitude and longitude of every location in one of Alexander's great world geographical gazetteers for insertion in the index – a most tedious task requiring meticulous attention, offset by the fact that they were more than fairly rewarded by Alexander on the basis of the hours worked. The author George Elliot apparently appreciated these labours, commenting in her *Life* about her copy of Alexander's *Handy Royal Atlas* and its 'glorious index being all the more appreciated because I am tormented by German historical atlases which have no index, and are covered with names, swarming like ants on every map'.

At one point, helping to compile the *Dictionary of Geography*, Alexander's wife, neglecting her beloved garden and greenhouse, mildly complained 'We are so busy, I think we shall soon turn into figures!' It appears that before Grace turned to writing on her own account she was much occupied in assisting her father in his cartographic works, but she continued after his death, presumably commissioned by the company. In 1875, she wrote about the labour of working on a condensed history of the Russo-Turkish War:

> I am breaking my back just now and nearly my heart over a most hopeless task! While waiting for proofs of the war, I am going over the whole letterpress, comparing it with the map and index and verifying all three. Think of examining three times and scoring off each name on the atlas of 32 maps, and you will have some idea of the labour...which had lost all its zest without the Father to direct and encourage.

Keith subsequently congratulated her on launching into literature 'it must be a very pleasant occupation when imagination and fancy are not barred in by square latitudes and longitudes and population figures and areas and boundaries, as in my particular nose-grinding'.

Keith himself must have been more than a competent draughtsman and cartographer by the time he was 22 when he was appointed by the renowned map-making and publishing firm of Stanfords in London as superintendent of maps in 1866, under the direction of Trelawny Saunders. Almost certainly this would have been due at least in part to the influence of his father who had collaborated with Saunders in the drawing of the maps for the very high quality *Stanford's Library Maps of the Continents* from 1858 onwards, engraved by W. and A. K. Johnston.[13] Over the next two years he produced a *Globe Atlas of Europe*, a *Library Map of Africa* and a revised edition of Murray's *Handbook of Scotland*. He stayed at Stanfords for just over a year but there is no record of his time there, other than an entertaining account of a farewell party given in his honour:

Our little dinner at Taplow, near Windsor, came off splendidly on Saturday…we had a row on the river as far as the Duchess of Sutherland's place…the dinner itself was everything that could be desired, and the champagne loosened the tongues wonderfully. Mr Saunders especially bursting into oration after oration, until he had it all his own way…

However, during his time at Stanfords, Keith had lodged with a Mrs Bruce in Islington and had fallen ill, according to his mother due to the lack of care or comfort which he received there; there is no doubt that her maternal instincts were to the fore when it came to the welfare of her beloved son.

Later, drawn by the attractions of the river, he moved from other quarters:

Last evening we got safely over the formidable task of giving notice to Mrs Ritchie, for whom we have the same sort of dreadful respect that Captain Cuttle had for Mrs MacStringer, tho' we can't deny she has made us most comfortable here in a rough way, or that she is properly insensible to any amount of noise, can cook a capital dinner and make gruel to perfection, if one is inclined that way.

The reference to noise is interesting as Grace refers to Keith's sensitivity to noise from early boyhood – at one point at March Hall he imprisoned a crowing cock in his bedroom till morning to attempt to silence its dawn wake-up call. In his London quarters he suffered from the various street callers shouting their wares – as a light sleeper he was easily disturbed by any unwanted noise. This sensitivity was later in Africa to be a cause for distress when he encountered loud drumming to accompany dancers, forcing him to run into his tent with his hands covering his ears. However, apart from that, there is nothing to convey Keith's reactions to living and working in the great metropolis of London, which at this time would have been noisy with the clatter of carriages and carts and, in many quarters, dirty, poverty-stricken and overcrowded. He would undoubtedly have longed at times for the tranquillity of Arran or the wildness of a Highland glen. He was in the metropolis at an interesting time, with major changes, particularly in the development of railways within the city, and the construction of the Southern Embankment along the Thames. (In Scotland, the first experimental pier was being constructed to support the proposed new Forth railway bridge.) While at home the new Reform Bill was wending its tortuous way through Parliament, abroad there was the impending Austro-Prussian war, and the signing of the contract for the construction of the Suez Canal.

Later Keith was much happier to take a room with the Moore family near Chiswick, where the two sons of the family were already Keith's friends, and shared many of his interests. One of these was rowing, and Keith established the local Grove Rowing Club, which he captained, becoming sufficiently proficient to compete in the famed Henley Regatta. He obviously impressed one of his sisters on a visit when she reported a race with a neighbouring club: 'Keith sent us up in a little boat to where

Henley Regatta (Source: Illustrated London News, 26 June 1869, p. 645, Trustees of the National Library of Scotland)

the steamer was moored, and after being hauled bodily up, we got a good place and saw the race well. Keith looked very handsome, pulling away with such vigour. The crew's costume was red, black and yellow stripes running round…'

Keith's visitors were often entertained on the river, and on their first visit to view his new quarters, his father and mother spent 'a delightful day on the river with a lavish picnic' before Keith and his father set off for the annual dinner of the RGS, where his father heard that he was to be the next recipient of the Society's coveted Gold Medal. During this visit, Keith and his father met many of his father's distinguished friends, dining with Admiral Sir William Hall, Sir Roderick Murchison and Lyon Playfair, 'the usual happy intercourse with his many scientific friends'.

With his restless nature, Keith frequently moved his quarters, albeit within the Kew area, and always within ready access to the river, where he spent virtually all of his free time. Later he wrote to his mother from Prospect House, Strand on the Green, about yet another move:

> I have had to leave my old rooms where because of problems with the landlord and because of imminent arrival of Sheriff's officers, greatest caution had to be observed in admitting only me to the house. Latterly one got expert in getting over railings though at first I used to congratulate myself in not being spiked!…I have come here to the third floor of a house which deserves its name, and has a splendid view over the river, up to Kew Bridge, down towards Barnes. It is an ancient edifice, and much out of repair: just now the painters are at work making the best of it from top to bottom. The view makes up for the discomfort, and for the sad want of 'nous' in the landlady.

A fortnight later he wrote 'I am tolerably comfortable in my new quarters, though the landlady is deaf to bells, but it is not by any means a serious matter to change if they don't suit, for I can now move almost anywhere in two hours, from the moment of heaving my old boots into the portmanteau at third floor No 1 to a peaceful pipe amid the perfect arrangements of No 2!'

Keith travelled to Germany in 1867, with many useful introductions from his father to distinguished colleagues, spending most of his year there in Leipzig, but also staying in Gotha and Berlin, to learn German and to acquaint himself at first hand with the much admired German scientific methods, notably in the field of geography and cartography. (His concern to study texts in their original language had even led him to take lessons in Russian from a priest in the Orthodox Church in London.) He spent much of his time at the famed cartographic house of Perthes in Gotha where Petermann was director. As expected he was very hospitably received by his father's old friends, who had assured him of a 'fatherly welcome', remembering their early days in Edinburgh. Alexander wrote approvingly: 'Your close friendship with Lange is most pleasing to all of us, but you have won golden opinions by your conquest of Petermann' – regretting at the same time that so many of his own contemporaries, such as Humboldt, Carl Ritter and von Buch, were now dead. The family at home strongly approved of his taking music lessons, and his father, writing to Keith, especially encouraged him in singing, while his mother said that she was 'anxious that you should still cultivate your "growl"...squeaks being predominant in our side of the house, it will form a fine contrast.'

From Berlin, Keith sent an amusing description of the Berlin Geographical Society's Meeting at which the large company, becoming bored with the speakers, simply conversed among themselves to while away the time before the substantial supper, which seemed to be the main purpose of the gathering. (It was incidentally the rise of this society which began to eclipse that of the institute at Gotha and was thought to have led to Pertermann's suicide in 1878.)[14] After a visit to Dresden and a climb up the Breslei for its glorious view, Keith returned to Leipzig for a farewell evening with Lange: 'We had a glass of toddy out of a real Scotch jug, to drink to Auld Lang Syne, and altogether spent the most happy evening I have had in Leipzig.'

At home, everyone was anxiously awaiting Keith's return, and some measure of their adoration of the only boy is reflected in Grace's remark: 'If you had only heard the plans and proposals *"when Keith comes home!"*' Keith did in fact spend the winter of 1868 at home 'which was a matter of great content to his sisters'. One of these was Berta, who was always in a state of delicate health; Keith's wrath at the mistaken methods of treatment by the family physician apparently came to a climax at this time, and caused a very unpleasant breach between the family and their long-standing doctor. Keith had for long been convinced that Berta's condition and continued suffering were due to ignorant or old-fashioned treatment, and that her youth and enjoyment of life were needlessly sacrificed: consultations with specialists later proved Keith's judgement to be fully justified.

Following Keith's return from Germany in February 1868, he was elected, at the remarkably early age of 24, a Fellow of the RGS, which was a singular feather in his cap. His father, under whom he had worked since his return to Britain, was of course one of those who seconded his application, but the great rival to W. & A. K. Johnston, John Bartholomew, declined to sign, indicating that he was not much known to Keith 'and besides I work chiefly for publishers that are rather in opposition to the Johnstons'.[15] (The first of the Bartholomews involved in map engraving was George, who started the dynasty as early as 1797. The company was to rival the Johnstons, producing comparable maps, although they surprisingly did not adopt the lithographic process until over 30 years after W. and A. K. Johnston.)[16]

In 1869, the family left March Hall for the city, eventually taking up residence at 16 Grosvenor Crescent, a fine Georgian building, typical of the solid, prestigious stone family houses of the New Town of Edinburgh, with its quasi-Grecian pillars and wrought iron balustrades. Apparently Alexander was tired of the daily travel from the outskirts into town, but his wife missed her garden and quiet life, and particularly regretted no longer having greenhouses – the greenery here being restricted to the crescent's small private park – she had loved every sight and sound of country life. However, in the manner of the times, she did not attempt to voice her own opinions in front of her husband, deferring to his convenience. The fashionable New Town, with its vibrant social life, would have made demands on hospitality which she did not relish, as she regarded socialising outside the family circle more as a penance than a pleasure – she was clearly much more at home at March Hall with her pots and plants.

In the same year, Keith, together with his cousin, Archie Johnston, left Edinburgh in the new steamer *Malvinia* for the last time to take up the position of head of the geographical department at W. and A. K. Johnston's new London office in the Strand. The sense of permanent departure was conveyed by his mother, writing to Grace:

> All morning I have been collecting our laddie's possessions…Molly is off to St. Andrews Square to meet him and make a few farewell calls… That evening, Keith stayed to dinner at Blackett Place (the home of his uncle and aunt) and I think · enjoyed his party, though he complained of headache from the immense amount of health-drinking he was subjected to. I suppose our poor laddie's safe in the great city by this time.

However, Keith was apparently a round peg in a square hole: 'His extremely reticent, sensitive nature and almost quixotic generosity made everything in the shape of business repugnant to him, and he soon drifted into solitary student life infinitely more congenial to him.' (His eminent friend Henry Bates thought that considerations of commercial or worldly success never entered his head.) All of this says a great deal about Keith, undoubtedly molly-coddled to an extent by both his mother and sisters, unable to face the rough-and-tumble of business life, no doubt slow to pursue debtors, and retreating into a semi-monastic existence. And yet it is not the whole story: among his own friends, he enjoyed a party – in the same year, he wrote graphically of a boat race between Oxford and Harvard, which he saw very luxuriously from the private barge of a Chiswick magnate whose supply of champagne and all sorts of good things to eat seemed limitless, while his captaincy of the local boat club indicates someone who could enjoy the company of others with a mutual interest. He was obviously fond of athletic activities and claimed that he did not feel right if he missed his regular gymnastic or fencing classes – the antidote, no doubt to an otherwise desk-bound existence. Indeed he was obliged to write to Henry Bates at the RGS[17] when he was employed there in 1872 asking for sick leave for a few days 'owing to damages received while playing football on Boxing Day' – an injured knee and two black eyes gave him 'a very unscientific appearance'. Things did not go well at the London Office, however, for in the same letter, referring to the need to attend to a court case against a debtor who had not paid bills to the firm, he says: 'This is the last flare up of the Strand House before it disappears from the stage.'

The mapping of Africa

For some time in the late 1860s Keith worked on a relatively small pamphlet which was nevertheless a very significant one, both in terms of his later career and, by a curious twist of fate, his eventual death. Exploration of Africa in the early and mid-nineteenth century had been dominated by the search for the origins and courses of the great river systems – the Nile, the Niger, and the Congo. Arguments raged fiercely in geographical and scientific circles concerning the sources and, with the exception of the well-known Nile, the outlets of these mighty waterways. Expedition after expedition was sent, frequently resulting in loss of life and considerable expenditure, ostensibly to verify or otherwise the claims of rival explorers, for whom this became an obsession, anxious to make their name by 'discovering' such sources. The question, following the discovery of several possible outlets, was whether these arose from a single vast lake or several water bodies, and the passionately held opposing views dominated many of the columns of the periodicals of the day, in arguments which are often exceedingly complex and difficult to follow, if not tedious. Indeed it was this obsession with river sources that may have in part resulted in the relatively unambitious maps, concentrating almost exclusively on the lakes and rivers, which were produced up to 1875.[18]

One of the reasons for this was the not unreasonable notion that these waterways would, with the recent invention of steamboats, provide the most obvious means of access to the interior for missionary or commercial activities. As Professor R.C. Bridges has argued, maps of East Africa in the nineteenth century largely ignored the scientific results obtained by explorers, focussing instead on topographic features and increasingly the political concerns of Europe in Africa.[19] However, there were different interpretations of 'scientific' since the discovery of the source of the Nile, for example, would be considered a 'scientific' fact, where its accurate latitude, longitude and altitude could be determined as the basis for locating it on maps, and particularly satisfied the scientific objectives of the RGS.

In 1870, Keith published this paper entitled 'A Map of the Lake Regions of Eastern Africa, showing the Sources of the Nile recently discovered by Dr Livingstone, with Notes on the Exploration of this Region',[20] a masterly summary, mainly drawn from Livingstone's communications, which for the first time brought together all the information which could be gleaned from the travels of many explorers over a considerable period. It was notable not only for its painstaking research and critical examination of narratives and notes, but also for the inclusion of reports from little known foreign travellers, including the early Portuguese and later Germans, as well as those of British explorers such as Livingstone, Burton, Speke and Grant.[21] The then president of the RGS, Sir H.C. Rawlinson,[22] referring to the question of the rivers in East Africa, stated:

> the British public will be much better informed than they have been on this subject when they examine a recent small work by Mr. Keith Johnston jnr...the

author has given a succinct history of all the explorations in South Africa and has also put together from the best authorities…a map which shows clearly to what extent the rivers from the southern highlands, on the south and south south west of Lake Tanganyika, are for the most part independent of that Lake, and may prove to be tributaries of the Congo.[23]

He subsequently described it as a 'signal service rendered to the cause of African geography'.[24] Burton was later to refer to Johnston's work in the continuing controversy over the Central African Lakes in a letter to the *Athenaeum* replying to a claim by the explorer Col. Grant:

> The Speke and Grant expedition alone must bear the blame for the errors of Messrs A. Keith Johnston, E Stanford, and E Waller. These scientific mappers could hardly believe in the superficiality of observation and the geographical ignorance which gave four outlets to one lake (Victoria). Consequently they divided the area into four, and they were fully justified in so doing.[25]

In a letter to the very first volume of *Nature* published on 27 January 1870,[26] Keith challenged a claim by Dr Beke in an earlier article that Livingstone's recent discoveries related to the Congo and not to the Nile. Keith went on to make a detailed scientific refutation of this suggestion (he actually put his meteorological knowledge to good use by calculating the likely volume of the catchments of these rivers), with the aid of references to these early explorations, and ended his letter: 'In this case the sources of the Nile would be side by side with those of the Congo: and the man who has the claim to be the greatest explorer that the world has ever known, has the double honour of having solved the two greatest of African problems.'

Dr Charles Tilstone Beke was noted as an Abyssinian explorer with a special interest in the source of the Nile and had published a paper on that topic in 1860, while at this early age, Keith had never left the shores of Europe – he was a mere 26 years of age at the time. In this case Keith's understandable admiration for Livingstone had led him into error, since it was subsequently recognised that the explorer Speke held that honour. Nevertheless his reputation was confirmed, not surprisingly, by the family friend, Livingstone, who commented: 'It was gratifying to find that, though my letters disappeared, Keith Johnston *secundus*, as he ought to be called, had, with the true geographical acumen of my lamented friend Keith Johnston *primus*, conjectured that the drainage went north-west, as I found it, and to the Congo, as I often feared.'[27] At one point Livingstone was to make the very complimentary and somewhat surprising remark – given his attitude towards 'armchair geographers' who presumed to interpret his observations – that Keith Johnston knew more about the catchments of central Africa than the great explorer himself.

Dr Beke had corresponded regularly with Alexander over his *Educational Atlas* and there is nothing to suggest that their relationship was other than cordial. Had

Alexander been alive in 1875, it is very doubtful if the libel case that was brought in the Court of Session in Edinburgh in that year by W. and A. K. Johnston against the *Athenaeum* for a review Beke had written in that periodical would have seen the light of day. The review concerned the *Edinburgh Educational Atlas of Modern Geography* published by W. and A. K. Johnston in 1874 and was highly uncomplimentary:

> The atlas now before us, though bearing the name of A. Keith Johnston, is the work of neither the *primus* nor the *secundus* [quoting Livingstone's appellation above] of that name, for the son is no longer connected with the house established by his late father, but is gone to seek his fortune in Paraguay. And not merely from the present work, but from others which have lately come to our notice, we regret to observe unmistakeable signs of the absence of that 'true geographic acumen' which Livingstone so justly lauded. This 'Educational Atlas', though nicely got up and in this and other respects following the traditions of the firm under whose name it appears, is scarcely a work likely to maintain the special character of the firm, it being one that might have been prepared at the work table of any map-maker of ordinary ability...the same atlas, published by the same firm twenty years or more ago, is to our mind, superior.[28]

The article goes on at considerable length to detail the errors relating to the presentation of the African lakes, quoting all the great explorers from Livingstone to Burton and ends: 'on the whole we miss in this Atlas the presence of the master-mind, in which both father and son, gave to the house of W. and A. K. Johnston the character it has so long enjoyed, but we fear is now losing in the world of science'.

In a reply in the same periodical[29] W. & A. K. Johnston claimed that the atlas was in fact designed and drawn under the superintendence of the late Dr Keith Johnston, but was not published in its present form until the beginning of 1874 and 'after it had received a most careful supervision by Mr Keith Johnston'. In reply, the editor of the *Athenaeum* apologises for its mistake, but does not retract its criticism, saying: 'We did not imagine that Mr Keith Johnston *secundus* would have made the blunders we pointed out last week.'(At this time Keith was in Paraguay and in no position to confirm or refute this.)

After the death of the two senior partners, Alexander and Sir William, the company was led by the youngest brother, Thomas Brumby Johnston, whose propensity for litigation (he took his own son Archibald to court for setting up a rival map publishing agency in London) was not approved of by the rest of the family. Although Thomas Brumby won his case, the family was more sympathetic to the *Athenaeum* when that publication commented 'though the jury had side with Mr T. B. Johnston, the world of science has pronounced in its favour'. Grace was pleased to record that the one mitigating circumstance was the unstinted praise which was accorded to both her father and brother – and that the periodical appeared to hold no grudges, since it later wrote favourable assessments of her own literary work.

The case had in fact generated considerable comment from both the local and national press. *The Times* of 26 March 1875 suggested acidly that it was unfortunate that the review in question had been handed over to 'the somewhat crochetty professional geographer, the late well-known Dr. Beke', who was elsewhere described as a man with a bee in his bonnet, and was much exercised by what they saw as a potential limitation to freedom of the press. The trial was by jury under Lord Justice Clerk Moncrieff and more than 230 pages of it were set out in a private publication by T. B. Johnston, after the original award of £1,275 was reduced to £100 in favour of the firm. The case revolved around the question of the real authorship of the atlas, since the article had implied that, while producing inferior work, the firm was now trading on the reputation of both Alexander and Keith.[30] Although by this time William had retired (under duress) from the firm, he was called as a witness in support of the pursuers and said that the mischief caused by the libel was 'incalculable'. For the defence, the renowned Clements Markham[31] was cross-examined closely on African geography, while Keith's mentor at Stanfords, Trelawney Saunders, was forced to admit that he had, as superintendent of maps, drawn only one insignificant map of the Black Sea in his professional life.[32] What is of interest is Thomas Brumby Johnston's claim, under cross-examination, that the firm had every intention of employing Keith on his return from Paraguay to justify his assertion that Keith was only temporarily absent from W. & A. K. Johnston.

Thomas Brumby Johnston was the youngest of the brothers who formed the partnership of W. and A. K. Johnston and, according to one of his sons,[33] was at odds with the other two elder brothers, but particularly with William. Things reached such a pitch that Alexander issued an ultimatum that the two brothers either resolved their differences, or he himself would resign. With the prestige and credibility that Alexander's professional reputation gave to the firm, this would have been disastrous and, recognising this, William wisely resigned in 1866. Later, after Alexander's death the brothers were to be involved in litigation over some marriage settlement, which greatly distressed Alexander's wife who claimed that she could not recall one kind act towards her husband or herself on the part of her brother-in-law William, who was noted for his 'ungovernable temper and selfish disposition'.

Whatever the difficulty was, it would have tortured the 'ever-gentle' Alexander and undoubtedly cast a long shadow over family relationships. After Alexander's death, Thomas Brumby Johnston took over the firm, which may have been the reason why Keith chose to work independently after 1875, on his return from Paraguay, although one of T. B. Johnston's sons, Thomas Ruddiman Johnston, claimed that both he and Keith had been forced out of the company for unspecified reasons. There was the suspicion that Brumby Johnston and his co-directors simply wished to retain total control and to reduce any financial claims on the firm which William and Alexander had built up to be one of the foremost cartographic houses in Europe. The *Athenaeum* review does give credence to Ruddiman Johnston's claim that, very soon after Alexander's death, the standards of the firm declined, although they were able for some time to trade on the unquestioned reputation of both Alexander and Keith. What is interesting, in relation to the production of a cartographic atlas, is the use of the term 'world of science' as the arbitrar of standards, clearly indicating that geography and associated map-making were now considered fully-fledged aspects of 'science' as it was then understood.

Following his father's death, Keith applied to have the honorary title 'Geographer to the Queen in Scotland' saying 'that it will be of some value to me in carrying forward my father's work which I hope to do'.[34] It is not known whether this request was acceded to, but it seems unlikely, since the Lord Advocate decreed that it could not automatically pass from father to son. What is known is that in 1877 Thomas Brumby Johnston also applied for the title, after Keith had allegedly been requested to leave the firm – he would have been very well aware that, if Keith himself had received the appointment, it would have been a serious matter for the company. The issue was left in abeyance until 1877 when Brumby Johnston was awarded the title, but his son, Thomas Ruddiman Johnston, who as indicated above had also been dropped by the firm, but had subsequently been asked to rejoin it to assist his father, suggests that this was fraudulent.[35] According to him, the factor at Balmoral, a Dr Robertson, a frequent visitor to the firm, made it clear subsequently to Ruddiman Johnston that he would have no difficulty in getting the Royal permission in favour of the senior partner, and that this was accordingly done, despite the fact that the recipient had no claims to the slightest geographical knowledge. It is worth remembering that Ruddiman Johnston published this information in his *Recriminations* when he was conducting a vitriolic campaign against the firm for what he claimed to be the denial of his inheritance, which is, however, substantiated by some remarks by Grace in her *Recollections*. All the indications are that beneath the surface of this eminent and highly respected family firm there was considerable turbulence and possibly even some skulduggery.

Keith wrote articles and letters for the main scientific and literary reviews of the day – his father had complimented him on both the tone and style of his first letter to *Nature,* but he also joined the staff of the *Academy* in 1871, a post he held during his lifetime for this very broadly based periodical. His father, ever anxious to promote his son's interests, wrote 'It would give me great pleasure to aid you in materials for the *Academy,* as it is clearly in the direction of your career' and undertook to make arrangements with the geographical societies of St Petersburg, Rome, etc. to supply materials. In the same letter he said how gratifying it was to receive news of the finding of Dr Livingstone and how cheering this would be for his old friend, Sir Roderick Murchison, the President of the RGS, then seriously ill. Keith himself had, no doubt like many others, volunteered to join the abortive Livingstone Search and Relief Expedition to 'rescue' the missionary/explorer, but was unsuccessful; however, in an obituary by his close friend Henry Bates, it was stated that he withdrew his application under pressure from his friends.[36]

In that year, Keith had followed up his interest in African inland routes by a commentary on the Rev. Thomas Wakefield's *Map of Eastern Africa* which was subsequently published as a separate paper by the RGS.[37] Wakefield[38] was a Methodist missionary who had very carefully recorded the known native trade routes to Lake Victoria and whose work had been strongly commended by several explorers; Keith was later to meet him in Zanzibar and to make considerable use of his experience in planning his own East African expedition. In 1876 The President of the RGS, Sir H. C. Rawlinson, acknowledged Keith's notes in commenting on Verney Lovett Cameron's[39] letters regarding the Livingstone East Coast Expedition in which he had made use of Keith's maps.[40] Keith was clearly now deeply involved with African geography.

Into the Royal Geographical Society

On 8 March 1872, Keith wrote to his mother, telling her of his application for the post of assistant curator and draughtsman to the RGS:

> I think I have a very good chance of getting it, and of being ultimately free of business altogether. The post is not worth 'salt to one's porridge', at present in respect of salary, but…the opportunities for study are most valuable. There is great opposition of most influential candidates, so please keep this in confidence till I tell you for certain that I have been successful, for we are not a lucky family, and I would not like it to be known that I had failed again.

This is a revealing confidence, confirming his distaste for commercial business and his inclination for academic work, which Grace had previously noted. The failure referred to may well have been his abortive application to join the Livingstone Search Expedition mounted by the Society, or more likely his inability to secure the Indian scientific post he had hoped for. In a letter to Clements Markham, the Secretary of the RGS, who was to play an increasingly important part in the Society's affairs over many years, Francis Galton said: 'I am heartily glad that we have so good a candidate as Keith Johnston – who as I now hear from Bates as well as from yourself, places his services *unreservedly* at our disposal, and that he is in fact, quite disconnected from the firm. I am sure we could not do better for the Society than to take him'.[41] He then refers to another candidate: 'I don't quite like to let Bauerstein wholly slip out of our fingers without further thought, though I quite agree with you that we must not through him, play into Petermann's hands'.[42] This apocryphal remark indicates some difficulty with the German geographer at this time who may have been supporting this candidate and might have thought that prejudice against one of his own countrymen had played its part in the selection process.

By April, Grace was able to record: 'It should perhaps have been said that Keith – without any difficulty – secured the post he desired at the "Geographical". He was now much in touch with travellers and men of science, and was closely absorbed in overhauling the map collection and bringing it up to date.' The maps bearing the imprimatur of the RGS carried considerable authority largely because the Society had access to the latest information from those explorers connected with it, such that Murchison described the RGS Map Room as the 'Map Office of the Nation'. (It did in fact receive a Government grant on condition that it made its maps collection accessible to the public.) The RGS had appointed map curators almost from its inception and, as early as 1832, had its own map draughtsmen[43] and had recognised the importance of mapping by awarding a number of its Gold Medals to cartographers, including Keith's father.

Keith had of course many previous connections with the Society, initially through his father, but also through the mapping work which he carried out during his time at the London premises of W. and A. K. Johnston, which would have stood him in very good stead in his application. The RGS had been founded in 1830, with its membership largely drawn from the Asiatic Society and the African Association. It had grown out of a gentleman's dining group called the Raleigh Travellers' Club established by Sir Arthur de Capell Brooke who had a desire to eat, in convivial company, the exotic fare he had encountered on his widespread travels as an army officer. The RGS had a distinguished membership – its first President was the Colonial Secretary Viscount Goderich, and its first chairman was John Barrow,[44] the Second Secretary of the Admiralty, who had instigated many expeditions to the Arctic and Africa (on which he had published works on exploration), almost invariably led by the naval officers who were surplus to requirements following the end of the Napoleonic War. It is hardly surprising that many of the RGS office-bearers and members were navy men, and the first meetings of the Society were held at the Admiralty.

It was John Barrow who had suggested to the Raleigh Club 'that a society was needed whose sole object should be the promotion and diffusion of the most important and entertaining branch of knowledge – geography; and that a useful society might therefore be formed, under the name of *The Geographical Society of London*.' He also proposed that the society should do everything in its power to facilitate the voyages of any explorer who came forward with good ideas as to how that branch might be extended.[45] The RGS was only one of a number of private associations which funded expeditions to support British overseas interests, but its influential membership, often drawn from the Establishment of the day, ensured that it had powerful backing from both commercial and governmental sources. Indeed, it came to be regarded as almost an arm of government, although overtly it tried to retain its scientific independence, supported by many leading scientists and geographers. It was held in high regard by comparable societies abroad who recognised that its accumulated store of information and expertise on matters geographical was probably unparalleled anywhere in the world, and by the mid seventies it had 3,000 members.[46] At least as important as the relatively few expeditions which the RGS sponsored directly was the influence that it had as an adviser and in oiling the wheels of other expeditions through its considerable prestige and accumulated collective knowledge.

The RGS was an important point of information exchange in the world of exploration and geography, particularly in relation to the development of Empire. As one writer has put it 'to map the earth was in this sense to know it. But it could also serve to sustain more directly colonial or imperial projects.' During the mid-Victorian period, the RGS had a high public profile and by the 1870s, when Keith was most actively engaged with it, it became the largest scientific society in London, even if there were considerable differences within its membership on its scientific and exploration roles respectively. It was in fact part social club – and a highly fashionable one at that – part imperial information exchange, and part platform for the promotion of sensational feats of exploration. Its historical context embraced both scientific exploration and Empire building, within which geography was increasingly regarded as the 'science of empire'.[47]

From the early nineteenth century, the world of exploration included a variety of official and quasi-official agencies, such as Kew Gardens, the Admiralty Hydrographic Office, the Royal Engineers, the Ordnance Survey and the Geological Survey. It is not surprising that the first two presidents of the RGS were government colonial ministers, and many of their successors were career diplomats.[48] One of Alexander's closest colleagues was Sir Roderick Murchison, the eminent Scottish geologist, who was a past master in the art of bringing scientists and government together and in turn linking these to the broader national policies of imperial expansion. His biographer has commented '…the context of science, like the style of an empire, is shaped by its cultural context. British geology and geography, as well as other sciences… were significantly influenced by Britain's possession of a colonial empire'.[49] Murchison was but one example, especially in relation to African exploration, of those who moved easily within the networks of geography, government, and at this time, of the influential anti-slavery movement, and who found the RGS a very convenient nodal point for making effective connections and exercising influence.

One of the most important connections between imperialism and science was in fact through cartography, and topographical mapping could be considered as the means for exercising power through territorial knowledge. This geographical knowledge linked to imperial authority was 'a powerful component of the rhetoric of cartography'[50] in which of course both Alexander and Keith were deeply involved. By the mid century, the RGS 'more perfectly represented British expansionism in all its facets than any other institution of the nation'.[51] The RGS even became associated with military campaigns such as that in Abyssinia in 1867, with its accompanying cadre of scientists, while military and civil servants made considerable use of the map room at the Society's headquarters.[52] Large-scale maps of Africa were a feature of the RGS and British Association meetings and of the great public gatherings which welcomed African explorers home, often embellished with the names of both explorers and other public figures who had been commemorated in place names given by such travellers.[53] There is no doubt that Keith would have been called on frequently to provide maps for many such occasions. Keith's obituary in the RGS *Proceedings* states 'he compiled and drew many of the fine wall maps in illustration of our papers at our evening meetings and also some of the best maps in the Journal'.

The only permanent member of staff at the RGS was Henry Walter Bates who was to become one of Keith's few close friends and mentors. Bates had spent 11 years in South America, seven of these on the Upper Amazon, where he had discovered 8,000 species new to science and was greatly admired by Charles Darwin for his scientific insights. Like many of his contemporaries, and probably influenced by Darwinian concepts, Bates did not subscribe to Christian beliefs. It is interesting to speculate in this area how he related to Keith, who came from a rigorously Presbyterian family, and to what extent Keith might have been influenced by Bates in this respect. His descriptions of his natural history explorations in *A Naturalist on the Amazon* were considered to be second only to Humboldt's work. He had been appointed assistant secretary to the RGS in 1864 and served the Society for 28 years, proving himself to be a very able administrator who effectively controlled the funding and mounting of all the expeditions promoted by the RGS and in addition very skilfully edited the Society's *Proceedings* and many other scientific works.[54] He appeared to be universally respected and loved: it was said of Bates 'He gave understanding help to little-known men setting out on their journeys, and when they returned famous, he was usually the first to greet them'[55] Undoubtedly he would have provided the first part of that generosity to Keith when he set out on his expedition to East Africa in 1878.

Despite the differences in their ages, Bates and Keith were not only close friends but had considerable respect for each other, sharing the characteristics of quiet modesty and scientific integrity. Although post-mortem appreciations are often eulogistic, Bates's appreciation of Keith after the latter's death is likely to be a true reflection of Keith's character, emphasising his thoroughness, his horror of all 'scamped' work, but also his total lack of consideration for material gain – in these respects he was undoubtedly his father's son. Bates recalls that when Keith was once told that publication of great usefulness would never pay, he had in all honesty replied that that was 'the last thing to think of'. (It is easy to see why the London branch of W. and A. K. Johnston did not prosper under his hand.) Bates comments on his fluency in German, such that the reading of the scientific literature in that language was a pleasure to him – according to Bates, he had acquired his habit of thoroughness from his time in that country. While he had endeared himself to his friends by his many excellent qualities, and excelled in a number of sports, significantly Bates also points out that 'if he had a fault, it was his exceeding reticence; for it was only to his oldest and most intimate friends that he would occasionally unbend and speak of himself and his aspirations.'[56] This was a characteristic noted by family and many of his friends and was later to greatly influence his crucial relationship with his deputy on his last expedition.

Keith would also have received help from an influential member of the Society, the Society's Honorary Secretary and Expedition Committee member, Sir Francis Galton. Galton was an experienced African traveller who, like the Johnstons, was especially interested in geographical education – he had in fact seconded Keith's application to become a Fellow of the Society. Perhaps more importantly, Galton constantly argued from the 1870s onwards that the RGS should become more scientific. By the time Keith took up his post, the Society's focus had largely been on exploration and survey – especially in eastern Africa. It had after all become quite closely involved with the great explorations of Burton, Speke, Livingstone, Cameron and Stanley in the twenty years which Bridges has defined as the 'classic' period of exploration between 1856 and 1876.[57] Within this remarkably short period of time, the blank space that was central Africa – one of the last great unknowns – had largely been filled in, at least in terms of its main features, especially regarding that obsession, the sources of the Nile and the Congo. But the president of the RGS in 1876, Sir Henry Rawlinson, emphasised the new direction of the society in commenting on Cameron's contributions to the map of Africa through his determination of longitudes: 'The Royal Geographical Society was not instituted for the purpose of merely registering personal adventures or sensational journeys; they had a higher object in view, that of the advancement of pure, substantive, scientific Geography.'

Keith had arrived at a very challenging time, with questions being raised about the Society's primary *raison d'être* now that the initial exploratory phase was ending. He was first faced with the daunting task of rationalising the Society's map collection, running into tens of thousands of individual maps resulting from these explorations, but one which would also give him unrivalled access to a remarkable cartographic resource, not least relating to Africa. Secondly, in a number of ways he bridged the gap between the factions within the Society, which argued on the one hand for the traditional emphasis on exploration and geographic survey, and on the other for greater emphasis on science. As late as 1893 the then President of the RGS stated: 'The first work of geographers is to measure all parts of the land and sea and to fix the relative positions of all places on the earth's surface.'[58]

To further this, and to attempt to standardise measurement methods, the RGS published at periodic intervals from 1854 onwards its *Hints to Travellers*, which were effectively instruction manuals to focus intending travellers on the gathering of information useful to science, rather than, as had often been the case in the past, to provide impressionistic sketches of the countries through which they were passing. Keith would have been well aware of this publication, the fourth edition appearing under the editorship of Francis Galton in the year of the RGS East African expedition.

The fourth edition included an explorer's outfit and its packing (with a chapter by the Zanzibar Consul, Dr John Kirk, on the carriage of instruments), surveying and methods of observation, and the collection of natural history objects by H. W. Bates, the last covering no less than 10 pages. His descriptions of some of the processes might dissuade some sensitive souls: 'a small piece of the skull is now cut away…and the brains and the eyes scooped out, the inside washed with soap and clean cotton filled in, the eyes especially being made plump'.[59] John Kirk even went to the length of strongly advising travellers to put down native names in print rather than script form since 'numerous errors and great loss of time now result in the attempt to decipher proper names written by travellers in their ordinary handwriting only'. There is great insistence on sextants as the key instruments and the need to become familiar with their use (an issue which was to arise critically in the 1878 expedition) with a detailed chapter on this by Francis Galton. In a sense, these *Hints* encapsulated the whole argument about the objectives and methodologies of exploration and scientific study respectively, with its emphasis on the need for accurate observation and instrumentation, for example. In another sense, it was an attempt by the RGS to exert some authority in this field, even if the latter was too diverse to be contained in this way.[60]

A brush with Henry Morton Stanley

The concern for the promotion of science was reflected also in the establishment of the British Association for the Advancement of Science a year after that of the RGS and which has been in existence ever since. Its annual meetings included a geographical section – effectively the summer meeting of the RGS – of which Keith was the Secretary, and which obviously involved a considerable amount of administrative work. Unable to join the family on a Lake District holiday in the summer of 1872, Keith wrote:

> The Association meeting (at Brighton) begins, according to the programme just arranged, on the 14th of August. Till then I shall be busily engaged in preparation for it, since the mainstay of the Section is in the papers gathered from the Geographical Society…we are also in daily expectation of a large budget from Livingstone which will give rise to a vast amount of work and will form a main feature of the Meeting.

It seems most likely that Keith was referring to the 'budget of news', i.e. the letters and journals of Livingstone, which Stanley had brought back after his famous meeting with Livingstone and which eventually were passed over to the geographers for interpretation.[61] It was known that Stanley and Livingstone had together proved that Lake Tanganyika did not have an outflow to the north and thus to the Nile, as Burton and his supporters had claimed, and which Stanley would describe: all-in-all this would be a very momentous meeting, not least for Keith who had deeply immersed himself in this very subject, as indicated both by his scientific papers and correspondence in the periodicals of the time.

However, Keith came into serious conflict with Stanley late in August 1872 as a result of a map which he had prepared to accompany an article in Clement Markham's publication *Ocean Highways*. In a speech reported in the press, Stanley accused Keith, among other things, of inaccurate recording of names of native villages, of being discourteous in not acknowledging his sources, of failing to credit Stanley with the route which he had pioneered and, most offensively, of making use of Livingstone's discoveries solely for financial profit. Keith was obviously shocked by this, to the extent that he felt obliged to make a very robust point-by-point rejoinder. In his unpublished letter of 3 September to the explorer, Keith expressed his concern:

> I have been compelled in self defence to write to the 'Observer' and 'Morning Post' in which papers your speech was reported in full, contradicting the erroneous impression which must be given by your words, and which if left unnoticed will be most damaging to me since every word you say is read with the utmost eagerness throughout the country.
>
> The position in which I find myself with respect to you gives me much greater concern than I can tell you, and I consider myself most unfortunate in thus having unintentionally come into collision with one for whose enterprise I have all along had the highest admiration.
>
> I do not wish in any way to connect the Geographic Society with this matter, for the Society has nothing to do with it and any blame must rest with me alone, but you will allow me to say that you are much mistaken in thinking that the Geographical Society as a body, has any other feeling towards you than gratitude for having saved Dr. Livingstone, and 'geographical' respect for your solution of the knotty problem of the north end of Tanganyika.[62]

Stanley's attitude towards Keith would have been coloured by a number of factors, not least that the editor of *Ocean Highways*, Clements Markham, a pillar of the RGS establishment, was antagonistic towards him and had written in derisory terms about the 'worst type of Yankee journalism'. Stanley saw himself as Livingstone's champion and, categorising Keith as yet another 'armchair geographer', would have resented the cartographer's work which showed that his hero was in error over the source of the Nile, a subject on which Stanley was sensitive. There is no doubt that, in turn, Keith's attitude towards Stanley would have been influenced by this unpleasant episode when he encountered him seven years later in Zanzibar.

Stanley himself attended the meeting to address the Geographical Section of the British Association, invited by a reluctant RGS which had to acknowledge his public acclaim following his 'finding' of Livingstone, although there were not a few in the Society who were fiercely opposed to his methods. But the RGS had become very strongly associated with Livingstone in the public mind, and indeed, like others, used the great man's name to further its own aims – it could be said that it was Livingstone, strongly supported by Murchison, who had made African exploration a national obsession. As the star attraction, Stanley drew an attendance of over 3,000 and gave his usual colourful presentation. However, the chairman, Francis Galton, in what could only have been a deliberate attempt to humiliate Stanley (and which the latter deeply resented) alluded to rumours concerning Stanley's birth and upbringing – while proclaiming himself as an American, Stanley had attempted to disguise the fact that he was illegitimate and had been brought up in a poorhouse in North Wales.[63]

The fact that Stanley was a journalist and engaged in what some derisively called 'sensational exploration' did not commend him to the more class-conscious RGS members – clearly Stanley was not a 'gentleman' in their terms. Neither apparently did they consider him a geographer: Clements Markham, in his unpublished history of the RGS, records his own words when faced with Stanley's apparent public popularity 'Damn public opinion – the fellow has done no geography!'[64] Keith, who was later to encounter Stanley in Africa, is more than likely to have agreed with this estimate, from the remarks in both his expedition diary and letters to his sister Grace. Significantly, following Keith's death, she was to judge Keith's deputy, Joseph Thomson, by very similar criteria: this form of snobbery provides the leitmotif of the times and perhaps especially of the gentlemen's club which was the RGS.

Perhaps in anticipation of the expected news from the great African traveller, Lord Tweeddale, an indefatigable traveller and noted ornithologist, wrote begging Keith to dine with him and meet 'young Livingstone' (presumably one of Livingstone's sons). Lord Haughton too extended his hospitality, showing that the son was not forgotten by his father's friends.

The restless cartographer

In these great debates regarding science, geography, and exploration, Keith was in the unusual position of being a highly professional cartographer but, as has already been indicated, with a broad interest in and knowledge of scientific subjects. Added to this breadth of interest he already had an explorer's instinct – that restlessness which was to lead eventually to both South America and East Africa. His father had pioneered physical geography and education in that field, to which Keith had also made considerable contributions. Keith was also entering a milieu dominated up to this point by the relatively wealthy and privileged who had regarded travel as an 'amusement' undertaken for interest, overlain by explorers motivated to a greater or lesser extent by the possibility of fame, if not fortune. The RGS was in many respects a somewhat exclusive social club, with a considerable leavening of affluent grandees from the shires of southern England. Many of these had an interest in the expanding Empire, either for overtly commercial reasons or because of the possibilities for positions of importance and influence for either themselves or their offspring. While the Society was not ostensibly a tool for imperialism, it undoubtedly furthered the ends of Empire building, if only through the results of the expeditions which it sponsored and the essential maps which resulted. In his work at the RGS and his leadership of the Society's 1878 expedition, not only was Keith very much part of this process, but it could be said that his intimate association with the Society would inadvertently lead to his early death.

The times in which Keith lived before the expedition were the years when Britain was probably at the zenith of its industrial and imperial power. It has been claimed that by the 1860s Britain was virtually the only truly industrial economy in the world, following its Industrial Revolution, and that it accounted for more than a third of the world's entire output of manufactured goods – the so-called 'Workshop of the World'.[65] It was also a leader in scientific and technological discovery and invention – the Babcock and Wilcox boiler for steam generation could power ships laden with 3,000 tons of cargo which could steam at 10 knots for more than 8,000 miles, cutting off a month from the return journey to China, for example. Queen Victoria had been declared Empress of India in 1877, the same year in which the Transvaal had been annexed by Britain, which had also secured its routes to the East by purchasing the most critical section of the Suez Canal two years previously. Communications were to be revolutionised by the laying of the transatlantic telegraph cable by the British *Great Eastern* as early as 1865 while, seven years later, England was connected by telegraph to Australia, which was the year in which the *Challenger* expedition explored the Atlantic, Pacific and Indian Oceans to establish oceanography as a serious science for the first time. In Britain, there were important advances in medicine and public health, with Lister's pioneering of antiseptic surgery in 1865 and the discovery that cholera could be contained by control of water supplies.

Many of these events and developments in science, technology and overseas expansion were at least partially stimulated by the scientific and exploration societies of the time, notably the British Association for the Advancement of Science and the RGS. These provided very influential networks of eminent men covering a wide range of disciplines and interests, not excluding the landed gentry who continued to regard travel as an acceptable occupation for gentlemen (women were not usually included) with a passing curiosity in observing the habits of exotic cultures, but others, such as Sir Roderick Murchison, a well-connected landowner, became highly respected scientists. In Keith's time, however, there was considerable tension at the RGS between those who espoused science at the expense of somewhat dilettante travel. The societies provided a crucial debating chamber and outlet for the many advances of the time, both in published papers and peer criticism. Anybody who was anybody in the world of science would either be a Fellow or a member of at least one of such societies, a position much sought after by anyone wishing to make a name for himself in his field.

Keith was especially privileged in this regard in being introduced to these relatively exclusive clubs by his father at a remarkably early age, and many of the well-known names of the time, such as Livingstone, Burton and Speke, would have been familiar to him. Backed by his father's reputation and his own scientific acumen, he would have moved easily and comfortably in such eminent circles, being brought up in a household where such names would be bandied about on a daily basis and where they would often be welcome visitors. Later, particularly in his position as assistant maps curator at the RGS, he would be required to prepare the maps for the meetings of the Society, listen to and contribute to the discussions of the explorers, and even help to edit their notes for publication – all this at a time when the Empire was continuing to expand, and when the doings of the explorers and missionaries were matters of great public interest.

In addition, as secretary responsible for the organising of the geographical section of the British Association's annual meeting, he was brought closely in touch with that important scientific society (the older Royal Society having atrophied somewhat), so that he was in a particularly favourable position, not only to be intimately aware of the major scientific developments of the time, but also to meet and have intercourse with those influencing such events. Based in London (at that time regarded as the pre-eminent capital of the world because of Britain's imperial power), Keith was very much at the hub of a Victorian world which was both exciting and enterprising, consorting with the relatively limited number of eminent geographers, explorers and scientists who constituted this network at the forefront of discovery. It is hardly surprising that he was restless and wanted to play a more obviously active part in it than being a desk cartographer, however valuable.

However, Keith was not entirely satisfied with his situation at the RGS and on 17 March 1873 he wrote to his mother:

> The news I have to give you is the prospect – still looming in the distance – of an improvement of my position at the Geographical. Stanford made me an offer some days ago of the Editorship of his publications, maps and books...I do not fancy going back to him at all unless under greatly improved conditions, but his offer has given me ground to go upon in an appeal to the Council of the Society, and I hope to decide one way or the other in a week or two...

In fact, it appears that Stanfords did not improve on their offer or that the RGS had met Keith's requirements, for his employment terminated with them in October 1873 when he had already made up his mind to accept a commission from the Paraguayan Government to carry out a boundary survey in that country.

In the early 1870s, Keith had been steadily extending his interests from the mapping of particular regions such as East and Central Africa into much more general geographic fields such as climatology and its relationship to the definition of types of landscape and vegetation on a world-wide scale. In 1874 he published *The Surface Zones of the Globe: A Handbook to Accompany a Physical Chart* whose objectives described by the *Athenaeum* review were to 'give the meteorological causes for the great effects visible on the earth's surface with regard to vegetable or non vegetable conditions'. In this work, Keith had divided the world into climatic zones from arctic to desert, incorporating the effects of altitude, etc. The review was glowing: 'We have seldom read a work that contains so much pleasant information conveyed in such simple unconstrained language, and yet bearing evidence throughout of careful study and thought.'[66]

The publication is in fact a highly significant piece of integrated geographical work, and was probably the first time that a scientific rationale had been provided for the relatively discrete biogeographical zones which occur world-wide, taking account of ocean currents, winds, altitude, etc. and incorporating the observations of many other travellers by way of field confirmation. He included, for example, the observations of his friend Henry Bates for his description of the primeval forest of the Amazon, together with a sketch from Bates's work. This anticipated by almost a century the more detailed biogeographical studies which were to become a foundation for global conservation planning in the World Conservation Strategy of 1971.

NOTES

1 National Library of Scotland, Edinburgh, W. & A. K. Johnston Archive. II.
2 Scott-Moncrieff (1966), 31–58.
3 Daiches (1980), 200–201.
4 Hutton (1875).
5 Gavine (1982) ii, 541.
6 *Merchiston Castle School Register* (1862), 665.
7 Murray (1915), 34–35.
8 Young (1933), 35–43.
9 Grierson (1909), 131.
10 Johnston, A.K. Snr (1869), 561–79.
11 Admiral Carl Ludwig Christian Irminger (1802–88) was particularly interested in geography and hydrography and was a foreign member of the RGS, co-founding the Danish equivalent in 1876. He collected large amounts of data from shipmasters' observations on currents in the North Atlantic commencing the first systematic hydrographic studies of the seas around Iceland.
12 Carpenter (1874), 367–8.
13 Smith (2000), 9–15.
14 Dreyer-Eimbecke (1997), 26.
15 Herbert (1983), 7.
16 Smith (1998), 23.
17 RGS Archives, fo. 25.
18 Bridges (1993), 13.
19 Bridges (1994), 12–16.
20 Johnston, A.K. Jnr (1870c), 122–41.
21 Keith writing to the RGS on 21 October 1872 indicated that he was working on a map for Captain Burton 'since he must see it before he goes' – this was following Burton's recall from Damascus and prior to taking up his consular post in Trieste (RGS Archives, fo. 25). Richard Francis Burton (1821–90), one of the most colourful of the nineteenth-century African explorers, became deeply embroiled in the bitter controversy with his expedition colleague John Hanning Speke over the sources of the Nile. His fraught relationship with Speke, which became a public scandal, may well have influenced the RGS in their reactions to the later similar difficulty between Keith and Joseph Thomson.
22 Sir. H. C. Rawlinson (1810–95) A distinguished soldier, Rawlinson travelled widely in India and the Near East and made his name as a scholar by interpreting important Assyrian inscriptions. He became Consul General of Baghdad in 1851, and was a member of the India Council till his death. He was President of both the Royal Asiatic Society and the RGS and contributed many learned papers to their journals.
23 *Proc. RGS* (1870), 330.
24 *Proc. RGS* (1872), 367.
25 *Athanaeum*, 11 Dec. 1875, 793.
26 *Nature*, 27 Jan. 1870, 330–7.
27 *Proc. RGS* (1874), 269.
28 *Athanaeum*, 11 July 1874, 53–4.
29 *Athanaeum*, 18 July 1874, 85.
30 Johnston, W. & A. K. (1875), 31.

31 Sir Clements Markham (1830–1916): Honorary Secretary to the RGS for 25 years and its President for 12 years from 1893. Following several years as geographer to the India Office, he was most active in promoting Arctic and Antarctic exploration. A prolific writer on geographical subjects, he was disinclined to favour the scientific approach over more traditional exploration.

32 Johnston, W. & A. K. (1875), 90.

33 Johnston, T.R. (n.d.) *Second Series of notes in Reply to a Circular issued by the Directors of W. & A.K. Johnston Ltd.*, 4. *The Recriminations of the Johnston Family* appeared as a series of privately published pamphlets (undated but probably around 1901) by Thomas Ruddiman Johnston while he was in business in Japan. In these, he bitterly accuses the partners of the firm (his brothers) and other directors of being deceitful and fraudulent regarding the financial position of the company and presiding over its decline since the death of Alexander.

34 RGS Archives, fo. 25.

35 Johnston, T. R. (n.d.), 3rd Pamphlet *What Security have the Shareholders of W. & A.K. Johnston?*

36 Bates, Henry in Thomson, J. (1881a), xvi.

37 Wakefield (1872), 125–9.

38 Thomas Wakefield (1836–1901): a United Methodist Free Church Missionary, ethnographer, naturalist and translator. Wakefield served the mission at Ribe in Kenya continuously for 27 years. His knowledge of the trade routes from the coast to the interior, gleaned from many sources, was highly respected by East African explorers. He was awarded a RGS Fellowship in 1889.

39 Verney Lovett Cameron (1844–94) was a naval commander who discovered the source of the Zambezi and was the first European to cross Africa from east to west.

40 *Proc. RGS* (1874), 127.

41 Francis Galton (1822–1911): an African explorer and a cousin of Charles Darwin. Galton was active in the RGS and many other scientific societies. He was noted for his research into human physical attributes and heredity, and confirmed the permanence of fingerprints for use in criminal investigations.

42 RGS Archives, fo. 25.

43 Bridges (1987a), 11.

44 John Barrow (1764–1848): Second secretary to the Admiralty for 40 years and co-founder of the RGS. Barrow travelled in China and South Africa. He was particularly influential in promoting exploration, especially in the Arctic and the attempts to find the North West Passage.

45 Fleming (1998), 275.

46 Bridges (1973), 220–32.

47 Driver (2001), 21–5.

48 Ibid., 41.

49 Stafford (1989), 222.

50 Driver (2001), 39.

51 Stafford (1989), 211–12.

52 Driver (2001), 44–5.

53 Ibid., 78.

54 Cameron (1980), 203–4.

55 Woodcock (1969), 257–8.

56 Bates, H.W. in Thomson (1881a), xviii.

57 Bridges (1987b), 9.
58 Ibid., 10; Galton (1878).
59 RGS Archives.
60 Driver (1989), 56.
61 Bridges, personal communication.
62 Koninklijk Museum voor Midden Afrika, Tervuren, Belgium. Archive of H.M. Stanley – Correspondence with Keith Johnston.
63 Driver (1989), 78.
64 RGS Archives.
65 Hyam (1993), 25–6.
66 *Athenaeum*, 25 July 1874, 117.

5

A Paraguayan Adventure:
the First Exploration

———

'No more "easy" or rather "uneasy" chair geography for a time' – so announced Keith on 10 October 1873 of his intention to assist a Paraguayan boundary survey early in 1874 – his first overseas geographical commission. The 'unease' almost certainly refers to his increasing distaste for sedentary and 'inky-fingered' work at the RGS and his desire for more adventurous action. Little did he know what he was letting himself in for.

Slightly larger than Germany, Paraguay has two contrasting parts – the rich rolling lands of the east with their wooded hills where most of the present population is concentrated, and the flat infertile plain of the Gran Chaco in the west, much of it savannah grassland, mainly used for cattle ranching. The country is entirely land-locked. Although part of the Spanish Empire from 1524, it was only lightly colonised by the Spaniards and became independent after a bloodless revolt against the Spanish conquerors in 1811. Paraguay in the nineteenth century was virtually closed to outsiders. In 1864, the President, Francisco Solano Lopez – who saw himself as the Napoleon of South America – declared a suicidal war, first on Brazil and then on Argentina and Uruguay, the so-called Triple Alliance. A ruthless commander, Lopez executed all who retreated, and even signed the death warrant of his own mother. It was not until Lopez was killed by Brazilian troops at the battle of Cero Cora in March 1870 that the war ended. For Paraguay, it had been an unmitigated disaster. Keith in his boundary commission work followed the exact line of Lopez's last march from his camp at Panadero to the wild and beautiful amphitheatre of Cerro Cora and graphically described the scene:

> The track tells too plainly of the miseries which accompanied this final retreat of his army, for all along it at little intervals lie the unburied and undisturbed skeletons of men who had lain down to die of weariness or starvation almost within sight of one another. Every little shade tree along the path had its heap of bones beneath it, sometimes with the rusty gun or sword, or weathered saddle lying beside.[1]

When Keith reached Lopez's last camp at Cero Cora, surrounded by its fantastic cones, cliffs and castellated towers of eroded sandstone, he noted: 'it remains as it was suddenly left: the wrecks of baggage carts and store boxes, broken arms, ammunition and gun carriages are thickly strewn about; bones of men too lie scattered in great numbers.'

It seems a remarkable coincidence, not least given Keith's later exploration in East Africa, that the outstanding African explorer Richard Francis Burton, for whom Keith had prepared maps in 1872, had been present at some of these battles in 1868 and 1869 (which he described in *Letters from the Battlefield of Paraguay* published in 1870) and might well have been present at the scenes of which Keith witnessed the aftermath. It is inconceivable that he would not have sought Captain Burton's advice on this area before his own departure.

The aristocratic Scottish explorer, Robert Cunninghame-Graham, who was in the country at the same time as Keith, described the rarity of encountering males: Lopez had recruited his army from men from the age of fourteen. Only just over half the population had survived the war, many dying of disease and starvation. Cunninghame-Graham records:[2]

> There were roads in the district of the Upper Parana, which I myself remember as a wilderness, uncrossed, uncrossable, where tigers roamed about and Indians shot at the rare traveller with poisoned arrows out of a blow-pipe, while they remained unseen in the recesses of the woods...The depopulation of the country, owing to the recent long war, had allowed the tigers to multiply to an extraordinary degree, and my guide and myself, after feeding our horses, had to sleep alternately, the waker holding the two horses hobbled and bridled.[3]

A more colourful description of the wildlife is given by Professor Leone, who was the Consul General for Paraguay in London, and to whom Keith was required to report:

> The chattering monkeys, the audacious jaguar, the spiteful tiger, the ferocious lion, are all there, there are the vulture and the ostrich, the crocodile and the chameleon, the viper, the serpent, and many other reptiles, whose presence is often far too near human habitations to be borne with indifference, while the mosquitoes are themselves a great nuisance.[4]

The same article promotes Paraguay as a land of untapped commercial resources: 'which England should help to develop...but internecine wars between her and other States continue to be, as heretofore, of frequent occurrence, or should bands of marauders or bandits still produce insurrections and confusion, there is nothing before Paraguay but misery and desolation'.

However, Cunninghame-Graham records that rather than danger, he was more at risk from hunger and extreme discomfort, with incessant rain bringing on rheumatism – which Keith was also to experience.

Despite these very unsettled conditions, Keith was anxious to leave his desk-bound existence behind. He wrote to his sister Grace:

> Till the end of the year I must give all my time to the Dictionary, to get it fairly back-broken. It drags along most woefully just now...I have today made an agreement with the Paraguayan Minister here to go out to his country as a geographer to a commission which will wander through the length of the land...the salary to be guaranteed at £500, a geologist plus botanist to accompany me.

In her turn, Grace records: 'From our father's splendid library, still housed with us, I was able to send him, at his wish, many books bearing on the subject of his coming travels.' He was in fact to be a geographer in a mixed party of Paraguayans and Brazilians responsible after the war for surveying and demarcating the boundary between their respective countries.

However, despite being scheduled to leave for Paraguay in January, even by mid-December, he had been unable to obtain a completed contract from the Paraguayan authorities. This tardiness was to plague all his dealings with the Paraguayan officials and caused him serious problems throughout his stay in that country. He consoled himself by having a Mr Twite to accompany him, a geologist 'who seemed a very agreeable and companionable sort of fellow'. Keith's mother, just before his departure, wrote very caringly:

> May our heavenly father watch over you all the way and grant me the joy of seeing you again...My dear son, you will send me a letter ere you go telling me, I hope, that all is well arranged for your safety and comfort...I can only think of your going...

(Keith's mother, who had been unwell, was travelling in Italy at this time and, early in 1874, he wrote to her in his final letter before departure from England expressing his concern about the catastrophic eruption of Vesuvius which he hoped she had not been caught up in.)

At Lisbon, Keith took time to visit his uncle Archibald's grave 'the place of the well-remembered picture which hung in Father's dressing room at March Hall'. This would have been the gravesite of the naval surgeon who died from typhoid. After getting along famously with his companions as far as Lisbon, he did not take kindly to the new passengers who boarded there, preferring more exalted company:

> A number of English passengers left us and in their place we have a crowd of Portuguese for the Brazils, dirty fellows, all of them, card playing, quarrelling and smoking...I spend the time over Spanish and playing chess with the Paraguayan Minister.

En route to Paraguay, he provided contrasting descriptions of St Vincent:

the most wretched and parched piece of desert one could well conceive, scarcely a blade of grass to be seen on it and the hot sun blazes down on it with suffocating heat...the negroes are miserable beings, and seem to live half their time swimming in the water, which is certainly preferable to the land if it wasn't for the sharks!

and Rio de Janeiro, which he was enchanted with, likening its botanic gardens to a garden of Eden.

Writing to his mother on 16 March, Keith complained about the interminable delays caused by the laid-back officials and the three weeks he had been forced to wait in Montevideo before he was able to get a steamer for Asuncion, the capital of Paraguay. On the way up the Parana River, Keith described the endless and monotonous forests, the brightly coloured birds, and the many alligators which 'are seen waddling down each bit of mudbank to hide all but the tip of their nose and eyes in the water'. But on arrival at Asuncion he found that his colleagues, Irvine and Balzano, were still waiting for the recently changed Government to recognise the Commission and grant supplies and transport. He wrote:

> The town of Asuncion plainly shows the wretched condition into which the long wars under Lopez, reduced the country. Most of its public buildings stand exactly as they were left after the Brazilian cannonade of the town four years ago. The streets once on a level with the house doors have been hollowed out by the rains till some are grass-grown ravines 10 or 12 feet below the bits of pavement which hang on the sides, here and there.

Keith referred to dereliction of the railway built by British engineers 15 years earlier:

> Till the day before yesterday one train a week was managed but a final rainstorm two days ago has laid a final straw on the camel's back... The government servants are paid by promissory notes which only yield 12 per cent of their value in the market, and the soldiers are being discharged unpaid for long periods... I write in my room in the 'best hotel in Asuncion' a little shed-like place with a window and a rickety door in which my hammock and boxes are the chief articles of furniture. The roof leaks rather, so that two nights ago I had to turn out as a pool was forming rapidly in the hollow of the hammock.

This incidentally is an evocative description by Keith, which conveys very economically both a picture of the town and his situation.

It was in fact only after Irvine's threat to resign, after waiting a full six weeks, that the Commission's work was finally approved. The Commission consisted of three or four Brazilian officers with about 40 men, and a Paraguayan detachment: a captain with 10 boy soldiers. Keith, who was generally disparaging about his military escort, remarked that the Brazilians had done all the work and provided the stores while the

Paraguayans looked on at a respectful distance and signed their names when required. Sometimes the work was arduous, such as cutting a path of over 120 miles through one stretch of dense forest. Although only wide enough to allow laden mules to pass, it required 6 months in cutting, and during this time the Commission suffered considerably from continual rains, losing many animals since the only food to be found for them in the forest was the succulent topmost leaves of the palms. The cutting of these paths raised the ire of the local natives who, headed by their military chief, appeared with 40 bowmen, demanding to know what the Commission was up to and why they were cutting paths which might allow their enemies access to their territory.

In the course of his survey work and his own explorations in the south of the country, Keith saw for himself the conditions described by Cunninghame-Graham, with the people in the most dire poverty and misery, remarking:

> It would be impossible to exaggerate the utter desolation which the long war has brought upon the southern part of Paraguay...in a few mud ranchos, often a league or two apart, some old women (for there is scarcely a man left in this part of the country) drag out a miserable existence, living on oranges and mandioca. [a cereal used for making bread]

He describes having to wade for two or three days along the edge of an endless waste of tall grass, skirting patches of impenetrable forest, often having to dismount in the mud to lead their tired horses, sometimes wading in mud and water up to their thighs.

Despite this, Keith thoroughly enjoyed himself in the country:

> You can fancy me generally jogging along on my jolly mule behind our string of carts which keep up a rumble-tumble, creak and squeak and groan as they move over tall grass and through pine clumps and little woods, and I up and down taking sights and notes right and left and as jolly and well as I have been in my life and as brown as a cigar.

However, to indicate that he was not enjoying himself so much as to be forgetful of home ties, he said: 'I have often, you may be sure, plenty of time when plodding along in the sun, to think back of home and of you all, one by one, and I can't help wishing now and then for just a glimpse of everybody.'

He was accompanied by an ex-Rugby schoolboy, Thornber ('well up to all manner and modes of travelling') and the two parties of soldiers from the Paraguayan and Brazilian sides, supported by ancient carts under which they slept, and whose axles were constantly breaking over the rough terrain, so that a tree had to be cut down to fashion another. The two sides kept out of each other's way, with the Paraguayans especially eschewing association with their conquerors. Food was frequently in short supply and Keith was obliged at one point to shoot some pheasants when they had entirely run out of rations. Referring to the first storms after a long drought, Keith noted:

> our soldier boys are huddled in the carts to keep themselves dry, and my companion Thornber is making the best of it beneath one of them. I write in my little tent in which one can scarcely sit upright, it is so very small, using my box for table, under difficulties, as the candle light is very much disturbed by the wind. But the rain seems as healthy and good for me as the old Arran soakings…

Nevertheless, they encountered more than simply tropical showers, Keith describing one of the frequent furious thunderstorms:

> One of these storms, more violent than usual, threw down the first mark [i.e. boundary markers] as soon as it was built and a second had scarcely been completed when a *tormenta*, accompanied with large hailstones, coming on at night, levelled our tents, and made the column a heap also.

But worse was to come:

> For us, however, the rain was far preferable to fair weather; for as soon as it ceased we were beset with clouds of little stinging flies…each one in biting left a blood blister on the hand or face; the horses and mules, tortured to madness by them, would break from their halters and run off in any direction to be free of the plague. This pest of flies afterwards became so bad that the hands and face swelled up from the irritation of their bites, and on fair days nothing could be done but to pray for sunset, since at that time they retired, giving way to the almost welcome ping of the ordinary mosquito.

While Keith seemed quite capable and resourceful under such conditions, and his rougher rambles in the West Highlands no doubt stood him in good stead, he did not spare those at home what he had to put up with. There was also something of the Boy Scout here, 'smiling and whistling under all difficulties' indicating a Victorian manliness which tries to avoid any suggestion of 'whingeing'. However, his later experiences would certainly give him something to whinge about: after returning to Asuncion to write his report following three months survey work with the Boundary Commission, he proposed to the Government that he should map the central part of the country.

In his published account of his travels in the *Geographical Magazine* of 1875, Keith gave a very detailed description of the country, not only of its physical features and vegetation, but also its condition and peoples, making perceptive comments on its economic potential. In his notes for the RGS[5] Keith demonstrated, from this first overseas exploration, that he was a very careful and assiduous observer providing a clear unadorned topographical description, including for example the delineation of the river catchments, the amplitude of the rise and falls of the river, and detailed comments on the meteorology of the country from the records of temperature, comparing this with equivalent latitudes in West Africa. Not content with a general description of the forests, he provided extended notes on individual trees and their timber properties. But he was also capable on occasion, without descending into purple prose, of evoking the experience of natural events, such as this accurate description of a tropical storm, which could hardly be bettered:

> The blackness spread up over the sky in wildly whirling clouds; a gust of chilly wind struck the river below us, lashing it up into waves and spindrift, raising great clouds of sand from a bank on the Paraguayan side, and bending over the palms and other trees of the banks. Quick flashes of forked lightning shot here and there, and the river assumed a strange dark olive-green colour, on which the white waves curled. Striking the *baranca*, the waves undermined and hurled down great masses of bank with a roaring sound, which added to the din of the incessant thunder-claps. In the next reach a blast caught the steamer and whirling her round broadside, drove her hard-and-fast on the bank.

In the meantime, Twite the geologist had resigned after three months, and Balzano was still believed to be in Paraguay, but completely destitute. It says much therefore for Keith that, under these circumstances, he decided to take the opportunity to explore on his own account and to persevere in his negotiations with the Paraguayan Government. There were the usual interminable delays in getting a response, and with a companion, a Royal Navy lieutenant called Congreve, he set off on several small independent explorations, always hoping that, on his return, he would have an affirmative answer to his proposals. Running out of both money and credit, he fell on seriously hard times, and they had to sell the last of Congreve's furniture to eat.[6] The government had not paid him for his official survey work, but neither were they enthusiastic about the prospect of him leaving the country, since he would undoubtedly reveal his shabby treatment at their hands – there was every indication that officials would attempt to detain him. In a letter to the Academy, Keith said:

> It would take too long to tell you of the months of revolution, changes of government and vexatious delays of the *Manyana* system which ultimately broke up our commission. We found Paraguay ruined and bankrupt, degraded materially and morally to an extent which can hardly be believed. It was not until after the Brazilians, who now virtually rule the country, had interfered to save the remnant of the Paraguayans from themselves, that it was possible to go beyond the dilapidated streets of Asuncion. The policy of Brazil seems to be to maintain Paraguay in a nominal independence, using the country as a buffer between the Empire and the Argentine Republic; but at the same time accumulating over it a load of debts and obligations from which Paraguay will never be able to shake itself free, and the garrison of 3,000–4,000 men in Asuncion is amply sufficient to ensure that the country will never again think differently from Brazil.

97

Keith had for some time wished to explore the River Tebicuari, and he and Congreve succeeded in slipping away without detection, reluctantly giving away their faithful horses and forwarding their luggage to Montevideo, while they themselves detoured around the Cordillera through very unknown country. At the head of the Tebicuari, they obtained a canoe, with the object of drifting downstream to the Paraguay, surveying by traverse as they went. They faced some formidable obstacles, since there was only one house between the headwaters and the mouth of the River Tebicuari – a distance of several hundred miles, so that they would have to hunt and fend for themselves. Then it was a question of getting clear of Paraguay by floating down as far as Corrientes – and either go all the way by canoe, or somehow get a steamer to Montevideo or Buenos Aires. What this indicates is that Keith was nothing if not adventurous, and even possibly foolhardy, but of course the circumstances created their own imperatives. At Itape, Keith saw the failed English colony with 800 immigrants sent out two years previously, and commented: 'A combination of bad management, bad faith on the part of the Government and bad material in the shape of the colonists, the most of whom had been gathered from the slums of Whitechapel, served to make a complete fiasco.'

The journey down the river took three times longer than expected because of its extremely tortuous course (which is readily confirmed by a glance at the map of the country), and it was not until 15 February that they reached Corrientes, but before they could reach Rosario, disaster struck:

> we were almost suddenly brought into a place where a strong current sets across the river from the high *barranca* [gorge] which, meeting the wind, raised a heavy sea which soon filled our canoe. We had managed to get within about 20 yards of the *barranca* before she completely filled, but then she rolled over, and out went all our baggage, instruments, maps, provisions and what not, sailing swiftly down the current, never to be seen again! For ourselves we had no fear. The canoe turned bottom up, and we could sit there alright. I managed to get hold of a paddle, and Congreve swam for our case of passports which happily floated near us.

Keith did not mention that he had also lost all his notes – in writing on 25 October 1875 to Captain George, the officer at the RGS responsible for collating explorers' scientific observations, Keith said: 'I find that only a few boiling-point observations have been saved: the rest have long ago been digested by the fishes of the Parana.'[7]

They bailed out the canoe and, with one paddle and a cane, managed to reach a friendly butcher who believed their tale. Apparently he got a pair of trousers for Congreve and put the benighted adventurers up for a few days. They managed to seal the canoe sufficiently to get them to a telegraph office to enable them to send a message to Montevideo for relief, and to pay their passage there. Like a couple of tramps, they took up residence on the public benches in the main square and were warned to keep clear of the police, who would arrest them, and always keep one step ahead – 'Congreve with a tattered shirt and a pair of "bombachos" – I with a jersey only and ragged flannels.'

Coming as he did from an ultra-respectable Edinburgh family, Keith's description presents an amusing picture of him and his companion as apparently disreputable hobos, down on their luck, and it is to Keith's credit that he could obviously see the irony of it. The remainder of the story is a sorry one of trying to get money out of the bank, while the British Consul was unhelpful. They then found that their luggage from Asuncion and transport to Montevideo, which had been paid for, had been embargoed, no doubt by the Paraguayan authorities. In the meantime, no money had been received from home – although Keith had submitted his report on the Boundary Commission four months previously, the Paraguayan Government had not paid a penny up to this point. Keith commented bitterly: 'It is all part of the bad faith which the Paraguayan Government and everybody connected with the country has acted during the affair...' Fortunately some friends accommodated him until he found a ship bound for England, landing there on 25 May 1875 to the great relief of his family, especially his mother.

The Paraguayan adventure, Keith's first foreign exploration, with all its ups and downs, would have given Keith invaluable experience for his later expedition, and given the circumstances, he appears to have coped remarkably well. Despite his treatment at the hands of the Paraguayan authorities and the extreme physical discomfort which he endured, he does not seem to have been dissuaded from seeking other opportunities for adventurous travel, and his account of his work was received with great approval. Keith the cartographer had now become Keith the explorer.

Notes

1   *The Academy*, 2 Jan 1875,14–15.
2   Cunningham-Graham (1901), 199, 288.
3   The reference to tigers is likely to be jaguars or pumas.
4   Levi (1875), 117–29.
5   Johnston, A.K. Jnr (1876), 494–507.
6   Johnston, A.K. Jnr (1875), 201–3, 264–73, 308–13, 342–5.
7   RGS Archives, Observations, No. 28.

6

'Only Waiting the Hand of Civilized Man'

Knocking at doors

On his return from Paraguay in 1875, Keith wrote to Henry Bates, expressing his disappointment that his application for a scientific post in India had come to nothing and that he would have to 'knock at some other door'. However, this was simply a prelude to a proposal for the redirection of the RGS which is remarkable for its breadth of thinking and modernity in relation to the broad scope of geography:

> the interest attaching to the Geographical Society…is derived from connecting the Society with the exploration of countries hitherto unknown. As soon as the general features and character of any country are tolerably well known, the interest in it sinks to the ordinary level. It is the unknown which forms the attraction; geography pure and simple and scientific geography have but a small share in the Society's programme. Such important work of exploration does of course require to be done, but the prestige of grand discovery will be wanting to it…the geography of the future must take on a new channel. It can only take two directions – that of examining more minutely the topography of the lands and seas or it may turn to the solution of scientific geography. The former direction promises no immediate sources of interest for the general mass of the people, or for the Society viewed as a popular body: to find attractiveness there must be something unknown, some question to solve, and topographical surveys, the more minute and perfect they become admit so much the less of discussion, but the latter part leads into an inexhaustible reserve and discovery of a higher order than that of outlining new lands…the geography on which the Society depends…must then turn gradually from that of discovery of new lands to the questions of physical geography.[1,2]

Keith argues for a 'centralisation of knowledge' to be undertaken by the Society because of the knowledge explosion. He says: 'Every branch of knowledge touches upon geography in some side…If you think anything of this scheme, and see any way in which a small, practical, gradual beginning could be made towards its accomplishment, I would willingly devote my life to the technical part of it.'

Read in one way, if 'physical geography' is broadly interpreted, Keith would seem to be advocating a more holistic and environmental approach, which was only to be fully adopted by the Society more than a century later, although anticipated by a paper by Sir Halford Mackinder in 1884 (in which he claimed that physical geography was the basis of all political geography, and that man was continually altering his environment).[3] In this respect Keith was well ahead of his time. The physical geography which he and his father had developed included not only the earth sciences of geology and physiography, but also climate, meteorology, hydrography, plant and animal life, etc. and the relationships between these – in other words what is now recognised as ecology in its widest sense. However, he was also somewhat naïve in proposing a centralisation of knowledge, given that effective information technology was yet to be invented, or that a private body could reasonably undertake this mammoth task. But it is more likely that he was advocating that the subject of geography – and therefore the future function of the Society – was to be an integrative one, taking aboard a much broader prospectus of topics, which he rightly says would be 'an inexhaustible reserve'.

He also saw this proposal as being tailor-made to his own talents and was obviously suggesting a job for himself ('I venture to ask your opinion of a scheme which has as its object...an increase or continuation of the utility and popularity of the Society.') although his final wistful sentence points to his continuing wanderlust: 'I would fain have seen something more of the world before settling down to any permanent task, but there does not appear to be any opportunity for this.'

During his time at the RGS, Keith had remained in touch with Augustus Petermann, who, from the Gotha Institute, had continued his links both with various geographic houses in Britain and with the RGS. Petermann expressed his grateful thanks to Keith for inserting notices in British periodicals from his own *Mittheilungen* and requested that he be sent 'any newspaper, or cuts from them containing early intelligence of your Arctic doings, with Captain Osborn at the head of it'. Petermann had been instrumental in promoting several Arctic expeditions and, perhaps surprisingly, had actively supported a new British initiative in this sphere. The references to Keith's involvement in Arctic exploration in 1875, following his survey work in Patagonia, are tantalising in their brevity. In a letter to Keith in Paraguay, Grace says 'Perhaps the news of this wonderful Arctic Expedition may induce you to turn homewards, tho' I trust you won't go off *there* next!' Was he contemplating joining the expedition, possibly as a cartographer or scientist, or was he merely assisting in its preparation? The RGS was certainly involved in advising on the Nares Expedition at this time, while Captain Sherard Osborn, one of John Barrow's naval protégés, had been on a previous Arctic expedition to rescue Sir John Franklin.[4]

In 1875 Osborn was much involved in promoting – initially against much public and official scepticism – his last major Arctic expedition, but had died suddenly a few days before the expedition's departure. The British Association for the Advancement of Science's summer meeting for 1875 contains a long paper by Osborn on routes to the North Pole, and it is more than likely that Keith was involved in the cartographic aspects of this.[5] It had been agreed that the expedition should be provided with all possible information on the Arctic in which the geography and ethnology should be written by the RGS and the remainder by the Royal Society.[6] Curiously there is another co-incidental family link to the Arctic – Keith's uncle William had, following the death of his first wife, married the widow of Dr William Scoresby, an Arctic naturalist explorer and curate who also developed a much improved ship's compass and whose published account of the Arctic regions in 1820 was a remarkable piece of work. It was Sir William's new wife who reported that Admiral and Lady Hall spoke very highly of Keith and hoped that he would not leave the RGS, as he was sure of promotion. However, Keith had confided in Grace that 'when this terrible gazetteer is finished [a new edition at which he was toiling] I have several things in view'. What these things were is not quite clear, nor which gazetteer was so terrible, but his remarks indicate that he was becoming exceedingly weary of the tedium imposed by such 'inky-fingered' work as cross-checking a host of place names, no doubt having also to insert their exact latitudes and longitudes.

The legacy of Livingstone

In the mid-nineteenth century, Africa was a continent which still represented a mystery: large parts of Central and East Africa remained to be systematically explored. Before 1856, East Africa was not an area which engendered much interest in Europe, but in the following twenty years it became a focus of intense concern, largely due to one man who embodied the high moral purpose of challenging the slave trade with the attraction of being an outstanding explorer, and made him the hero of the day. The Scottish missionary David Livingstone had become the first European traveller to cross the continent from the Atlantic to the Indian Ocean, an historic march between September 1854 and May 1856, which captured the public imagination as perhaps the greatest feat of African exploration.

Although his original modest background was quite different, Livingstone had many of the Victorian attributes demonstrated by the Johnstons – a belief in progress through development and trade, a powerful work ethic and sense of duty, a wide interest in many facets of science, and a morality based on his Christian beliefs. He was raised to heroic status by that first extraordinary journey, and his dedicated opposition to the slave trade, becoming a symbol of the great age of African exploration and missionary endeavour. But nothing stirred his vast popular audiences at home more than his description of the evils of the slave trade – 'this open sore of the world' – and its bitter fruits: the demoralisation of whole populations, the brutalisation of both slaves and slavers, the barbarism which reduced whole regions to a state of permanent poverty and fear.

Albeit probably the most famous of African explorers, he was simply one of a legion of Scots who were disproportionately represented in African discovery, trade and mission endeavour, not to mention administrators, educators, soldiers, and hunters. Scotland had been connected to North Africa from mediaeval times, but the enslavement of Sir John Henderson of Fordell by the Arabs of Zanzibar in 1628 is the earliest recorded connection with East Africa. Elsewhere, Mungo Park was the best

103

known of the Scottish explorers in West Africa, while Mary Slessor of Calabar became its most renowned missionary. The literally towering figure of James Bruce dominated the exploration of the Blue Nile in the latter half of the eighteenth century, and at the other end of the continent, Thomas Pringle from the Scottish Borders led the first party of Scottish emigrants to South Africa in 1820. In the latter half of the nineteenth century, the stage is crowded with Scots, almost too numerous to mention, from Dr James Stewart of the Livingstonia Mission on Lake Nyassa, to Grant on the Upper Nile. It was Col. Grant who symbolised the many soldier/explorers, in this case representing the powerful connection between East Africa and India, where so many Scots established their military careers.

While explorers and missionaries were 'at the sharp end', many Scots were more indirectly involved, particularly the Scottish businessmen and entrepreneurs who supported expeditions, missions, and development enterprises. Sir William Mackinnon,[7] the great shipping magnate, recruited the Moir brothers, Frederick and John, to survey and construct the first road into the African interior from Dar-es-Salaam. (Staunch evangelical churchmen, the two brothers, in the arduous trials of building the road, consoled themselves in their lonely evenings by singing Moody and Sankey hymns together.) James Stevenson from Irvine, together with a group of west of Scotland businessmen, who were also Free Kirk supporters, dedicated a considerable portion of his fortune to the opening up of the Central Lakes through the establishment of the Livingstonia Central Africa Company (later the African Lakes Corporation) and the commencement of a road link between Lake Nyassa and Lake Tanganyika in the early 1880s. The great missionary endeavour at Livingstonia on the shores of Lake Nyassa, and subsequently the Church of Scotland's mission at Blantyre, were stimulated and largely staffed by Scots, so many of whom had been inspired by Livingstone's example.

This last is an important pointer to the question of why it was that Scots offered their money, time – and in some cases literally their lives – to African exploration and development. While there had been Scottish involvement in Africa before Livingstone, there can be no doubt about his influence on a whole generation of Scots to whom he embodied much that they valued in the national culture of the time – the thirst for knowledge, the power of the will to overcome obstacles, Christian principle manifested in practical action, and a sense of duty. It was the sense of duty which impressed Stanley, who claimed that the English were contemptuous of the notion of duty, while the Scots took it seriously: above all else, it was not their intellect or physical attributes which motivated them 'but they have been educated in one thing more than all others…that one thing is duty'. Something of that sense of duty, combined with the notorious national pride of the race inspired Joseph Thomson, following Keith's death, to claim that he had been supported by the great roll-call of his illustrious compatriots, in his determination to carry his leaderless expedition forward.[8]

Another commentator has put a more psychological if not nationalistic slant on this motivation in suggesting that African exploration also provided an outlet to those whose psychology was affronted by, alien to, or incompatible with, mainstream European civilisation. Within the context of Great Britain, this often meant Celts who felt themselves to be outsiders in terms of the dominant Anglo-Saxon culture. If they did feel this, it is difficult to harmonise it, in the case of Scotland, with its long-standing association with and absorption of European culture, if not an exclusively Anglo-Saxon one.[9] What is also apparent is how completely the Scots had identified with Great Britain as a whole in its imperial ambitions and methods, including the justification for exploration, not least in being a prerequisite for bringing 'civilisation' to unenlightened parts of the globe. In post-devolution Scotland today, with its re-emerging sense of identity, what strikes a discordant note is the use of 'English' and 'Englishman' in the Scots explorers' references to themselves, not only for national identification, but clearly laying a claim to a set of standards attributable to the dominant partner in the Union. It has to be said that, on a number of occasions, this was simply a form of shorthand at a time when England was, in the minds of others, synonymous with Britain.[10]

The enthusiasm for nineteenth-century African exploration and development was not confined to the Scottish establishment or its wealthier merchants, but was shared by many ordinary people who were linked by the belief in the power of Christian evangelism to convert the heathen to more civilised ways – again with Livingstone as their inspiration, combining the explorer, scientific geographer and missionary. William McEwan, an aspiring engineer, wrote this in his diary before offering himself for work in Africa, with which he has been fascinated since boyhood: 'The name of Livingstone completed the spell, and from admiration to desire for imitation there is but a thought, and my ideal life has ever been Livingstone's work, Livingstone's religion, Beaconsfield's perseverance, and God's help.'[11] That religious fervour and dedication underpinned the philanthropists in the Scottish commercial community, who had little hope of seeing early, if any, returns on their substantial investments in missions and trading stations. James Young, the Scottish entrepreneur whose discovery of the economical method of extracting paraffin from local oil shale had made his fortune, financed Livingstone's last journey, and likewise funded the costs of bringing Livingstone's servants, Suzi and Chuma, back to Britain. It could be said with some justification that Scottish Christian missions provided the example for other nations in the prosetylisation of Africa.[12]

Opening up a continent

Livingstone's descriptions and those of others painted a picture to the Victorians of a continent which was now ripe for the civilising influence of western – and essentially Christian – culture, which in the minds of many was most likely to be achieved by replacing slavery with 'legitimate' commerce. It also had the dual attraction of a high moral purpose combined with the lure of adventure, and the real possibility of personal fame for those who responded to his call. There is no doubt that Livingstone's written descriptions of his experiences, and his public lectures, which were enormously popular, had a great appeal for the general public and stimulated both missionary and commercial endeavour, apart from geographical exploration. Nothing would advance this cause more than improvement in communications, requiring investigation of the most feasible routes from the East African coast to Central Africa.

It was Cameron, after making the first European crossing of Africa from east to west, who stated: 'the only thing that will do away with slavery is opening up Africa to legitimate commerce, and this can best be done by utilizing the magnificent water-systems of the rivers of the interior'.[13] With Livingstone's death in 1872, the great period of East African exploration began to tail off, and ended with Stanley's return five years later. The mystery of the interior had been cleared up – the ancient 'sea' which had been reported from the time of Ptolemy was now known to be a series of vast freshwater lakes. Nyassa and the Shire River had been explored by Livingstone, Lake Tanganyika by Burton and Speke, while Victoria and the outflow of the Nile had been identified by Speke – all of these 'discoveries' had been made by British explorers in a matter of four years between 1859 and 1862, when Britain was undoubtedly at the forefront of African exploration.

By the early 1870s, many of the blanks in the maps had been filled in, at least in outline, through the efforts of a relatively small number of explorers: in a review of Thomson's narrative of the 1878–80 Expedition and the preceding expeditions *The Scotsman* claimed that 'each in his different ways shows evidence that the palmy days when a great reputation might be made by anyone who had the hardihood to plunge into the unknown interior of Africa are drawing to a close'. Later in the same review, it hinted that civilisation had perhaps already arrived in describing Thomson finding, on 25 December 1879, two English clergymen and a French priest camped on the banks of the Lukuga River and about to sit down comfortably together to their Christmas pudding and other materials for a 'capital dinner'. By May 1878 the RGS African Exploration Fund Committee, referring to the importance of the return of Stanley and the discovery of the source of the Congo, suggested that the greatest of the problems of African geography had now been solved, and the area of discovery had therefore become more restricted.[14] Subsequent ventures were primarily undertaken by traders, missionaries and empire-builders. Much later, Thomson was to take serious issue with the way in which the often-used phrase 'legitimate commerce' was used to justify a form of commercial imperialism in some cases amounting to quite immoral activities.

There was considerable competition between the Germans, French, Belgians and the British for a stake in East Africa.[15] In September 1876 King Leopold II of the

Belgians, who, like other European countries, felt that his country was missing out on involvement in Africa, hosted a congress in Brussels which established an 'International Commission of Exploration and Civilisation of Central Africa'. Britain regarded this with some suspicion, although it did not formally object to the setting up of a commission which was ostensibly humanitarian. In fact, it was Stanley who had supported Leopold to promote an 'independent' state in the Congo, but with the king as personal ruler. (Keith was later to meet up with Stanley when he was starting out on his fact-finding mission for this purpose.) King Leopold had visited Britain in May 1876 and had apparently secured the support of the RGS, who sent a strong delegation to the conference, including its President Sir Rutherford Alcock, past presidents Sir Henry Rawlinson and Sir Bartle Frere, in addition to a number of eminent explorers, philanthropists and businessmen.[16] All of these eminent men were leading members of the RGS, having served on its governing council, an indication of the depth of involvement of the Society in this topic.

Leopold suggested the establishment of a chain of European stations across Africa as launch pads for exploration, research and trade, to be manned by the international organisation – the International African Association. Although the RGS was initially enthusiastic, and indeed made a substantial contribution to what was regarded as a very successful conference, the British Government later woke up to the possibility of being outvoted on matters which might concern Britain's national interest. It was agreed that Britain's contribution from then on would be largely confined to exploration, which would be consistent with the charter of the RGS, who perhaps used this to avoid becoming too closely involved with the Association, and to retain their independence in this field. Leopold had perhaps inadvertently forced the hand of the RGS in having to decide their further involvement in Africa, and in Professor Bridges's words 'Leopold's influence had weaned the RGS from its customary refusal to become concerned with non-geographical matters.'[17]

Sir Bartle Frere's position was particularly interesting in relation to the Scottish interest. He had formed a close association with William Mackinnon, a Scottish shipowner, and with him had promoted the opening up of the African interior as a means of curtailing the slave trade and advancing the cause of missions and 'civilising trade'. (Frere had been deeply involved with John Kirk, the consul at Zanzibar, in concluding the treaty to end the slave trade in the sultan's dominions and introduced him to Mackinnon.) It was undoubtedly Frere's influence which secured a place for Mackinnon at the Brussels conference, where he became committed to the vision of developing East and Central Africa through communications along its waterways and linking roads. Frere was impatient to get things moving in this direction and on 9 November 1876, using Mackinnon's influence, he convinced a meeting of Glasgow magnates to support the proposal for a road between the East African coast (originally from Kilwa) to Lake Nyassa. A number of those attending were members of the Glasgow Livingstonia Committee, staunch supporters of the Free Church Mission established there in Livingstone's memory, including the influential James Stevenson, who also had a particular interest in developing transport links. On the basis of a further meeting on the following day with the Glasgow Chamber of Commerce, a Scottish branch was established, anticipating the formation of a 'British National Society' in the wake of Leopold's International Commission. When this did not materialise, despite Frere's best efforts with the RGS, the Scottish branch withered, but Mackinnon and Stevenson, supported by the chemist James Young, the missionary James Stewart, and the philanthropist Sir Fowell Buxton, were determined to go ahead and made their plans for roads to and between the Central African Lakes.[18]

The African Exploration Fund

The response of the RGS to the International Commission's proposals for national associations was to set up the African Exploration Fund on 12 March 1877 for 'the exploration of the regions as yet unknown to civilized Europe, the attainment of accurate information as to climate, the physical features and resources of the country, the character of the inhabitants, the best routes of access, and all such matters as may be instrumental in preparing the way for opening up Africa by peaceful means'.[19] The Fund, under the patronage of the Prince of Wales, had a very distinguished membership, including Sir Rutherford Alcock, President of the RGS; Sir Thomas Fowell Buxton of the evangelical family; Sir William Rawson, former Colonial Secretary of the Cape Colony, and Governor of the Bahamas and Windward Isles; Sir Harry Calvert Verney, who had trekked across the Andes; Francis (later Sir) Galton, geneticist and explorer of South West Africa; Col. James Augustus Grant, who as an explorer had accompanied Speke; and General Christopher Palmer Rigby, formerly British Consul at Zanzibar – truly a gathering of the 'great and the good'.

On 19 July 1877 a large meeting was held in London to hear the Archbishop of York move a resolution on the suppression of the slave trade including the obtaining of 'further information regarding the less well-known region of central Africa, and ascertain the best routes thereto from the coast'.[20] Sometimes, however, the euphoria and verbal exhortation were not matched by practical and financial support for such ventures – here is Keith's ironic description of the event:

> I was in hopes on Thursday, when I got it [a hand-knitted Kilmarnock bonnet from Grace] that something was to be done that day towards deciding about an African Expedition and then I might have had a chance of taking it with me to the 'Dark Continent' to astonish the natives, for there was a grand meeting at the Mansion House then to pass resolutions about civilising Africa. There was the Lord Mayor, who thought that er-r Africa should certainly be civilised somehow, er-r he had heard say that there were a great many people there who had very little clothing, er-r who didn't know what it was to have coats and trousers, or even boots and shoes, and that it was a great shame er-r and must be seen to at once, and

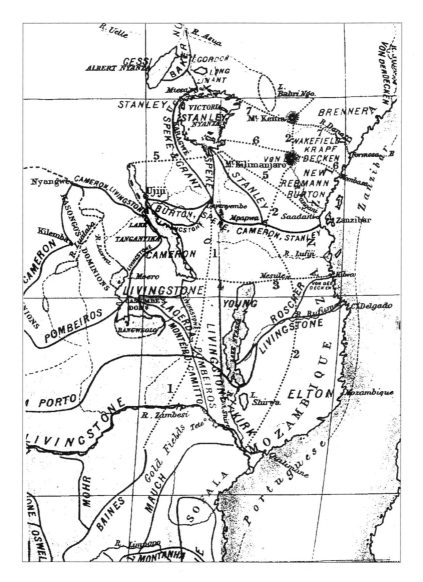

Proposed RGS exploration routes 1877
(Source: Royal Geographical Society)

he proposed the first resolution that Africa should be civilised. Then there was the great Archbishop of York, who had crammed up startling statistics of the Slave Trade, but who wasn't very sure if it was hundreds or thousands he had to deal with – anyhow there were a great many, too many slaves about in Africa and his resolution abolished them all – also carried. There was a whole heap of other resolutions and harrowing speeches and appeals to the City pockets, and everybody on the platform looked as if he would have given his 'bottom dollar' to the poor down-trodden African. I went out almost the last, and looked to see the millions which had been cast into a huge silver platter which had been ostentatiously placed in charge of an official at the doorway for offerings – so therein was a single solitary satire of a *shilling* – nothing more nor less! This seems to have been too much for the African Exploration Fund Committee which has spent a whole year drawing up a programme of what it intends to do, and so its members have resolved to postpone the 'civilisation of Africa' till the grouse shooting is over.

In a lengthy Presidential Address to the RGS in November 1877, Sir Rutherford Alcock set out his comprehensive arguments for maintaining the momentum of African development, especially in the field of communications: 'A telegraph line from Khartoum…to the nearest point of our own line in the Cape Colony, and a practicable road, or still better a light rail, to the three great inland seas from the East Coast, would work more wonders than Aladdin's lamp…' and then went on to reveal one of the purposes, commenting on the possible unwillingness of the Americans to take an equivalent amount of British goods for their enormous exports of sugar, cotton and tobacco, saying 'should we not deal much more advantageously with a new country, and in all probability on more favourable terms and without hostile tariffs?'[21]

Later that year, the African Exploration Fund reported to the Council of the RGS, carefully defining the limited remit and resources of the Society, before proposing a small-scale expedition. After discussion of various routes to the African interior, they recommended a route from the coast to the Central Lakes, emphasising the benefits of subsequently linking these by road.[22] However, the extent of navigable water, apart from the lakes themselves, was much more limited than at first thought, and the problem was how to reach these Central Lakes. One of the great impediments to East African travel was the difficulty of using pack or draft animals because of the prevalence of tsetse fly, so that bullock-carts, which had been used with such success in South Africa, could not operate under these conditions. Donkeys, as Keith was to find out in due course, were almost an embarrassment, while an experiment by the Belgians with Indian elephants was a disastrous failure.[23] But the attraction of being able to use steamboats on the great lake system was compelling, and there were many proposals in the subsequent years for different routes to reach these water bodies and indeed to connect them by road. If this could be done, there would be a prospect not only of trading around the shores of these vast waterbodies, but also of connecting the lakes with the coast.

Despite its ostensible function of geographical exploration, the pronouncement from the RGS indicates that British interests in East Central Africa were now focussed largely on potential commercial or missionary activities, even if the RGS itself was still mainly concerned with geography and science. (Out of 109 medals awarded by the RGS by 1880, 98 had gone to explorers.)[24] It recognised that new 'discovery' in the topographical sense, which had effectively started with Captain Burton's expedition in 1857, was now restricted. By the late 1870s, the earlier individual explorers had been replaced by well-organised groups of traders, missionaries and concession hunters. There was no doubt that the preliminary explorations supported by the RGS would pave the way for the expansion of British influence and trade, which needed new markets for the huge amounts of manufactured goods now being turned out by the home factories.[25] Thus the RGS concentrated its attention on finding the most economical and safe route to the Central Lakes as the primary object of the African Exploration Fund in its first year. But the Committee of the Fund expressed its ultimate aims in resounding prose: 'vast tracts capable of supporting an agricultural and industrious population, if cultivated, are only waiting the hand of civilised man, and a Christian spirit, to establish with willing aid from native tribes, peaceable communities over the greater portion of Central Africa; from the Equator to the Zambezi and from sea to sea'.[26] But the scale of the problem was to be kept in perspective: 'from eighty to one hundred millions would not be an overestimate of the population cruelly oppressed and kept in hopeless barbarism by the tyranny and violence of comparatively small numbers of predatory and bloodthirsty tribes'. It was suggested that under European guidance and defence, those millions would be quite prepared to form villages and communities capable of defending themselves. With all of this blood and thunder, it seemed necessary for the Chairman to remind the Committee that any expedition leader should go in peace and only have recourse to force in self-defence.

Between the euphoria of the Livingstone era and the mid-1870s, public interest in African exploration, and certainly financial support, appeared to evaporate, coinciding with the beginning of a 20-year period of economic depression. Despite a major campaign by the RGS, none of the captains of industry responded in any meaningful way, the great city corporations contributed nothing, and the appeal to Fellows of the Society was so disappointing that, at its meeting to report to the Council in May 1878, the African Exploration Fund Committee had to admit that contributions which the Fund has received to date had not exceeded £2,000 – raising the question of whether it should in fact still consider undertaking expeditions, or whether it should simply concentrate on collecting and disseminating geographical information. The appeal to the public had resulted in the amount subscribed to the fund being, in the words of one committee member 'so trifling, that any grand scheme of Exploration was out of the question'. Part of the problem was that the sort of careful, well-organised expedition the Society had in mind lacked the romance of previous African explorations, and certainly the drama of some urgent rescue bid which would have rapidly attracted more funds.

Although the public may have been generally in favour of bringing 'civilisation' to Africa, this period between the renowned geographical exploits searching for the Nile and Congo sources and the later activities of traders and missionaries no longer had the same emotive appeal. The explorer Col. Grant expostulated that during six months he had spent in the north of Scotland (he came from the county of Nairn), having mentioned to friends there his wish to start an Exploration Fund Branch, he had not the slightest difficulty in raising £200 in a few months, or one-tenth of the sum collected since the Fund was originated.[27] He challenged the costs involved, basing this on the cost of previous expeditions averaging out at about £1.10 shillings (i.e. £1.50 pence) per mile.[28] At these rates, the cost of exploring all the seven routes proposed would have been in excess of £11,000; in the event the Society raised only £4,000, of which half came from the Society's own funds. The same Col. Grant later in the discussion commended the notion of exploring the feasibility of an overland telegraph line along the route, which could then connect with South Africa and Europe. Referring to the barbarism and slavery of Africa, the Committee acknowledged that 'it was impossible to avoid a painful impression of the sacrifices entailed on those who undertake the perilous work' (one of the unmentioned sacrifices was monetary – the payment given to the explorers was laughable) '...many risk not only health and fortune, but the perils of martyrdom...'. The last statement was to prove a prescient one in this case.

Appeals were also made to the universities of Oxford and Cambridge to establish fellowships to promote geographical study, including one in the memory of Livingstone with the avowed purpose of bringing forth young men prepared to follow his example by dedicating their lives to African exploration and development – with similarly disappointing results.[29] Keith had previously shown his willingness by seeking to join the Livingstone Search and Rescue Expedition while Joseph Thomson, who was to accompany him on the RGS expedition in the following year, had apparently pleaded with his mother to persuade his father to provide the necessary funds to allow him to join the rescue bid – at the age of ten![30]

Late in 1877 Keith confided to Grace his dissatisfaction with his sedentary occupation, and his restlessness: 'often do I wish that I kept cattle on the plains of Paraguay, rather than sit here, inky-fingered on a stool all day. You see my wandering mania still clings to me. Sometimes I think it is sheer, stark insanity, but whenever I think of settling down here respectably, the longing comes on with double force to be away.'

Deciding a route

Early in 1878, Keith submitted a 'Memorandum on a proposed Geographical Expedition, from the East Coast of Africa near Mombas to the shores of Victoria Nyanza, via Mt. Kenia'[31] to the Secretary of the African Exploration Committee, to which he also appended a sketch map showing the routes of all former European travellers and the caravan routes of the traders between the east coast and the lake region – a subject on which he was an acknowledged expert. In order to take advantage of the experience gained by earlier explorations of the missionaries Krapf, Rebmann, Wakefield and New, he proposed that the expedition should start 'towards the snowy mountains near the Equator', from the mission station at Ribe near Mombasa. Keith had presented to the RGS a paper by Wakefield on the caravan routes and clearly held a very high opinion of his work.[32] He also commended Wakefield as an adviser on stores required, selection of reliable porters, and if at all possible, his recruitment to the expedition, especially in view of his knowledge of native languages.

Keith indicated his preferred route in considerable detail, commenting: 'no part of Africa appears to present more attractive physical features for examination than this plateau between Mount Kenia and the lake regions and none could be more interesting from an ethnographic point of view, as it is the debatable land in which the great races of eastern Africa meet and interlace'. He was in fact talking not only about the land occupied by the Great Rift Valley but also that area that came to be known as the White Highlands. However, in his memorandum Keith continues:

> On this very account however the region in question is perhaps the most dangerous of any in the Continent. All these various tribes are at enmity with one another and according to Mr Wakefield, thirst for each other's blood…the Wamasai and Wakwavi hate each other mortally…these wandering and insatiable robbers appear indeed to be also the constant scourge of the more settled agricultural or pastoral peoples scattered over the country under consideration.

Keith notes that the Swahili traders from the coast have great difficulty in crossing this dangerous tribal land, and for security, travel in caravans from 600 to 1,000 men strong, armed with muskets, 'but are often nearly all slain'. In fact in 1879 a Swahili caravan of 2,000 men had been almost entirely annihilated.[33]

There is considerable irony in the fact that, in 1884, Thomson, Keith's deputy on his subsequent East African Expedition, gained fame for being the first European to cross Masailand without serious incident, albeit with the aid of his own brand of 'wizardry', including the simultaneous firing of a small but hidden cannon while dropping a tablet of fruit salt into a tumbler of water and fascinating the tribesmen by removing and replacing his false tooth. The only real attack his caravan suffered was from a very determined pride of lions.

*Masai warrior (Source: J. Thomson, **Through Masailand**, 1885,*
Trustees of the National Library of Scotland)

Finally Keith proposed that, apart from its leader, the expedition should have one other European, particularly to take astronomical observations, declaring that the assistance of someone who is competent to 'take time' is almost indispensable and proposed 'that a man of some such standing as a Sergeant of Engineers should be engaged for the journey, at a small salary, say of £150 or £200'. In the event, what he got was someone very different, who ironically, despite his many other talents, was not trained in the taking of astronomical observations.

One of the main purposes of this memorandum was to indicate what budget might be required for such an expedition and Keith provided considerable detail on the weight (about 2,000 pounds) and costs of trade goods, the number of porters and soldiers (*askari*) required – 100 and 30 respectively – calculating their pay for the return journey at £1,800. He built into his costings the assumption that the War Office, as was often their practice for quasi-official expeditions, would supply the necessary armaments and that the Society would obtain its usual 30 per cent travel discount for RGS representatives. Astronomical and other instruments would be provided from the RGS stores, but Keith, a keen photographer, also budgeted for photographic apparatus and developing chemicals. An interesting proposal, which appears to have been usual practice, was for these costs to be based initially on a one-way journey, but with the expedition having the facility to draw on whatever funds might be necessary for the return trip, after it had passed a certain point or longitude on the line of exploration, to be determined by the RGS Committee. Such funds would be held by the British Consul at Zanzibar, Dr John Kirk, but no indication is given of how in practice these would be made available when the expedition was many months into the interior of Africa.

After Johnston's death, Thomson was to claim that the calculation of the funds required to spend the rainy season at Lake Tanganyika and then return to the coast as his leader intended would have taken far more time than the funds allowed for, and complained about the lack of instructions on the financing of the expedition; he was in fact in the same position as Dr Kirk, as indicated by the folio of correspondence in the RGS archives, which is replete with confusing correspondence on this question. It reflects again the penny-pinching approach of the Society which Thomson railed against when he said: 'for want of a few hundred pounds I must simply take a view of the promised land and turn away'.[34] In fact, Thomson commended himself to the RGS Committee by keeping well within budget, by losing not a single bale of trade goods, and by considerably reducing Keith's estimate of the average cost per mile of travel.

As far back as July 1877, no fewer than seven possible routes had been suggested for consideration, including one from South Africa to Lake Tanganyika and several to Lake Victoria from the east coast.[35] There were strongly expressed opinions about the merits of these various routes (especially from those explorers such as Col. Grant claiming a knowledge of the country and his promotion of a trans-Africa telegraph line), hanging on the question of the security of the caravan and its cost if many armed soldiers were required – money which the Committee did not have. It appears that Stanley had some influence in deciding on the most appropriate route for the RGS expedition, which, given Keith's preference for the Kilimanjaro–Mt Kenya route, might explain some of his subsequent antipathy towards him. However, another reason for the final choice was that the roads from the coast, which Mackinnon was sponsoring, and the road between the lakes, proposed by Stevenson, required preliminary survey, given that both were started without any real idea of where they were leading.

Stanley opposed Keith's preferred route, paradoxically – given his own reputation for using any force he thought expedient – on the basis that the tribes inhabiting the northern routes were totally hostile and would require the use of force. Because of his reported treatment of Africans in the course of his travels, the involvement of Stanley in giving advice to the Committee was strongly resented by some members of the RGS, several of whom resigned over the issue.[36] The final route decided was the shortest one, to the south-west of Dar-es-Salaam aiming at the southern end of Lake Tanganyika, both for its scientific interest and for its potential as a trade route, and because it offered the possibility of combining two proposals, including the link between Lakes Nyassa and Tanganyika.[37] One committee member, Frederick Holmwood, commended this route on the basis that it 'was one of the finest elephant countries in that part of Africa, and every year a large number of Makuas were in the habit of going there to hunt the elephants and take the tusks down to Kilwa... the chief of Dundanguru would be delighted at any moment to assist Mr. Keith Johnston, and even go with him to the forest'. Holmwood (whose house Keith would temporarily occupy while in Zanzibar) declared that the route which it was proposed for Mr Keith Johnston's expedition was through agricultural tribal country 'and any man who knew the languages might pass along, as far as his personal safety was concerned, with only his carpet bag and an umbrella'.[38]

Among Keith's objectives was to elaborate the courses of the still mysterious Rivers Rufiji, Ruaha and Uranga.[39] Further, if a path could be made between Lake Nyassa and Lake Tanganyika, the Committee suggested, and a steamer placed on each, then 'a long line would be opened through the central regions, while the return journey through the intervening country to the east and the west would go far to complete the line of communication...'. This was in fact an ambitious objective – the Committee obviously wanted maximum value for money, while at the same time avoiding unnecessary loss of life or conflict with the local population. It was perhaps typical of such Victorian enterprises that they were visionary in scope, but in other ways hard-headed and cautious, especially with regard to expenditure.

One of the reasons for selecting this route was that the first section of it was in process of being considered as the so-called Mackinnon Road, after the Scottish shipping magnate Sir William Mackinnon, referred to previously, who together with the

PROCEEDINGS

OF THE

ROYAL GEOGRAPHICAL SOCIETY

AND

MONTHLY RECORD OF GEOGRAPHY.

PUBLISHED UNDER THE AUTHORITY OF THE COUNCIL, AND EDITED BY
THE ASSISTANT SECRETARY, 1, SAVILE ROW.

NEW MONTHLY SERIES.

VOL. III., 1881.

LONDON:

*Proceedings of the RGS, which recorded the successful completion of the 1878–80
Expedition to the Central lakes (Source: Royal Geographical Society)*

philanthropist Sir Fowell Buxton had committed finance to this project to encourage indigenous trade near to the coast. Mackinnon's shipping service was well known throughout the orient, and he provided not only the first steamship and mail service to Zanzibar, but also linked the latter by telegraph to Aden. He conceived the first organised economic penetration and development of the East African interior, and attempted to negotiate a major trade concession with the Sultan of Zanzibar – a proposal welcomed by the humanitarian Buxton who fervently believed in commerce as a way of ending the slave trade. By midsummer of 1877, six miles of good road had been completed and as many as 100 local people were using it to bring their goods to the coast each day.[40] Some four years later, despite great difficulties in construction, it extended to 73 miles, but its use after the first 40 miles by oxen or horses was pre-empted by the presence of tsetse fly. By coincidence, James Stevenson, from west Scotland, was prepared at the same time to finance a road between Lakes Nyassa and Tanganyika forming the final extension of the proposed expedition – and could therefore be seen to be fulfilling the RGS role of exploration to support development which was being actively planned. Keith quite clearly hoped to be the leader of such an expedition.

On 26 May 1878 Keith's mother wrote to Grace to tell her that the East African Expedition was now approved and that Keith had been chosen as its leader but also: 'I am thankful his first route is abandoned, as the tribes are so hostile: it would have been martyrdom to attempt it …dear Keith! I rejoice for him, but I do dread the going.' Keith should not have concerned himself about his appointment, since the committee were in no doubt about his suitability stating that they

> could not have a better officer for such an undertaking than Mr. Keith Johnston, who was a thoroughly practical traveller and geographer, and whose heart was in the work. If Mr. Keith Johnston carried out the present as a preliminary expedition successfully (as doubtless he would), that would be proof that something could be done, and the public would then, in all probability, open their purses and subscribe the funds for the more enlarged undertakings.[41]

The Resolution was seconded by Sir H. Rawlinson, saying that the Society 'might reserve its geographical aspirations for great results until some future occasion. Let them commence in a practicable, workmanlike way, and when Mr Keith Johnston returned, and told them about the country, the public interest would be more excited, and ample funds would be obtained for carrying out larger undertakings'. Later, a past President of the Society, Sir Clements Markham was to write: 'in point of fact he would have been selected if he had not volunteered…No man in England then combined such an amount of scientific knowledge with such qualifications as a traveller.'[42]

Introducing Joseph Thomson

In agreeing that Keith Johnston would be well fitted for this task the Committee recommended that 'a second person might be associated with him, duly qualified, with medical experience perhaps, to attend to various branches of science other than pure geography and general survey, which would be the special duties of the leader'. The committee believed 'that the work required must be of a progressive and steady character, and not too ambitious at first, or beyond the real exigencies of trade and civilising efforts to which geographical exploration is the pioneer'. The person chosen was Joseph Thomson, who ironically was later to emphasise on a number of occasions his view that the claimed riches of Africa were a mirage and not based on any sound evidence regarding its natural resources or the obstacles in the way of their exploitation.[43]

What of Keith Johnston's 20-year-old assistant, Joseph Thomson? Thomson's background and personality could hardly have been more different from Keith's, and the story of the relationship between the two men, much of it derived from the correspondence between Keith's mother and the wife of the British consul in Zanzibar, stems directly from this. Born in the small rural village of Penpont in Dumfriesshire, Thomson was the son of a quarryman, who nevertheless, like so many artisans of his day, was both literate and studious, with an interest in astronomy and geology.[44] Young Thomson appears to have been a born leader among his playfellows and schoolmates, with a fearlessness and enthusiasm which was attractive.[45] At the same time he also seemed happy on his own, enjoying the fine pastoral landscapes of his native county, which brought out his distinctly romantic streak. He had received a solid if limited education at the local schools, where he was described by his headmaster as a favourite of the school throughout his time there,[46] 'always the soul of fun and mischief, the champion of smaller boys'.[47] A great reader, he was stimulated by the narratives of the great African explorers at an early age, but his romantic view of adventurers would have been would have been heightened by the many colourful descriptions of other lands by authors such as R. M. Ballantyne.[48] Following his youthful decision to become an African explorer, he prepared himself by sleeping on bare floors and in other ways toughening up his constitution.[49]

Apart from his natural charisma, he had an avid interest in natural history, especially geology, and was a keen collector of rocks, encouraged by a local doctor with a wide-ranging interest in science. Thomson encountered Archibald Geikie on one of his rambles, and the learned professor was sufficiently impressed by Thomson's knowledge to invite him to become one of his students at Edinburgh University. (Coincidentally, Geikie was a long-standing friend of Alexander, who supported Geikie's canditure for the first chair of geology at Edinburgh University.) Thomson, in his time at the university, sat at the feet of a number of eminent scientists: apart from Geikie himself, he studied botany under John Hutton Balfour, and natural history under Thomas Henry Huxley, the distinguished evolutionist. Thomson seems to have particularly enjoyed field work and was renowned for striding ahead of his class to scale a crag to identify its strata, apparently with a very quick eye for geological structure, but also displaying his strength and daring.[50] But Thomson was also a diligent scholar, taking many of the class prizes and medals, particularly in geology and natural history, and when almost by chance he applied to join the 1878 RGS expedition, these attainments and Geikie's personal support would have recommended him to the interviewing committee, perhaps helped by the fact that he did not request payment.[51]

During the autumn of 1878, both he and Keith made intensive preparations for their expedition. Thomson, searching among the various London institutions for relevant information, discovered how little data there was on the geology of East Africa, and took instruction under the renowned botanist, Sir Joseph Hooker, to improve his knowledge of African plants at Kew Gardens. He even went so far as to take swimming and boxing lessons to prepare himself for the physical challenges ahead.[52] (In fact, his physical feats were prodigious. James Barrie claimed that he once walked from his home to Edinburgh – a distance of over 70 miles – in one day, and still had enough energy, after supper, to visit an exhibition in the city.[53]) Thomson was to claim that, throughout the 1878 expedition, he marched on his own two feet, sometimes to the point of total collapse, disdaining either donkey or litter. He neither smoked nor drank and it was said that his most notable feat was bringing back from an African expedition an unopened bottle of brandy.[54] During his preparation time in London, he was greatly helped by the kindly assistance of Henry Bates, the Assistant Secretary at the RGS and an old friend of Keith's, describing him as 'an exceedingly pleasant old gentleman, ever ready to be of service and continually priming me with valuable confidential hints'.[55]

However, even at this early stage, he clearly had difficulty with Keith. Writing to his elder brother, he confides that he 'came prepared to stand on the most loyal and kindly footing', anxious to develop a sense of comradeship, but apparently not with obvious success. He thought Keith 'a very nice fellow, hating all fuss, but his conversational powers were not very remarkable which made it somewhat difficult to get along sometimes, but hoped this reserve would wear away, once they got together on their expedition'.[56] This is a typical Thomson ironic understatement, since Keith's withdrawn and uncommunicative personality is entirely consistent with the views of others who knew him well, but there is no indication that the younger man was seriously discountenanced by this.

Thomson himself was somewhat overawed by his assigned title of 'Geologist and Naturalist to the Expedition' commenting in some embarrassment that 'I was about as much surprised by my good fortune as doubtless were most of my friends'.[57] He was in fact truly overwhelmed:

Great Fire of Edinburgh, 1824: the fireman in the centre of the picture is attempting to extinguish the fire in Old Assembly Close (Source: sketch by W. Archer; courtesy of Edinburgh City Libraries)

Zanzibar: old British Consulate and plaque (Source: author/Mike Shand)

The prize-winning globe showing its physical geography constructed by Alexander Keith Johnston for the 1851 Great Exhibition (Source: Royal Geographical Society)

Examples of atlases produced by W. & A. K. Johnston (Source: Trustees of the National Library of Scotland)

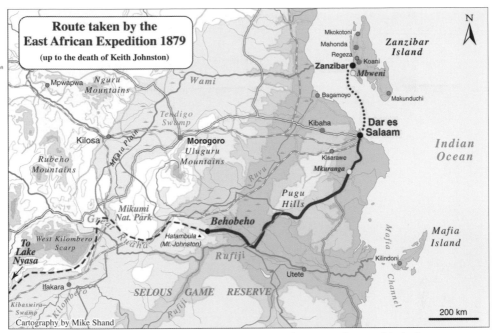

Route of the Royal Geographical Society 1878–9 Expedition, up to the time of the death
of Keith Johnston (Source: Mike Shand)

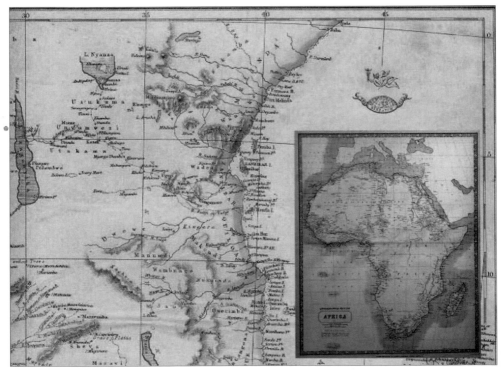

Mapping of Africa in the 1850s (Source: Mike Shand)

2001 expedition: dhows at Zanzibar (Source: author)

The great Rufiji River (source: author)

2001 expedition: Campi ya Fisi in the dry bed of the Behobeho River (Source: author)

2001 expedition: 'fly camping' – less claustrophobic than Keith's tent (Source: author)

Cycads in John Kirk's garden at Mbweni (Source: author)

2001 expedition: Behobeho River near presumed gravesite (Source: author)

2001 expedition: Mike climbing aboard a modern 'caravan' (Source: author)

The author in a dugout canoe, exploring the tributary
of the Rufiji River in 1961 (Source: author)

2001 expedition: approaching Hatambulo
(Source: author)

Water-logged trail through swamp forest
(Source: author)

The Selous has the largest conecntration of crocodiles in Africa,
some up to 5 metres in length (Source: Jonathan Willett)

River crossing in 1961 (Source: author)

Porters on the march: forest survey expedition, 1961 (Source: author)

now what is a poor unfortunate to think who is next to be launched on the ocean without a compass at the age of twenty…and with no experience. Don't you think it really too hard to raise expectations of such a brilliant character? I am continually asking myself if I am not like a mushroom which appears suddenly in the night and disappears nearly as rapidly under the light of day…May heaven grant that all expectations be realized.

His plea might have been even more heartfelt if he could have foreseen what totally unexpected responsibilities all too soon he would have to carry on his young shoulders.

NOTES

1 RGS Archives, fo. 25.
2 Prof. Roy Bridges (personal communication) has commented that this statement reveals the dilemma which geographers of discernment faced at this time. One reason for turning to the Poles was the realisation that pure discovery was now possible only there. Clement Markham's failure as the RGS leader for most of the next thirty years was not really to confront the issues raised by Keith. Others ducked the issue by trying to make geographical societies commercial or even imperial organisations. In his view this was a large element in the emergence of the RSGS in 1884, which wished to ensure that Scottish enterprise should profit from work in Africa and, equally, to ensure that Scots should be able to offer the benefits to Africa which they were in a position to provide.
3 Crone (1950), 536.
4 Osborn had been stripped of his command and put under cabin arrest by the notorious Sir Edward Belcher, but had been completely vindicated on his return.
5 *Proc. RGS* (1875), 7.
6 Freeman (1980), 17.
7 For a full account of this important entrepreneur in this region see Galbraith, J.K. (1972) *Mackinnon and East Africa* Cambridge, and also the forthcoming publication on his world-wide maritime empire, Munro, J. F. (2003) *Maritime Enterprise and Empire: Sir William Mackinnon and his Business Network, 1823–93*, Boydell & Brewer Ltd.
8 Thomson (1881a), 150.
9 McLynn (1992), 345. McLynn makes several references to 'Celts' embracing all Scots explorers, who may or may not have had 'Celtic' ancestors. He deals at some length in Ch.16 on the psychology of explorers in particular.
10 Prof. R C. Bridges (personal communication) suggests that this use was simply to denote the fact that they were English speakers.
11 McEwan, unpublished letter, RSGS archives, 1883.
12 Shepperson (1982), 7.
13 *Proc. RGS* (1876), 325.
14 *Proc. RGS* (1878), 463. This lengthy address by the President of the RGS is a remarkable summary of East African exploration and British aspirations there, which by the end of the year was to be developed into a specific proposal for an RGS sponsored expedition.
15 Rotberg (1971), 24.
16 *Proc. RGS* (1877), 16–17.
17 Bridges (1963a), 25–35. This paper provides the most comprehensive account of the involvement of the RGS with the Leopold initiative and the subsequent mounting of the 1878–80 East African Expedition at a time when the Society was probably at the height of its power.
18 Munro (2003) *In press.*
19 *Proc. RGS* (1877), 603–5.
20 *Proc. RGS* (1877), 601–22.
21 *Proc. RGS* (1878), 26ff.
22 Ibid., 463–75.
23 Bridges (1963a), 30–1.
24 Bridges (1987a), 2.
25 Bridges (1963b), 22.

26 *Proc. RGS* (1878), 465.
27 By contrast, the renowned explorer Cameron had contributed a mere £2 to the African Exploration Fund. RGS Archives. African Exploration Fund Cash Book.
28 *Proc. RGS* (1878), 471.
29 Freeman (1980), 12.
30 Thomson (1896), 17.
31 *RGS Journal* mss (1878).
32 *Proc. RGS* (1872), 125–9.
33 *Proc. RGS* (1878), 466.
34 RGS Letters files, Thomson to Kirk, 12 January 1880.
35 *Proc. RGS* (1877), 388–94.
36 Bridges (1963a), 25–35.
37 *Proc. RGS* (1878), 472.
38 *Proc. RGS* (1878), 47–72.
39 The riverine forests of the latter, now named the Kilombero, were first surveyed systematically by the author in 1961–3.
40 Coupland (1939), 300–2.
41 *Proc. RGS* (1878), 474.
42 Markham, in Johnston, A.K. Jnr (1909).
43 Coupland (1939), 371.
44 Thomson (1896), 3.
45 Ibid., 16.
46 Alexander Hewitson, quoted in Thomson, J.B. (1896), 11.
47 Waugh (1905), 85.
48 Rotberg (1971), 16.
49 Thomson (1896), 18.
50 Geikie, quoted in Thomson, J.B. (1896), 42.
51 *Proc. RGS* (1885), 476.
52 Thomson (1896), 48.
53 Barrie (1926), 108.
54 Ibid.
55 Thomson (1896), 48.
56 Ibid., 49.
57 Thomson, J. (1881a), 3.

PART III

JOURNEY INTO AFRICA

7

African Travel: 'A Chaos World'

Survey and equipment

What was being asked of Keith in the 1878 East African Expedition was no mean challenge, for the RGS Committee gave explicit instructions on what was expected of him. Not only was he to gather data to construct a map of the route and to make a special investigation of other routes for future communications, but he was also required to make observations on meteorology, geology, natural history and ethnology, and to obtain information on the region, its inhabitants and products. He was instructed to examine the range of mountains at the north-east end of Lake Nyassa and obtain information on their extent, elevation and condition of routes and passes, and to enquire into the practicability of constructing and maintaining a telegraph line, with special attention being paid to the uses of the lake shore of Lake Tanganyika.[1] This was a very tall order indeed, but not atypical of the almost obsessional attention to detail which was characteristic of RGS-sponsored expeditions and their concern to get value for money.

The general methods of survey employed are succinctly described by Speke thus:

> My first occupation was to map the country. This is done by timing the rate of march by watch, taking compass bearings along the road, or on any conspicuous marks – as, for instance hills – and by noting the watershed – in short all topographical objects. On arrival in camp every day ascertaining, by boiling a thermometer, of the altitude of the station above the sea level; of the latitude of the station by the meridian altitude of a star taken with the sextant; and of the compass variation by azimuth. Occasionally there was the fixing of certain crucial stations, at intervals of 60 miles or so, by lunar observations, and distances of the sun from certain stars for determining of the longitude by which the original timed-course can be drawn out with certainty on the map by proportion.[2]

This continuous recording was an onerous chore, especially under the demanding conditions of an expedition, whatever the weather, and especially if the explorers were unwell, when it required a considerable act of will to attend to the discipline of time-keeping and recording of compass bearings. (An example of the detail of this is given as an extract from Keith's expedition diary in Appendix 1.) It also inhibited exploration away from the prescribed routes, however interesting these might be – Burton indicated his distaste and boredom with this constraint, much preferring a more spontaneous approach: he was in fact a good example of the old-style literary traveller, relegating 'science' to discovery pure and simple. Thomson, who was inclined to go off on unscheduled side tracks for light relief, delighted in being able to escape from beaten paths and getting away from the responsibilities of leading a large caravan and always having to keep a watch on both his men and his surroundings. On his last journey in the Atlas Mountains of Morocco he failed to measure up to the standards of observations of the RGS, and the Society penalised him by reducing his expenses.

The high standards also meant that explorers had to be competent in the use of instruments, some of which, such as the sextant, were by no means easy to use. Again, Thomson appears, most surprisingly, to have received no training in the basics of this essential instrument before his first expedition with Keith, and at one point after his leader's death, he actually wrote to the Society asking for instructions. By contrast, Keith had been inducted into the mysteries of astronomical instruments by his father at an early age. Certainly, reading Keith's expedition diary with its page after page of almost unrelieved route directions, often taken every 15 minutes, it is easy to understand why the explorers became very impatient with this time-consuming chore, often extending over months of travel. The wonder is that they were able to make the many other observations on the country and its inhabitants which were expected of them.

The cumulative labour involved in mapping is well described by Stanley, referring to his journey to rescue Emin Pasha in 1887:

> Mine have cost me more labour than the note-taking, literary work, sketching and photographing combined. In the aggregate, the winding of the three chronometers daily for nearly three years, the 300 sets of observations, the calculation of all these observations, the mapping of the positions, tracing of rivers, and shading of mountain ranges, the number of compass-bearings taken, the boiling of the thermometers, the records of the varying of the aneroids, the computing of the heights, and the notes of temperature, all of which are necessary for a good map, have cost me no less than 780 hours of honest work, which, at 6 hours per day, would make 130 working days.[3]

The list of instruments recommended to be taken on expedition was formidable and, being made of the highest quality materials and workmanship, the instruments were expensive. They usually included sextants, azimuths, compasses, astronomical telescopes, chronometers, aneroids, pedometers, barometers, thermometers, anemometers, and sometimes theodolites (the full tally of instruments carried by the RGS expedition of 1878 under Keith's leadership is given in Appendix 2). In case of loss or damage, or simply to cross-check accuracy, instruments were sometimes replicated – it was something of a disaster if instruments were lost (as had happened on Keith's Paraguayan journey) or damaged beyond repair. Special precautions were taken to avoid this – they were carried in specially constructed boxes which would remain in the personal charge of the explorers throughout the expedition, although the sheer weight of these (often due to brass construction) meant that they might have to be distributed within the caravan. On Thomson's subsequent expedition across Masailand, the volume of scientific instruments in total required no fewer than six porters and, at the start of every expedition, there was usually a noisy and acrimonious scramble to avoid these loads, not because of their weight (which was carefully calculated to be as equitable as possible) but because the porters disliked the hard-edged and awkward boxes compared with the more manageable bales of trade goods.

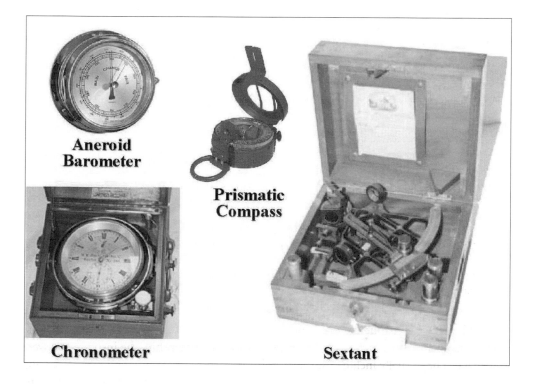

Survey equipment used by the 1878–80 Expedition
(Source: Mike Shand)

Personal clothing and equipment at the time of the RGS expedition could be expensive and, although an outfit allowance was provided, it was expected that explorers would make up any deficiencies from their own pockets. While this would not have been a problem for the affluent Keith, Thomson was obliged to complain to the Society secretary that the £50 allowance was insufficient and requested a further £40.[4] The most expensive single item was a double-barrelled rifle at £22, but his outfit also included three tropical tweed suits, six flannel shirts (to soak up the sweat) and no less than three sets of 'sleeping pyjamas'.[5] Norfolk jackets were favoured, with long trousers and socks tucked into oversized boots to allow for swelling. In continuously wet conditions, rotting boots could be a considerable problem. The whole ensemble would often be topped with a coal-scuttle shaped helmet of white rubber or cork. The personal outfit also included an individual tent – the only item of equipment which Keith, despite his meticulous planning, complained about, since these were so small that it was not even possible to sit upright in them: incarceration in these leaky shelters for any length of time, especially during extended periods of sickness, would have induced acute claustrophobia if nothing else.

'Insolent violence and unjust demands'

The personal armaments would extend, as they did in Thomson's case, to a further single-barrelled rifle and a Colt revolver, but the total armoury carried by caravans could be formidable: some 30 Snider carbines and 20 old Lee Enfields were provided by the War Office for the 1878 expedition, and often the porters were augmented by armed guards in the most dangerous areas. A number of the men brought their own muzzle-loading flintlocks.[6] For Keith's original proposed route across Masailand, it was estimated that a minimum of 30 armed askari would be required. To 'soothe the savage breasts' of hostile natives, Keith had another proposal which he broached to Henry Bates at the RGS:

> Revolving your idea of fiddling one's way into central Africa, thinking better of it at every turn and also the difficulty of finding a Paganini and a gallant explorer rolled into one, it occurred to me why should not the expedition be provided with a small but powerful barrel organ, the performance of which would not involve any mental exertion on the part of the traveller. If arranged to play various loud jigs, strathspeys...it would put life and mettle into the heels of any savages and would doubtless make the party very popular. The white man might easily preserve to himself the mysterious power over the spirit of the chest by simply abstracting the handle. For the sake of the Arabs, a book of music might be added.[7]

The threat from hostile natives was not an empty one – there are numerous records of attacks upon caravans by the more warlike tribes. Stanley's expedition in

1874 to Lake Victoria suffered several determined attacks by the Waturu, despite the size of his well-armed caravan. Following a series of murders of individual members of his party, the caravan was systematically attacked several times, forcing Stanley to build a stockade from which he carried out his own attacks using squares of men in formation to avoid being cut off. Although this was successful, he lost no fewer than 22 men in these pitched battles.[8] During this expedition, out of 347 persons with which he had started, Stanley lost 181 through battle, famine and desertion.[9] (However, Stanley regarded this as a credit, reflecting the obstacles to be overcome in seizing a worthy prize.)

In the year before Keith's arrival in East Africa, Arthur Dodgshun, heading for Ujiji with his ox-wagons through the territory of the murderous and notoriously scheming chief Mirambo, described the killing of a missionary, Mr Penrose (the skin of whose face was carried off as a trophy.) Despite being a missionary himself, Dodgshun was in no doubt about his line of action:

> Of course I object to fighting, but in this case we are two defending ourselves against the unjust demands and insolent violence of bloodthirsty wild beasts and if I shoot, it will be as against wolves…though we have no great store of ammunition, we are well armed, and have no great reason to fear bodily injury as the savages will probably retire if half a dozen of them fall.

(Nevertheless, Dodgshun suggests that his mourners should confine their mourning symbol to a band of crepe.)[10]

However, the 1878 RGS expedition was less likely to be held up by marauding warriors than by rapacious chiefs demanding gifts, in the form of what was known as *hongo* or trade goods. Such trade goods included bales of cloths of various colours and designs, likewise beads of different colours and sizes, and copper or brass wire, dependent on the preferences of local tribes. Caravans would traditionally set out with about 10 days food supply, but thereafter expected to barter such trade goods for whatever the local population could offer in the way of food, including fowls and rice – a constant problem for large expeditions. There was in fact a going rate for certain items: for example, a sheep would cost 10 yards of cloth and an ox 24–40 yards, while three eggs would cost 6 inches of beads (enough for a necklace) and a hen would raise this to 18 inches. The most popular cloth was the strong *mericani* from the USA, which at this time was ousting the much poorer Manchester cottons, but indigo dyed cloth from India was also popular in some districts.[11]

All of these goods were packed carefully into conveniently sized bales for carriage, about 5 feet long by 2 feet wide, each of the bales carefully marked and containing a range of goods, so that the whole of a caravan's load did not have to be opened to satisfy the desires of individual tribes and villages. Each bale would be wrapped in a form of matting for protection, especially for crossing rivers.[12] The beads, of up to 400 varieties, were packed into 50 pound bags, although on the 1878 expedition, the explorers found that these were useless for trade in many areas, where the people preferred cloth or more useful items. This was a universal practice of explorers round the globe, which Jonathan Raban refers to in the handing out of beads to North West Pacific Indians: 'They were the chief symbol of the universal white assumption about natives, that they were childish and feminine; irrational lovers of worthless trinkets, governed by their foolish eye for anything that sparkled, when what they wanted was copper, chisels, saws, iron – even in 1778.'[13]

In addition to legitimate barter for food and services, a number of local chiefs engaged in a form of blackmail, demanding increasingly large gifts in return for allowing an expedition to camp, use local water, or to pass through territory. Those chiefs with experience of expeditions disdained the customary trade goods, and sought more valuable items, such as watches and guns, and in some instances resorted to robbery. Many explorers recorded their anger and frustration at being held up by the rapacity of such chiefs, disregarding the fact that their caravans represented unimaginable wealth to the villages through which they passed and offered an irresistible temptation. The cost to caravans was immense: on Thomson's expedition through Masailand, it required 75 porters to carry the necessary trade goods, out of a total caravan strength of 123 men.[14] By 1890 it was costing £130 a ton to transport a caravan from the coast to Lake Victoria, and on the main road to Tabora, it was reckoned to cost approximately a pound a mile in trade goods. Even on settled mission stations, trade goods were essential to obtain food and other services, and in one year the mission at Livingstonia expended no less than 15 miles of calico for all its local purchases. Forty years later, when trade goods were no longer required, the number of porters and other servants being recommended for game safaris was astonishing: one expert suggested a headman, a boy, a gunbearer and two askaris, a cook and no fewer than 30 porters for each person, the volume of the game trophies and the life style requirements of tourists substituting for the previous trade good volume to be carried.[15] This, however, pales into insignificance when compared with Stanley's 1886 expedition to rescue Emin Pasha: 600 porters to carry over 27,000 yards of cloth, 3,600 pounds of beads and a ton of wire, all defended by over 550 rifles and a Gatling gun.

The porter – 'this useful person'

Each of the men carrying these bales had themselves to be fed and, if food was unlikely to be available locally on certain stretches of the caravan route, then a sufficient stock had to be accumulated in advance, and extra porters recruited to carry this over deserted areas. Stanley's 1874 expedition suffered terribly from shortage of food, with men actually dying from starvation. At one point Stanley was obliged to open his medicine chest to broach his emergency supply of 10 pounds of oatmeal with which, with 25 gallons of water, he made a thin gruel, just sufficient to give each man two cupfuls.[16] Explorers complained that porters often emptied or greatly reduced the water in their calabashes to avoid carrying this extra weight, with obvious consequences when traversing waterless country. Each march therefore became a logistical challenge, if not a nightmare, not helped by often misleading reports of the condition of the country ahead. Frequently porters would be unwilling to travel far beyond their own villages if they had to return without the protection of the caravan and, demanding to be paid in advance, often absconded.

This situation would have been eased greatly if draft animals such as oxen or even horses could have been used, but in East Africa this was pre-empted by two factors: the presence of tsetse fly carrying sleeping sickness, which killed such beasts, and the ground conditions which more often than not precluded the use of carts. Donkeys were used, but were temperamentally unsuited to expedition work, panicking at river crossings and generally being considered more bother than they were worth, especially as they required a man each to control them, and no fewer than ten men to load and unload them, while the animals themselves carried only the equivalent of two men's loads. When the last donkey died on the RGS expedition Thomson viewed its demise with something like relief.[17]

However, since ox-carts had been used successfully in South Africa, several attempts were made to experiment with these animals under the more difficult conditions of East Africa in the mid 1870s. The journal of Arthur Dodgshun, of the London Missionary Society, gives a graphic account of one such expedition, led by the Rev. Roger Price attempting to reach Ujiji in the year before the RGS expedition. The result was a tragic failure, with many of the ox-drivers falling ill, the oxen themselves dying, and almost insurmountable problems with road making in advance of the grossly overloaded ox-wagons.[18] It became clear very quickly that travel in East Africa would depend on human muscle power. The experience of explorers differed widely: while Keith and Thomson had little difficulty with their men, almost certainly due to the personality and leadership of their African caravan leader, others such as Henry Drummond, referring to the main recruitment point at Zanzibar, had a much more jaundiced view:

> Here these black villains, the porters, the necessity and despair of travellers, the scum of old slave gangs, and the fugitives from justice from every tribe, congregate for hire. And if there is one thing on which African travellers are agreed, it is that for laziness, ugliness, stupidity, and wickedness, these men are not to be matched on any continent in the world...but this singular avidity (to be recruited) is mainly due to the fact that each man cherishes hope of running away at the earliest opportunity.[19]

In fact, although desertions were not uncommon, partly because of the custom of paying advances of wages to purchase their food and personal equipment, the rate of pay on expeditions was far above what the ordinary villager might expect, and therefore these were much sought-after positions. Wages were approximately £1 a month for ordinary porters, rising to double this for the caravan leader – it is interesting to compare this with present day rates for porters accompanying climbing parties up Kilimanjaro at just over £1 per day, carrying less than half of what those of 100 years ago carried. Apart from the pay, considerable prestige attached to being a porter, or *wangwana*, who ran the considerable risk of not returning alive to his village; of the 708 who left Zanzibar with Stanley in February 1887 on the Emin Pasha expedition, only 210 returned in December 1889. Stanley, who very much appreciated their worth, described the African porter as 'This useful person is the camel, the horse, the mule, the ass, the train, the wagon and the cart of East and Central Africa. Without him Salem would not obtain her ivory, Boston and New York their African ebony, their frankincense, myrrh and gum copal. He travels regions where the camel could not enter and where the horse and the ass could not live' – before going on to refer to his cheapness.[20] Keith attempted to reduce desertion by having formal written contracts drawn up, and by threatening to inform the *akidas* or local administrators for the Sultan so that the offenders would be arrested or would be denied their 'leaving certificates' and would be less likely to be employed on future caravans. The last could also be used as a deterrent to unsatisfactory service or behaviour.

At the time of the RGS expedition, the Sultan of Zanzibar was building up his army under British leadership and pressing into service any idlers he could find, so that the expedition was overwhelmed by the many who wished to avoid conscription, including some slaves. Of all those recruited to an expedition, the western tribe of the Nyamwezi were much preferred as they had built up a tradition of porterage, and to a large extent at this time had something of a monopoly. They understood the rules, had the equivalent of 'unions' to express their grievances and were immensely strong: they were capable of carrying 90 pounds on their heads or shoulders, sometimes the load being split into two parcels suspended at either end of a carrying pole. By the time of Keith's expedition, the bales were reduced to 60 pounds, but with the addition of a rifle, cooking pots, etc. the load could total 80 pounds – still a very considerable weight to be carried over difficult terrain for several hours each day on minimal rations: a tumblerful of the staple rice was standard.[21] They could expect on average to cover 10 miles a day, but with half that weight, they could carry this for 30 miles. Because of their reliability, the Nyamwezi would be entrusted with the more valuable loads, such as scientific instruments; such was the importance of the profession of porterage to the Nyamwezi that the males were not allowed to marry until they had carried a load of ivory to the coast and brought back a load of calico or brass wire, as the tribal stamp of manhood.[22]

The relations between the porters and the explorers depended to a large extent on the influence of the African caravan leaders and their headmen, but also to a considerable degree on the personality and attitude of the explorers themselves. Despite his often very brutal methods, Stanley was regarded in some quarters as being the most effective leader because he combined a genuine sympathy for his men with a robustly authoritarian approach when necessary, while Burton, who despised Africans, had such trouble that he could only complain about their quarrels, sickness, theft, disobedience, laziness and desertion, which meant that his greatest problem was keeping his ill-disciplined caravan on the move. But the last word perhaps belongs to the perceptive Thomson who generally maintained good relations with his men: 'I cannot express, in too appreciative terms, the honesty and faithfulness which characterised my men, and the really genuine character which lies at the bottom of their semi-savage nature…the Zanzibari porter is infinitely better than he is usually represented…we hear frequently about their troublesome conduct, desertions, obstinacy, etc. But we are never told how much they have to bear from their masters.'[23]

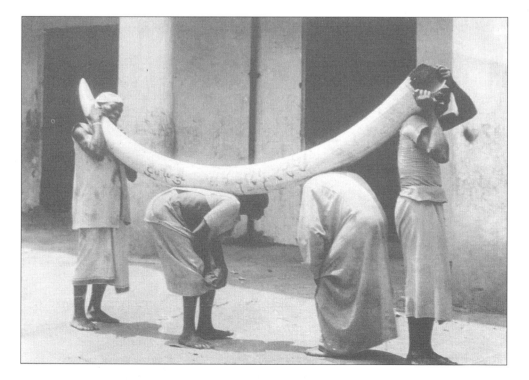

'Black and white ivory', Zanzibar around 1895 (Source: original source unknown; published as postcard from National Archives of Zanzibar)

The hazard of wildlife

Apart from the dangers from other humans, there was the wildlife to contend with, although it has to be said that a large caravan was more than likely to frighten away any animals in its vicinity. This was one reason why Thomson reported that, after his first expedition covering a distance of 5,000 miles, he had to go to a zoo to have his first sight of an elephant, despite the fact that the area he crossed, immediately before and after Johnston's death, now boasts over 60,000 elephants, the largest concentration in Africa.[24] However, the area was also known as the haunt of ivory hunters who may well have significantly reduced the populations of elephant. On his subsequent expedition through Masailand, he did report a sustained attack on his caravan by a pride of six lions which caused panic among the porters. On Thomson's same expedition a lion was heard sniffing around his tent and actually carried off one of his men. He himself was thrown by an angry buffalo, considered by many hunters to be the most dangerous of African game animals, which resulted in a six-inch wound in his thigh. (A Parisian lady viewed an illustration of Thomson being tossed into the air for some time and solemnly asked: 'Ah, M. Thomson, but how could you pose like that?'[25])

*Thomson being thrown by buffalo (Source: J. Thomson, **Through Masailand**, 1885, Trustees of the National Library of Scotland)*

Thomson recorded a very close encounter with a crocodile during the 1879 expedition:

> According to my usual custom I went out one morning to enjoy a good splash in the lake. Wading out a considerable distance, but not out of my depth, I observed what appeared to be a block of wood a short distance from me. Taking no notice of this I went on laving the cool water over myself. Looking up after a few minutes, I observed that the apparent log had floated nearer to me. Noting it more closely, I made out the outlines of a crocodile's head, with its ugly snout, wrinkled skin, and glittering eyes. I stood for a moment aghast at the sight, for I was a considerable distance from the shore, and still it came nearer. Regaining my presence of mind I made the welkin ring with a shout of 'Mambo! Mambo!' (crocodile). The cry instantly brought my men with their guns to the water's edge, and they seeing my imminent danger and desperate efforts to reach the shore, rushed in a body to meet me, making the waters boil. When they reached me the crocodile was within a few feet and would have seized me in another minute. But seeing the porters in such numbers, yelling and shouting, and firing their guns, it evidently thought that an empty stomach was better than a feast of bullets, and wisely disappeared. If I had been out of my depth at the time my chance of surviving the rencontre would have been a poor one.[26]

(Crocodiles apart, bathing in such waters would have made Thomson vulnerable to bilharzia, the waterborne disease transmitted by snails from which it was said he eventually died.) River crossings were made a nightmare by the presence of crocodiles, which in their depredations, exceeded all the other predators in the deaths and mutilations which they caused – Thomson himself was lucky to escape one attack when a crocodile tail almost swept him off his canoe. The area which Keith and Thomson traversed around Lake Tagalala, together with the nearby Rufiji River within what is now the Selous Game Reserve, has the largest concentration of freshwater crocodiles in the world.[27]

The water held other dangers: at the Murchison Falls in 1864, Samuel White Baker shot a crocodile, but the noise of his weapon so disturbed his boatmen that they allowed his canoe to drift into nearby reeds where a large bull hippopotamus apparently 'charged the canoe, and with a severe shock striking the bottom, he lifted us half out of the water'.[28] On the Shire River, the hunter Fred Moir records his boat being attacked by a hippopotamus which bit clean through the bottom of the boat and upset it, throwing everyone into the water, from where they were lucky to escape with their lives.[29] In fact, hippos came to be regarded with some justification as a real danger, especially the large aggressive bulls whose huge mouths could readily destroy a canoe.[30]

The incident in which Livingstone was quite severely wounded by a lion is well known, but one of the most astonishing encounters with the species occurred on the Scottish missionary Frederick Arnot's Zambezi safari in 1881 when his guide was awakened by the unmistakeable – and very loud – roars of a lion nearby, but apparently coming from under the ground near where they had recently been sleeping. The lion was in fact trapped in a camouflaged game pit which the travellers had not seen: they had inadvertently acted as bait and the beast was quickly despatched.[31]

Contrary to popular myth, snakes were unlikely to be encountered in any numbers, tending to avoid humans wherever possible, although Thomson caused pandemonium in one camp when in his own words he 'scattered a whole village, and my men besides, by coming amongst them holding by the neck a large green snake, eight feet long, which I had stunned and then picked up. It wriggled around my arm and body, though of course it could not bite, and when I appeared in this fashion, the people broke and fled in astonishment and fear'.[32] The reaction of the local population was, in my own experience, typical of the African's healthy fear of potentially lethal animals which in some districts are encountered on a daily basis. Africans have traditionally had a horror of snakes, estimated to kill thousands of people in Africa even at the present time.

Nor was it the more obviously lethal or larger forms of wildlife which the explorers had to contend with. Jiggers penetrated the feet and caused serious infection, guinea worms raised large blisters on the legs and had to be carefully extracted by unwinding with a straw, and the ever-present attentions of flies by day and mosquitoes by night were a major problem. An invasion of small black beetles into Speke's tent resulted in one penetrating far into his ear. His attempts to remove it with a penknife caused severe lacerations which became seriously and painfully infected and ended with a tumour which left a hole between his ear and nose.[33] Thomson records in the Usambaras how he woke up covered by fierce biting ants, 'like a million needles …I danced and writhed about as did Johnston and our men' dancing around frantically for two hours to get rid of them. (However, while the others dealt with the ants by lighting fires round their hut, it being a clear night, Keith calmly took the opportunity to obtain a latitudinal fix on a star.)

Later the same night, Thomson records: 'I was just on the point of sleeping for the second time, when an ear-piercing yell rang out through the air, and made me spring to my feet and instinctively seize my umbrella…a leopard had carried off a dog from within a few feet of where we lay'.[34] He was in fact confirming what many others before and since knew, that the leopard was one of the most dangerous and boldest of predators, with a particular appetite for dogs, and would even enter huts to attack sleeping women or children in particular. Samuel Baker considered the leopard far more dangerous than the lion.

Illness and disease

Of all the hazards presented to explorers, none could compare with the threat of illness and disease, which claimed so many European lives within a short time of landing in Africa. One commentator has put it dramatically: 'The recital of their sickness is horrifying. Collective and various fevers whose effects ranged from hallucinations of dual identity to toes that curled and looked one in the face. Troubles with insects that bit and burrowed into flesh and bone. Cuts and scratches which instead of healing normally remained inflamed for weeks. Dysentery-like visitations which lasted for months and left each traveller exhausted, and often too weak to move.'[35] The medical outfit is unrecognisable today, with considerable use of tincture of opium and port wine – the use of alcohol, especially in the tropics, would now be frowned upon, and the lack of recognition of the dangers of dehydration, for example from dysentery, must have led to numerous deaths.

Undoubtedly the greatest scourge was malaria, usually referred to as 'fever' which was debilitating and prostrating, to the extent that explorers were unable to move for considerable periods.[36] The proportion of Europeans who died of this disease was frightening: apparently, over 60 per cent of the men sent out by the Church Missionary Society in West Africa died of this, and the proportion elsewhere was not dissimilar. It was in fact the greatest killer of explorers, traders, soldiers and missionaries, with a 50 per cent or greater mortality rate.[37] The area traversed by Keith and Thomson immediately west of the coast was low-lying and swampy (malaria was often designated 'swamp fever'), providing an ideal breeding ground for the malaria mosquito *anopheles*. 'The great malarious coast-belt must be crossed, and one simply has to take his life in his hands and go through with it' stated Henry Drummond.[38] It was the same author who commented 'The climate is so pestilential that when two go, you and your friend are simply nursing each other time about, and the expedition never gets on…there is a stage in African fever – and everyone *must* have fever – when the watchful hand of a friend may make the difference between life and death.[39] Every single explorer suffered from malaria, including both Keith and Thomson. By the end of his travels, Thomson had also picked up cystitis, dysentery and bilharzia. Livingstone suffered from malaria from the beginning of his travels, and three of his companions died of it in the three successive years from 1861 to 1863, while it was responsible for the death of his wife, Mary Livingstone. Subsequently, he issued controlled doses of quinine daily as a prophylactic, with remarkable success. Following a bout of malaria, Kirk remarked that Keith was much better since he had taken quinine regularly.[40]

Apart from malaria, dysentery was one of the commonest causes of serious illness, resulting in acute diarrhoea, with weight loss, chronic sickness and anaemia, and according to Livingstone, the condition was aggravated by eating native porridge. What was not appreciated was that the condition required rest and rapid rehydration because of fluid loss. Unfortunately the robust Thomson, in company with others, believed that 'the only way to resist successfully the enervating effects of a humid tropical climate is by constant exertion, and by manfully fighting the baleful influence…hard constant work is the great preserve. Sweat out the malaria and the germs of disease, and less will be heard of the energy-destroying climate of the tropics.' However, Thomson himself, on his journey through Masailand, suffered a violent attack of dysentery which he admitted nearly killed him.[41]

Against this litany of afflictions, the explorers travelled with a veritable pharmacopoeia, most of which was useless. For malaria, whose source was attributed to the 'miasma' arising from the swamps, quinine was effective in relieving the symptoms, and was sometimes taken in massive doses.[42] The explorer Grant's medicine chest contained Brown's blistering tissue, plaster, lunar caustic, citric acid, julap, calomel, rhubarb, blue pill, colocynth, diachlon plasters, laudanum, Dover's powders, and emetic essence of ginger – a somewhat pathetic collection of pills and powders with which to combat tropical scourges. According to *Hints to Travellers* these should be contained in a long lacquered cylindrical tin to be divided into upper and lower compartments, clearly separating and identifying poisons.

There are pages of instructions on the use of these medicaments, but it is interesting to note the wide range of ailments which each was used for: opium pills were recommended not only for colic and diarrhoea, but also for rupture and spasms, while morphia was recommended for colds in the head! The recommendation to use ipecacuanha for dysentery would almost certainly cause vomiting, which would result in loss of fluids, and yet the instructions were to reduce fluid intake – quite the opposite of what would now be recommended. Purges were frequently favoured for a variety of conditions, again likely to cause dehydration. Some of the treatments appeared worse than the affliction: gunpowder was exploded on snakebites, while a charge of the same in warm water made an effective emetic according to Francis Galton, and haemorrhaging was stemmed by the application of a red hot ramrod. One explorer eased the pain of rupture by strapping an opened sardine tin over the painful spot. Medical comforts which were to be used only in emergency include brandy, milk, tea, sugar, salt and pepper, which would indicate, at least for the last four items, an unusual degree of abstinence.

Recording the journey

It was the general practice to plot the astronomical observations as the expedition progressed. When the conventional narrative was published on return, tables of positions and altitudes were included after they had been checked by specialists. In fact, because Livingstone had lost track of the dates on his last explorations, all of his latitudes and longitudes would have been quite inaccurate.[43]

Normally the first records were made in the expedition diary as the journey proceeded. On the basis of this, a journal would sometimes be constructed (and published in newspapers or other periodicals, sometimes as a series) and reports would be made to the sponsoring body, often simply in the form of correspondence, before the final narrative – the definitive account of the expedition – was written up, complete with illustrations and maps, for publication. In addition, the expedition diary would frequently be complemented by detailed data in notebooks containing astronomical observations for latitudes and longitudes, meteorological data and boiling point temperatures to ascertain heights, while some would contain scientific data on geology, plants, animals, etc. Livingstone jealously guarded his notebooks and journals – the former he regarded as confidential, fearing with some justification that others might steal his ideas about where the true sources of the Nile lay. He generally felt that he knew more about scientific matters and African affairs than some of the 'stay-at-home African experts' who would presume to interpret his work.

These initial reactions to what the explorer actually saw at the time were important, as they often provided a revealing contrast to the edited version which would appear as the published narrative, the editing partially carried out by publishers and others. This published account would often leave out much that was originally contained in the field notebooks and diaries, including comments on individuals (for example, Livingstone on John Kirk at Zanzibar[44]) or to local groups encountered, which might not be to their advantage, throwing light on the writer's attitudes. Where descriptions of African life are given, these are rarely complimentary, reflecting very much the attitudes of the age and the European sense of superiority.[45] Keith was certainly not immune from this, and even his descriptions of the physiognomy and dress of villagers encountered on his expedition often imply 'primitiveness'.

The final polished narrative could gloss over incidents or misrepresent situations where convenient, but this was less likely to happen where there were two or more explorers travelling together. While some such as Livingstone seemed to prefer to travel without the companionship of other Europeans, in the words of Henry Drummond: 'An unutterable loneliness comes over one at times in the great still forests... on the whole the solitary course is not to be commended.'[46] Often the vocabulary used was altered to avoid giving offence to Victorian sensibilities, but more significantly the narrative might attempt to give the impression that the European explorer was more in control than he actually was. Not only were they dependent to a high degree on their native caravan leaders and headmen, but also to their interpreters, and in the case of East Africa, on Swahili and Arab traders, including known slavers. Nothing would be revealed in these narratives which might impugn their own honour or reputation.

Apart from Keith's diary and Thomson's subsequent published narrative, other records of the 1878 RGS expedition, such as Thomson's diary and any notebooks of the two explorers, have not been found. Almost certainly, Keith would have kept a notebook for his detailed observations, since his diary (recently transcribed by me) is too bulky to have been written up *en route*, while the organisation of the entries indicates that it must have been written up at the end of each day. A heavy calf-bound standard Lett's diary for the year 1879, it includes an almanac which itself gives a flavour of the times, including the birthdays of no fewer than 16 members of the

Royal family and their children, 'Directions for Making a Will', and advice that 'An Englishman travelling on the Continent seldom needs a passport except in times of war...' Perhaps the most arcane inclusions are the Alimentary Tables giving not only the amount of nutrition per 1,000 parts of common foodstuffs but also the time needed for digestion – from raw oysters to apple dumplings. More seriously, as the background to commercial activity, it identifies important events such as the 'The Eastern Question' and the invasion of Turkey by Russia, the ceding of Cyprus to Britain as part of the condition for guaranteeing Turkish sovereignty, while Austria was attempting to invade Bosnia and Herzegovina.

Each subsequent ruled foolscap sheet is assigned to a day, with entries from 1 January to 12 June 1879. In two instances, the diary is extended by notes (for example, on the proposed expedition route) running over several days. Joseph Thomson, as deputy leader of the expedition, would have kept his own diary from which he compiled the final expedition narrative. Both the diary and the separate geographical observations (including astronomical readings) would be the property of the expedition sponsors, the RGS.

Exploration diaries of this date and earlier are notoriously difficult to transcribe, though in this case Keith was at least systematic in confining himself to a bound volume, whereas Livingstone, for example, apparently was inclined, when he had exhausted his formal stationery, to write on any piece of scrap paper which came to hand. In the case of Keith, several problems became apparent from the outset. Apart from the handwriting, it is obvious that he was writing for his own purposes, in the first instance in the form of cryptic notes, with minimal punctuation, and sometimes with abbreviations: for example, 'dist.' can mean both distance and district, while 'm.' can mean miles or minutes. His sister Grace, transcribing his Paraguayan diary, commented 'we all weave away at crewel work in the intervals of attacking a certain South American journal written in very minute characters with unstable Republican ink. When we flounder into a tremendous bog we apply an immense magnifying glass to the spot, and when *that* fails, imagination comes to the rescue!' (This is identical to my own experience.) As an acknowledged linguist, Keith clearly learnt Kiswahili readily, and not infrequently used that language in the diary for items such as cloths, food items, etc. His spelling created greatest problems with place names, where it is not always consistent – many of these locations are ephemeral since they relate to settlements which no longer exist.

Deciphering Keith's script proved a considerable challenge where either he has been using a broad-nibbed pen, or more likely, as has been noted in other diaries where liquid ink has been used, the ink has over time spread into the fabric of the paper so that it can at times become illegible. For some reason, this becomes most apparent in the section dealing with the trial expedition to the Usambara region. Here only occasional words could be deciphered with the result that the transcription became meaningless. Fortunately, Keith succeeded in completing and forwarding his formal notes for this journey, which were published.[47] It was assumed that for ease of transport powdered ink would have been taken for mixing with water, but there is an entry shortly after the start of the main expedition to the interior which contradicts this, when Keith notes 'find that Souza has omitted ink from the boxes; two large bottles were ordered', Souza being one of the suppliers of the expedition in Zanzibar.[48] I had reason to be grateful for Souza's negligence since, from that point, Keith was obliged to use a relatively sharp pencil, producing a much clearer script, and incidentally confirming the suggestion above concerning ink spread.

Life on the march

Life on an expedition would follow a routine dictated by light, with an early start, the camp rising as early as 4am when the night fires would be re-stoked, the tents struck, and the first meal of the day eaten. It would often take a considerable time to get a large caravan on the way, the loads having to be assigned, weapons checked and the various groups sorting themselves usually according to tribe and language. The *kiringosis* or guides would head the long file, with their flamboyant red cloaks and feathered headdresses, carrying the red flag of Zanzibar, accompanied by a drummer – all of this of course to impress the local inhabitants. They would certainly have been impressed by the noise, whether of the kudu horns or the marching chants of the porters. After walking for several hours, there would be a meal about 8.00am, with a further march until the early afternoon. Wherever possible, a camp for the night would be made near to a village, where food and water could be obtained, each man (or woman, since it was not unusual for wives to accompany their husbands) being given a portion of cloth to trade for food with local villagers.

The final meal of the day would be taken in the late afternoon before the light faded. If there was thought to be a threat from either wild animals or equally wild humans, a *boma* or stockade of thorns would be built around the encampment, and fires would be maintained throughout the night. The evening would be punctuated by the songs of the porters and *askaris*, as well as the drums and other musical instruments to accompany the dancing that was a feature of camp life, often hosted by the local villagers. The morale of the caravan depended on the quantity and quality of the food and on the experience of the day's march, whether it had been an exhausting march up steep hills with dense undergrowth, a floundering passage through swamps with interminable river crossings, or conversely a speedy crossing of open plain with abundant game for the pot. Few if any of the porters would have footwear, and although the thick skin on their feet would have given some protection, they were not immune to the scorching heat of the ground or the sharp thorns which were a feature of much bushland. The European explorers, whatever their condition, would attempt to write up their notes in daylight, and before retiring to their tiny tents. With darkness falling quite suddenly around 6.30pm, unless they were inclined to observe the socialising of their men, it would have been a long evening, and because of the lack of illumination and the dangers from wild animals, there would be no inclination to explore their surroundings. In any case, they might well be exhausted by a gruelling march under difficult conditions.

> On the whole there was an excess of everything. When it was hot it was unbearably so, and as dry as dust. When it was wet it was like a steam bath most of the time, with sudden plunges under a cold shower…going through the forests was like crawling through a series of damp dark cellars, embraced by monstrous vegetable growth…[49]

The problems of progressing through dense bush is well described by Stanley on his 1874 expedition where at one point he states:

> The day brought us into a dense jungle of acacias and euphorbia, through which literally we had to push our way, by scrambling, crawling along the ground under natural tunnels of embracing shrubbery, cutting the convolvuli and creepers, thrusting aside stout thorny bushes, and, by various detours, taking advantage of every slight opening the jungle afforded…[50,51]

The motivation of explorers

African exploration has been described as 'a chaos world…all travel in the interior depended on human muscle…Africa's climate was also inimical to the white man and all his works. The heat with temperatures frequently over 100 degrees F, produced weird effects. Screws worked loose from boxes, horn handles dropped off instruments, combs split into fine laminae and the lead fell out of pencils…hair ceased to grow, nails became as brittle as glass…flour lost more than eight per cent of its weight…'[52] Given what has been said already about the problems of African travel, the threat of disease, of attacks by humans or animals, the problems with porters or terrain, the question has to be asked 'Why did they do it?' It certainly cannot have been for material gain: apart from their expenses and a modest honorarium of a few hundred pounds, neither Keith nor Thomson were paid anything. A first clue is given by Rotberg:

> Each added in his own way to the excitement of Africa's discovery…their different adventures were followed avidly by a public obsessed as is today's with exploits in space – with the drama and glory of the conquest of the mysterious dark continent. All received the medals and plaudits of the world's leading geographical societies, the praise of statesmen, and international recognition of a most gratifying kind. Celebrities of a romantic, evangelical age, they were much sought after in metropolitan society, and were heroes to several generations of men and boys.[53]

Fame was indeed the spur for many, if not the sole reason for embarking on ventures which were as likely as not to claim their lives; it has even been suggested that some subconsciously sought martyrdom and a sanctification through death in Africa.[54] But the reasons for engaging on such potentially lethal expeditions were as numerous and varied as the personalities of the explorers. Nor can altruism be discounted with Livingstone's high moral call to young men of Christian principle enthusing so many. He himself was at least as much an explorer as a missionary (it was said that he disguised the former by the latter) and many other missionaries trod the same path, often making important geographical and ethnological contributions. Thomson hero-worshipped Livingstone from childhood, but was also a romantic – a characteristic shared with nearly all explorers – for whom Africa had a special appeal.[55] It presented an opportunity for action in a personality which could not abide inactivity.[56] But he was also motivated by the intellectual challenge, manifested in his collections of specimens and scientific writings. Like so many others, once he had tasted the adventurous life of an African explorer, he admitted that life in Britain, with all its restrictions and Victorian mores, including its social hierarchies which would have left him at a disadvantage, held no appeal.

It is more difficult to assess Keith's motivation, albeit that he had a longstanding association with Africa through his cartographic interests. Having through his father a direct connection with Livingstone, he too would have been inspired by the great man's example, although it is doubtful if he shared with Livingstone the latter's sense of being divinely ordained with a powerful moral purpose. Through his map work and scientific studies from an early age, he would have been familiar indirectly with the geography of many countries, and for his compilations, thoroughly researched the detailed records of other explorers – there could hardly have been a better intellectual grounding. His fellowship of the RGS and subsequent professional map work there, together with his father's associations, would have brought him into direct contact with some of the greatest explorers of his day, including such luminaries as Burton. But his confidences to his mother and sisters indicated that at least as compelling was a very simple reason: sheer restlessness. He shared with Thomson a strong desire for adventurous action: while in London he complained on a number of occasions about the tedium of often mechanical deskwork. Keith would not of course have been immune also to the attractions of anticipated future fame and public acclaim, both social and professional, although perhaps he needed this less than Thomson.

Other deeper, often subconscious, motives have been attributed to explorers, especially in Africa. Many were considered obsessives, driven by a need to find their own identity; Stanley said that only in Africa could he be himself.[57] He claimed that Scots were impelled by a powerful sense of duty, fuelled no doubt by a Presbyterian ethic and morality. Others sought a sense of freedom, not least from the materialistic urban and industrial society of western Europe in the mid nineteenth century to live a more simple and naturalistic life, if only temporarily. Still others were perhaps testing their manhood and attempting to gain satisfaction from personal achievement against the odds, with the strong pull of initial discovery and the claim to be first.[58] What seems clear is that the motivations of explorers were often very complex, barely recognised by the majority of them, and rarely explained by their own statements. One commentator has gone so far as to claim that all of them were neurotic to a degree and that nearly all of them were liars.[59] Certainly most were egocentric: even Keith's notorious shyness could be ascribed to this.

The degree to which explorers took an interest in the appearance, culture and customs of the indigenous communities through which they passed varied considerably; Livingstone and Burton gave detailed descriptions of Africans.[60] That did not prevent some from taking an interest for other purposes, including sexual liaisons, which were not infrequent. It has been suggested that one of the motivations for at least some explorers, characterised by Burton, was to be able to escape the restrictions of civilisation – particularly a Victorian one, with its special prudery – and to be able to indulge in sexual freedom at a convenient distance from home. However, this in turn could mean that those with moral scruples or inhibition about promiscuity between Europeans and African women could suffer deep anxieties, and even depression.[61] A certain titillation would be aroused by the narratives of the explorers themselves in their frequent allusions to undressed African women, such as Thomson's description: 'I found myself surrounded by a body of undraped damsels, whose clothes and ornaments consisted of a string of beads' or on another occasion 'in this place [the Usambaras] clothes are manifestly at a discount, especially among the ladies, who have nothing but a small piece of cloth hanging from their waists. Hence this "dress" is generally one of simple shreds and tatters, kept together no one knows how…one young damsel sported as the sole apology for a garment the remnant of an old fishing net'. He had led up to this by indicating that 'gauze was not considered too airy a fabric' – surely an invitation to erotic speculation.[62]

The interest of others was sometimes quite different. Before his departure, Grace wrote to Keith:

> I have been asked by the secretary for an Asylum for Idiots if you would take notes of any imbeciles you may meet in your African adventures! I suggested the sane savages would be quite bad enough, but this enthusiastic Secretary indignantly declared that the study was profoundly interesting – that it had not yet been proved that idiocy existed among African tribes, and pointed out the boon you might do to science…so don't fail to take notice of the 'silly' folks you meet…

In October, Keith let the family know of his engagement to a Miss Ida Chinnery from London of whom they had often heard, but had never met – when they did, it is clear that they were not over-impressed, considering her too shallow and falling below Keith's intellectual standards. Following Keith's death, her behaviour was to be a cause of much distress to Keith's mother. An engagement just before a potentially hazardous expedition which might last for up to two years may not have been unusual in Victorian times, but at least the prospect of a lengthy separation presumably could not have been attractive to the couple.

Grace records:

> When he came to us, late in October, he was so full of happiness, expanding in his shy way, as he talked of his new hopes, that we could not but be glad for him. It was a hurried visit and during the daylight hours he and I were making calls on all the friends he wished to see. We lunched – or dined – I forget which – at Kirkhill, and I remember what great and wonderful prophecies our lively aunt made as to his future. Mother, in sad depression, could not go with us.

From her contact with explorers and missionaries, Keith's mother would have been familiar with the dangers and obstacles her son would have to face, so well summed up by Stanley:

> Fatal Africa! One after another, travellers drop away. It is such a huge continent, and each of its secrets is environed by so many difficulties – the torrid heat, the miasma exhaled from the soil, the noisome vapours enveloping every path, the giant cane grass suffocating the wayfarer, the rabid fury of the native guarding every entry and exit, the unspeakable misery of life within the continent, the utter absence of every comfort, the bitterness with which each day heaps upon the poor white man's head, in that land of blackness.[63]

The family were only too well aware of how fatal Africa could be and how readily 'travellers drop away':

> The last evening of all, we sat by the fire and tried to talk cheerfully, but Mother could not be comforted. He was leaving by the night train for London and having forgotten to provide himself with a travelling cap, I manufactured one out of a discarded sealskin coat, and we laughed over the fitting of it...mother said goodbye to him alone; I went to the station. When the express crept along the platform he leaned from the window to wave to me: then it entered the tunnel and was swallowed up in the darkness. And that was the last I saw of his dear face.

NOTES

1 *Proc. RGS* (1879), 63.
2 Crone (1964), 4.
3 Stanley (1890), II, 306–7.
4 RGS Letters file, Thomson to Bates,1 November 1878.
5 Rotberg (1971), Appendix 1.
6 Even in the early 1960s, some porters carried their own flintlocks on my forest surveys.
7 RGS Letters file, Johnston to Bates, 12 January 1878.
8 McLynn (1992), 221–2.
9 Ibid., 224.
10 Bennet (1969), 113. Dodgshun wrote in the strongest possible terms to the British Consul in Zanzibar, Dr John Kirk, about the latter's support for Mirambo – see Bennet (1969), 100–14.
11 Simpson (1975), 89–97.
12 Thomson (1883), 138–9.
13 Raban (1999), 197.
14 McLynn (1992), 138.
15 Dugmore (1900), 198.
16 McLynn (1992), 217–18.
17 Ibid., 133.
18 Bennet (1969), ix–xii.
19 Drummond (1889), 5.
20 McLynn (1992), 151.
21 Ibid., 144.
22 Ibid., 142.
23 Ibid., 170.
24 *The Scotsman,* 28 May 1881.
25 Barrie (1926), 104.
26 Thomson (1881b), 143.
27 The speed with which unprotected men crossed rivers in the course of the author's forest surveys was noticeable.
28 Bradnum (1970), 261–2.
29 Moir (1923), 69–70.
30 For a very useful explanation of the travel records in East Africa at this time, including a note on 'Armchair geographers' see Bridges, R. C. (1987b).
31 Lawman (1960), 61.
32 Thomson (1881a), 131.
33 Bradnum (1970), 85–6.
34 Thomson (1881a), 42.
35 Bradnum (1970), 24.
36 For a very detailed and horrifying account of the nature and symptoms of these tropical diseases, see Liebowitz (1999), 42–5.
37 Liebowitz (1999), 44.
38 Drummond (1889), 7.
39 Ibid., 10.
40 National Library of Scotland Kirk Archive Acc.9942/31 Diaries and Notebooks.

41 Shepperson (1982) 26. Letter of Thomson to Lord Aberdare, 26 July 1884.
42 Such was the claimed efficacy of the modern anti-malarial drugs by the 1950s that the author's African troops were automatically placed on a punishment charge if they contracted the disease, on the assumption that they could not have been taking their daily pill.
43 Bridges (1987a), 12.
44 National Library of Scotland Ms. 10728, Notebook XV, 59–61.
45 Rotberg (1970), 6–7.
46 Drummond (1889), 10.
47 *Proc. RGS* (1879), 545–58.
48 McCarthy, J. (2000), *The 1878–80 Royal Geographical Society Expedition to East Africa: The Diary of Keith Johnston.* NLS mss.74.
49 Bradnum (1970), 23.
50 McLynn (1982), 219.
51 This description tallies exactly with my own experience in emulating in 2001 Thomson's attempted ascent of Mount Hatambulo which he renamed in honour of his deceased leader.
52 McLynn (1982), 8.
53 Rotberg (1970), 1.
54 Klein (1975), 351.
55 Rotberg (1970), 305. This work is probably the most systematic attempt to describe the methods and motivations of European explorers in East Africa.
56 Rotberg (1971), 302.
57 McLynn (1982), 340.
58 Ibid., 343.
59 Klein (1975), 334–4.
60 Rotberg (1970), 5–6.
61 McLynn (1992), 355.
62 Thomson (1881b), 38.
63 McLynn (1982), 7.

8

Zanzibar

———

'The cesspool of wickedness'

Keith and Thomson left for their East African Expedition from Victoria Docks, mid-afternoon on a day of drenching rain on 14 November 1878 on the steamship *Assyria*. They were provided with a free passage by Sir William Mackinnon, a staunch supporter of development in East Africa and owner of what became the British India Line.[1] In the worsening weather conditions of the Bay of Biscay, Thomson suffered the agonies of seasickness, with the ship rolling through the Atlantic surge. In a letter to his mother, Keith said that 'the captain is a very jolly fellow and has made me quite at home in his cabin'. They reached Aden on 12 December, where the ship to take them to Zanzibar was not expected for a further two weeks. Underneath the great baking and barren rocks above the town, the explorers had their first real taste of desert heat – a torrid atmosphere that made them listless. Here Keith, again writing to his mother, said he was 'longing now to hear what you three dear people have been doing since the beginning of the month, and that my dear lassie is safe and happy with you...' referring to his fiancée, Ida, then on an extended stay with the Johnston family in Edinburgh.

Across the Gulf of Aden in Somalia lay the port of Berbera, its colourful annual market then in full swing. While the eager Thomson made his way there with many adventures *en route*, more cautiously Keith, anxious about missing his connecting vessel, stayed behind. Leaving Aden in the SS *Punjab*, Keith recorded in his diary meeting William Beardall, who was then engaged on building a road westwards from Dar-es-Salaam, and discussing with him the country the expedition was to travel through. He noted the French ship, the *Vortigern*, grounded off the Somali coast, which was to cause the British authorities some anxiety: it was reported to have quantities of gunpowder and ammunition which might have fallen into the hands of the Zulu chief Cetawayo, then threatening British forces in South Africa.[2] The *Punjab* itself grounded at the entrance to Zanzibar Harbour before the explorers were able to disembark on the exotic island where they were to spend the next four months.

Zanzibar is the second largest island on the East African coast roughly about the size of Hertfordshire, 53 miles long by 24 miles broad, some 22 miles off the mainland. The first record of the island is about AD 60, but it would have been visited by ancient races of Assyrians, Sumerians as well as Egyptians, Phoenicians and Southern Arabians. Vasco da Gama visited in 1499 and early in the sixteenth century the Portuguese became masters of both Zanzibar and East African coast, but by the end of the seventeenth century they were displaced by Arabs from Muscat and Oman.[3] By the middle of the nineteenth century it was the most important depot for the slave trade. Travellers at this time describe a town of the utmost squalor contrasting with the opulence of the Sultan's palaces – Seyyid Said bin Sultan, the founder of modern Zanzibar and its clove industry, transferred his capital from Muscat to Zanzibar in 1840. Following Seyyid Said's death in 1856, after two treaties for the restriction of the slave trade in the Sultan's dominions, and other commercial treaties with USA, Britain and France, the Imam's possessions in Africa became independent of Muscat and Oman. Zanzibar was brought into close contact with Europe by the opening of Suez Canal in 1869, and by the inauguration of a monthly service between Aden and Zanzibar in 1872 by the British India Steam Navigation Company, while the Eastern Telegraph Company laid down a cable in 1879.

Largely because of its status in India and its domination of the off-shore island of Zanzibar, Britain was at this time the most influential European power in East Africa. Much of this involvement came from commercial and missionary enterprise, rather than directly from the British Government which tried to avoid overt entanglement in African affairs, even if the missionary societies and traders sought its help in containing Portuguese and Arab opposition – the latter especially in relation to the Indian Ocean trade in slaves and ivory. The important connection with India was demonstrated by the dominance of Indian traders in Zanzibar, not least in the fitting out of caravans through their capital and credit facilities. However, the British interest in East Africa was also connected to its strategic involvement with Egypt and the Nile Valley, so that there were a number of quite complex inter-related strands of commercial, imperial, and proselytising factors in Britain's interests in the latter half of the nineteenth century in East Africa and Zanzibar.[4]

What sort of place had Keith and Thomson come to? Historically, it had an evil reputation: 'closely packed, reeking suffocation of dirt-caked stone and coral-lime houses, divided into a crossword puzzle of dark, fetid alleys whose open drains, abundant night soil and busy vermin helped erase any image of oriental glamour'.[5] Ten years before Keith's arrival, the Scots physician Dr James Christie wrote 'Countless millions of ants and beetles, millions of rats and armies of wild dogs aid in removing the garbage of the town...' Not surprisingly, disease was rife, with cholera claiming a total of 50,000 lives in the outbreaks of 1858 and 1869. Livingstone, who named the island 'Stinkibar' claimed that no one could enjoy good health there.[6] However, the sight and smell which most revolted Europeans were those of the rotting corpses of slaves on the beaches, brought in by the tide after being thrown overboard from the dhows of Arabs who had no further use for them, if for example they had been found to have disease,[7] – or they might be those unfortunates – men, women and children – murdered by the roving gangs of northern Arabs who terrorised the town at night.[8]

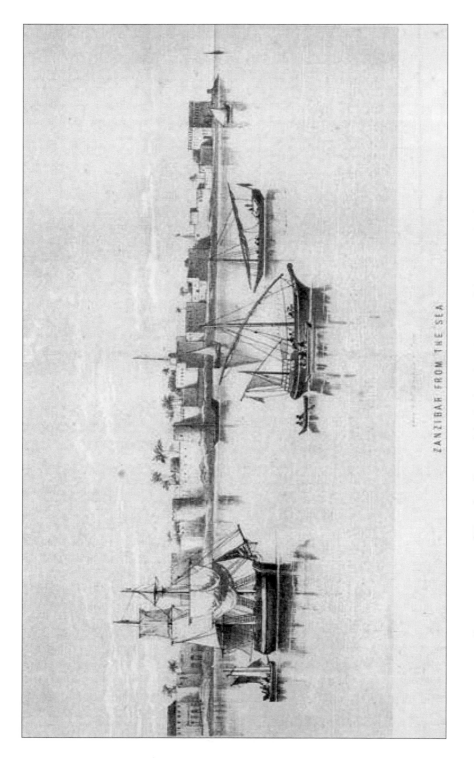

ZANZIBAR FROM THE SEA

European quarter of Zanzibar (Source: John Kirk Archive, Trustees of the National Library of Scotland)

Yet the initial impression gained on approaching the port might be that

out of a sapphire sea rose a coral island of incandescent green, studded with groves of coconut and mango, and orchards of cloves, the palm forest decked with pink convolvulus, a thin line of creamy surf beating languidly on the milk-white sand. Approaching across the shimmering lagoon, one saw a city that might have been summoned by Aladdin's lamp, its arches and colonnades, towers and turrets, flags and flagpoles, refracted upwards in the frenzy of a mirage...[9]

In fact, Zanzibar had changed considerably from the mid-1870s and, by the time the explorers arrived, Thomson was not unfavourably impressed: he was enchanted by his first sight of the green island after the barrenness of the north-east African coast, especially at sunset on a beautiful night. He commented on the changes which had taken place in recent years:

Dead animals, filth and garbage are no longer allowed to be thrown out into the streets to rot and fester in the sun; and dead slaves are at least placed below the soil instead of being thrown upon the beach... No starved or ill-used slaves are to be seen, for on cases of inhumanity being reported to the Sultan, the sufferers are at once set free, and made safe from the brutality of their masters. Indeed this class seem to have a remarkably easy time of it, and have ten times more liberty than thousands of our clerks and shop girls. They are commonly allowed to engage themselves out to work; and no caravan ever goes up the country without a number of slaves among the porters. A jolly-hearted crew they are, whose motto in life is, 'beer, women, and ease.'[10]

One of the most obvious buildings was the recently built Anglican Cathedral where the Universities Mission to Central Africa (UMCA) was based, constructed symbolically above the notorious old slave market, at the instigation of the famous linguist Bishop Steere of that mission. (The massive and rather ugly cathedral still stands in its somewhat unkempt grounds.) However, Thomson, who described the Bishop as 'that genial and laborious gentleman', was scathing in his condemnation of the money and energy spent on this, claiming that it could have been much more usefully directed elsewhere.[11,12] Thomson notes that:

Everywhere there are gorgeously dressed Arabs, riding on horseback...Negroes dressed in white shirts, or women with more highly coloured stuffs carrying huge pots of water on their heads. With those are mixed Hindus, Banyans, and Parsees, and not infrequently a European lady or gentleman goes riding or walking past... the square, prison-like houses are devoid of ornament and all whitewashed present little variety. They form narrow crooked lanes whose only recommendation is their shadiness during the greater part of the day.[13] There is nothing European in the scene with the exception of the ships in the harbour and an occasional white man in the streets...the Arabs are the dominant race, and form the upper and ruling class.[14] Each nationality has its own separate quarter in the town... Pass along some lanes, and but for the houses you might imagine yourself to be in India…Wander towards the palace, and you leave the business thoroughfares behind and enter Arabia in a twinkling…from Arabia we seem suddenly to enter a purely African scene…there is a gabbling crowd of natives in all degrees of undress – the wild-looking Somali from the far north of the Sultan's dominion, Wanyamwezi porters waiting for a return caravan to Unyamyembe, representatives of the coast tribes, and finally Waswahili slaves and freed men from every tribe.[15]

However, writing even 10 years later, the Rev. Henry Drummond was distinctly unimpressed:

Zanzibar is the focus of all East African exploration …oriental in its appearance, Mohammedan in its religion, Arabian in its morals, this cesspool of wickedness is a fit capital for the Dark Continent. An immense outfit is required to penetrate this shopless and foodless land, and here only can the traveller make up his caravan…. the ivory and slave trades have made caravanning a profession and everything the explorer wants is to be had in these bazaars, from a tin of sardines to a repeating rifle.[16]

Zanzibar Cathedral (Source: W. & A.K. Johnston Archive,
Trustees of the National Library of Scotland)

About 80,000 people lived in the grossly overcrowded port of Stonetown, dominated by the Sultan's palace and the larger homes of wealthy Arab and Indian merchants, known as Banyans. The Indian merchants had developed a virtual monopoly over the island's trade in cloves, India rubber and ivory, and largely financed the so-called Arab slave trade. It was estimated that two-thirds of the black Africans living on the island were slaves, many of them working on the plantations, as domestic servants, or as porters at the harbour. By the middle of the nineteenth century, this trade in people was worth 100,000 dollars annually to the Sultan in duties imposed on each slave passing through the Zanzibar market.[17] When Keith arrived in Zanzibar, the slave trade in the Sultan's dominions had officially been terminated with the Sultan's agreement, under considerable pressure from the British Government. This did not, however, mean that slavery had ended (it still exists in Africa and elsewhere in the world) nor was the trade ended – in 1879, there was evidence all around, not only of an illicit trade, but of toleration of 'domestic' slavery – after all, Keith recruited slaves to his caravan as volunteers under contract to their masters. Although the closing down of the Zanzibar slave market was a serious impediment to the sea-borne slave trade to Arabia, and between the mainland and Zanzibar, the British were unable to challenge slavery *per se*.

The Sultan's writ was only effective on the coast and the immediate interior; the trade still thrived inland.[18] Closely associated with this human trade was the export of ivory, as this was brought from the interior to the coast on the shoulders of the slaves, giving rise to the term 'black and white ivory' since the ivory was also used to purchase slaves – the white variety considered to be the more valuable item of commerce. Slaves were used to carry ivory, but ivory was also used to purchase slaves and vice versa, i.e. they were another form of currency,[19] hence Livingstone's idea of replacing this with legitimate trade by development of an infrastructure and production of other goods to export, which led to mission plantations of agricultural cash crops. It was estimated that, at the time of Keith's expedition, some 400,000 pounds of ivory was being transhipped from the island *en route* to the warehouses of Europe, North America and the Far East.[20]

Reliable figures of the numbers of slaves taken from East Africa are difficult to obtain, but one estimate is of 2 million slaves exported between 1750 and 1867, mainly to Arab lands, but also to the Caribbean plantations and Brazil. A conservative estimate was of 100,000 slaves being exported from East Africa annually, many of these from around Lake Nyassa and Lake Tanganyika to which the RGS expedition was headed.[21] The effect on local populations was devastating, bringing a reign of terror and, in the most affected areas, a complete destabilisation of the social and economic structures. A number of African chiefs, tempted by the offer of guns and trade goods from Arab slavers, did the latter's work for them by carrying out slave raids on neighbouring tribes, creating an atmosphere of suspicion and fear, which the RGS expedition encountered on many occasions.[22] The acquisition of firearms by these chiefs simply meant that their raids were more effective and, in the process of capturing a few slaves, many more villagers might be killed or injured, while the same guns were also used to acquire ivory. Retaliatory raids created a situation of constant tribal warfare which prevented development, forced whole movements of settlements and decimated local populations. There were enormous losses through starvation, exhaustion and ill-treatment on the way to the coast and beyond: Livingstone estimated that, for every slave sold in the Zanzibar market, five died on the way.[23,24]

The prices paid by the Arab or Swahili traders to chiefs varied according to the sex, age and health of captured slaves. W. P. Livingstone, writing around the time of the RGS expedition, records the going rate around Lake Nyassa – one of the most heavily raided areas – as ranging from 2 yards of calico for a toothless old man to 56 yards for a young unmarried girl, or 32 yards for a young woman with baby unweaned – with 4 yards for the baby.[25] Horace Waller, who had served for five years as a missionary on Lake Nyassa and was a close associate of Livingstone, was a vociferous opponent of the slave trade all his life. He remarked 'I have seen children from the age of eight to ten years being bought for less corn than would go into one of our hats.'[26]

Although Keith did not himself encounter any slave caravans, Thomson gives a graphic description of one he met shortly after his leader's death:

> Half-way up the ascent a sad spectacle met our eyes – a chained gang of women and children. They were descending the rocks with the utmost difficulty, and picking their steps with great care, as, from the manner in which they were chained together, a fall meant dislocation of the neck. Truth compels me to say that this was the first slave caravan I had yet seen in Africa, though I had heard of a number which had kept out of our path for fear of our liberating the slaves. But though it was the first, it exhibited all the well-known horrors of the cursed traffic. The women, chained to each other by the neck, were carrying many of them their children on their backs, besides heavy loads on their heads. Their faces and general appearance told of starvation and utmost hardship, and their naked bodies spoke with ghastly eloquence of the flesh-cutting lash. Their dull despairing gaze showed that all hope of life and liberty was gone forever. Even the sight of an Englishmen gave no hope to them; for, unfortunately, the white man has more the character of a ghoul than of a liberator of slaves in the far interior. Saddest sight of all was that some little children reduced to perfect skeletons, looking up as if they beseeched us to kill them and put them out of further torture…the most I could do was to stop them and give the little things such a feed as they had not had for weeks.[27]

On the whole question of the effect of slavery on native populations, Thomson makes an interesting generalisation from his own experience travelling along the expedition route where the slave trade had previously been rife. He contrasts his own impression of the psychology and state of development of several tribes near the coast with those of Burton, who had also passed through the area some years earlier. Although Thomson acknowledges that Burton's very derogatory remarks were typical

Slave caravan (Source: H. Waller, Last Journeys of David Livingstone, vol. 1)

of his whole attitude towards Africans, Thomson's own observations indicated that there had undoubtedly been a marked improvement in the state of agriculture, the absence of warfare and a generally welcoming attitude on the part of the local population. He ascribes this partly to the recent consolidation of the Sultan's authority and to the increase in trade, particularly in rubber and gum copal.[28] Significantly, however, he suggests this activity was due to the increased sense of security resulting from the decline in the slave trade, backed by the Sultan, and the consequent stability and interest in legitimate commerce. Of course, since the whole purpose of the RGS expedition was predicated on the improvement of communications to further this object, Thomson would naturally make the supporting argument, but at least these were based on his own quite perceptive observations of apparent change.

John Kirk: Consul extraordinary

On arrival in Zanzibar the explorers were warmly welcomed by the British Consul John Kirk, who allowed them the use of rooms at the consular residence until their accommodation was made ready in the old consulate, which had been vacated by the Vice Consul Frederic Holmwood, then on leave in England.[29] The Kirks were to feature largely in the lives of the explorers during and after their time in Zanzibar; John Kirk was to prove a most reliable source of expert advice and practical support, while his wife Helen took almost a maternal interest in the explorers' welfare, becoming a particular confidante to Keith. Even after their move to the old consulate, Keith and Thomson visited the Kirks on a daily basis and accompanied them regularly on evening strolls, Keith reporting that 'nothing could exceed their hearty kindness'.

From 1870 onwards, Kirk, a Scottish doctor born in 1832 near Arbroath, was a dominating influence in the life of Zanzibar and the whole British political and strategic involvement in East Africa at this time. Kirk was educated in medicine at Edinburgh University, with its strong foundation in natural sciences, especially botany (he was elected a fellow of the Royal Botanical Society while still a student). He was one of the first Europeans to investigate the use of native African plants as potentially useful crop species, leaving behind an agricultural 'garden' which became known throughout East Africa, and he exchanged plant material with botanical institutions throughout the Empire. Among his many accomplishments, he was good at photography (having taken photographs as a schoolboy in the 1840s) and was producing high-quality prints as early as the 1850s: he is noted for his historic photos of the hospital where he worked in the Crimea.

Kirk embodied the energetic broadly based educated Scot of his time; in 1858, at the age of 26, following medical experience in the Crimean War, he had joined Livingstone's expedition up the Zambezi as botanist and doctor – he was perhaps the only officer to emerge from the Zambezi expedition with his reputation intact, renowned for his reliability.[30] He returned to Zanzibar in 1866 as medical officer on

Livingstone's recommendation and was worked to exhaustion by the great cholera epidemic of 1869–70, before being appointed Vice Consul, then Political Agent and Consul on the island. In this he was unusual, since such appointments were normally granted to Oxbridge graduates or those with a military background, at a time when the Indian Government had considerable authority in East African affairs before the subsequent gradual ascendancy of the Foreign Office in this area.

Sir John Kirk in consular uniform (Source: John Kirk Archive, Trustees of the National Library of Scotland)

As an all-round and very knowledgeable natural historian, Kirk frequently sent specimens of flora and fauna to the British Museum from where he received regular requests for particular species. He was a first-class shot, and sent many bird skins to that institution, but he also asked other explorers and missionaries to collect on his behalf. Live animals procured included a dwarf antelope discovered by Kirk in Somali country and named after him – the Museum (which was also a zoo at that time) even went so far as to ask him to obtain a wild African elephant. On his many trips into the mainland, Kirk used his photographic skills to send back pictures of a wide range of fauna, many of these never previously described. He also made notes on the abundance of animals (such as the large numbers of elephants at the junction of the Ruaha and Uranga rivers on Keith's expedition route), the state of agriculture, use of trade routes, and the attitude of the tribes. He was in fact a most important repository of any information which might be useful to travellers and the British Government.

Kirk was renowned for his hard-working application to his very many duties as the highest ranking British official in Zanzibar and, throughout his time on the island, he had a very genuine concern for its welfare. One of Kirk's strengths was his ability to get on with people, and he became a firm friend and confidante of the Sultan Seyyid Barghash-bin-Seyyid, who did nothing of importance without consulting Kirk. He was known for his direct manner and meticulousness in everything he undertook, voicing his views politely but with precision, maintaining an even temper.[31] It was a considerable advantage that he spoke Arabic and had absorbed much of the Muslim culture from his time in the Middle East. Perhaps his greatest accomplishment was to persuade the Sultan in 1873 – albeit with the ultimate sanction of force by threatening a naval bombardment – to outlaw the slave trade in his own domain, against all the prevailing economic and cultural forces. Britain, largely in the person of its consul, effectively protected the Sultanate from external enemies, as it had done for over 80 years. Some would say that Kirk was the *de facto* Sultan of Zanzibar, but it was his personality, allied to his patient diplomacy, which convinced the Sultan that the slave trade would not be tolerated.

By the time Keith arrived, Kirk had been in East Africa for over 20 years, 14 of these in Zanzibar, so that he was very experienced in the ways of Africa and in particular, the requirements for a successful expedition. The British Consulate received all persons of consequence and was very much the centre of social life. Thomson records that he and Johnston were met with such a welcome by Dr Kirk 'as at once put us quite at our ease...Mrs. Kirk also charmed us by her graceful and hospitable reception'. Kirk's wife Helen was the daughter of a general medical practioner from Worcestershire and seemed to be the perfect partner to her husband, having been married on a British Man o'War in Zanzibar 10 years before Keith's arrival. The missionary Horace Waller[32] was to describe her as 'so nice, refined, hearty, good and very genuine... Kirk a man of great taste, could not well choose anything else.'[33]

Mrs Kirk and daughters at British Consulate (Source: John Kirk Archive,
Trustees of the National Library of Scotland)

From her correspondence, she comes over as a warm, thoughtful, humane person, devoted to her family; Keith describes her as 'a most charming little body, always active and energetic, like her husband'. She also had considerable personal accomplishments, not least in music. Keith records her playing the harmonium for the Sunday church services and many musical evenings when she sang and played the piano for soirees at the consular residence – 'she sings and plays exquisitely' Keith wrote to his mother. It appears that she shared John Kirk's enthusiasm for botany and gardening, but also kept something of a small menagerie including two mountain cats, a lemur, and a young leopard, which the children's nurse took for walks attached by a string until it apparently became too strong for her. Particularly during the early period of the Kirks stay on the island, it would have required a person of considerable robustness to cope with living conditions there. Yet she was also obviously expected to act as a consular hostess on very many occasions and even as secretary to her husband for a time. She was to be seen regularly on horseback and used to send Christmas turkeys and other delicacies to the Universities' mission from her own table to tempt the appetites of the sick there.[34] She was equally solicitous for the health of the explorers, sending them gifts of cake, fruit and jam and arranging for the consulate physician, the Aberdonian Dr Robb (formerly of the Indian Army Medical Service), to call when they fell ill.[35]

An expatriate club

After all the explorers had heard about the malodorous and disease-ridden island, they were astonished to see the Kirks' four apparently healthy children, and Thomson comments further on the general health and welfare of those he met: 'We found to our surprise, that the Europeans were a most select company of gentlemen, full of health and spirits and that etiquette and fashion were as dominant as in England'[36] Thomson, however, did acknowledge that there appears to have been a very marked change in the climate of the island since the earlier reports, with a considerable drop in annual rainfall.[37] Later, in correspondence with Keith's mother, Mrs Kirk told of much disease and many deaths of Europeans in Zanzibar.[38]

Zanzibar Harbour when Keith arrived would have been a hive of activity. Apart from the coming and going of mailboats, all sorts of other craft from across the world, both steam and under sail, would be loading their cargoes of cloves, rubber, gum copal, pepper and other exotic spices, and unloading the many stores required by the Zanzibar community. One of the most imposing ships was not connected with any of these commercial activities: HMS *London*, moored in Zanzibar harbour was used both as a base and as a supply depot for anti-slavery operations. It had a chequered career: built in 1810, it had seen service as a wooden sailing ship in the Crimea before being converted into a steamship with auxiliary sail, one of the last of the wooden steam battleships. Despite its vintage, at 2,626 tons, it was a potent symbol of British authority, and when it was withdrawn a few years later, it was claimed that there was a resurgence in the slave trade as a result.[39]

HMS London (Source: Chrysalis Books Ltd)

*Mrs Kirk and others with naval officers on HMS **Forte** (Source: John Kirk Archive, Trustees of the National Library of Scotland)*

Descriptions of slaving, especially those of Livingstone, left a deep impression on the British public, and the anti-slavery movement was a very popular one. The Government was committed to stopping this human traffic: since the 1820s the British navy had been attempting to limit the slave trade and subsequently to put an end to it by intercepting dhows suspected of carrying slaves from the mainland to the Middle East and India. There was therefore constant patrolling of the Indian Ocean around Zanzibar by fast corvettes usually commanded by naval lieutenants, all keen to gain their spurs by a successful apprehension of slave-carrying dhows. The freeing of the slaves could be a traumatic business: the dhows crammed with as many as 600 doubled-up men, women and children in conditions where a total lack of sanitation not only bred disease, but caused the hardened British bluejackets to faint from the overpowering stench down below. It could also be hazardous, as the dhow captains were not always willing to give up their valuable human cargoes without a fight: one captain of HMS *London* was killed in such an encounter off the island of Pemba in 1881.[40]

Bounties were paid to Her Majesty's ships for capture of dhows and slaves, and on tonnage of prizes. For example, HMS *London* received £885 (at £15.10/- per ton) for captures between October and December 1878 (when Johnston was sailing to Zanzibar) while, in the same period, all ships based on the island received £3,591 in total – a very considerable sum. There were many disputes on bounties due, according to Kirk, to the inveterate lying of slaves. Among his many other duties, Kirk was judge of the Consular Court at Zanzibar and was responsible for 'condemning' dhows and freeing slaves, involving a huge amount of investigative work on paper, much of it going back to Whitehall. One particularly tricky case resulted when one of Keith's sporting companions, Captain Earle, injudiciously boarded an American barque and apprehended three suspected slaves, creating a veritable snowstorm of diplomatic correspondence with the Foreign Office.[41] (Shortly after Keith's arrival, Kirk's court was given full jurisdiction for all civil and criminal cases, including capital offences such as murder.) From his frequent visits to the wardroom of the *London*, Keith became very familiar with the whole operation of dhow chasing and the peccadilloes of the individual officers, several of whom regularly attended events on shore with him. (Perhaps significantly, there is no record of Thomson visiting the ship.)

Officers were allowed a month to savour the fleshpots of Zanzibar after each month at sea on patrol, and the ship also served as a social centre in Zanzibar – its officer cadre also enlivened the social scene on the island, participating in polo matches, tennis, riding, and socialising at the consulates. Keith's diary often refers to fraternising with the *London's* navy complement at dinner parties and other occasions. (There is no mention of how the ordinary seamen entertained themselves.) One of the young naval officers, Lieutenant Lloyd Mathews, reorganised the Sultan's nondescript army into an efficient fighting force, and went on to have a long and distinguished career as First Minister to the Sultan. Another, Lieutenant O'Neill, went during Keith's time on the island to become the British Vice Consul in Mozambique and was the model for Captain Good in Rider Haggard's *Alan Quartermain*.

Middle-class Europeans in Zanzibar formed something of an expatriate club on the Indian model. There was a varied round of activities, although men predominated with their sports, including polo and lawn tennis. It is unlikely that Thomson participated in these as he was known to be so uninterested in games that according to his friend J. M. Barrie, even in later life, he did not know the basic rules of cricket, but he was frequently observed shooting birds, probably for identification. The Kirks hosted many dinner parties for residents and visitors, at which Mrs Kirk would entertain with piano playing and singing – Handel's Water Music was a favourite of Keith's. The standards of these dinners is indicated by one guest[42] who noted 'the great treat of the meal was the abundance of ice and iced dishes, making my unaccustomed teeth almost ache with their exquisite coldness'.[43] There were courtesy visits between the consulates – with his knowledge of the language, Keith was particularly welcome at the German consulate. Many of these would be quite formal occasions – Keith records a Major Brown apologising to the Kirks for his absence since he had dressed for dinner, but had to undress again 'to fish out a coolie' (presumably from the sea) so he could not dress again'.[44]

The style of more relaxed occasions are indicated by Thomson: 'What could be more delightful than to stroll on band days down the promenade, and listen to wonderfully well-played operatic selections and to study the marvellous collection of divers races in their infinite variety of costumes.'[45,46] Although the Sultan kept a number of carriages, which were readily made available to the European community, and which resulted in the broadening and straightening of a number of roads on the island, the area accessible was limited, and there were constant encounters between members of this community on daily walks or going about their affairs. Everyone knew everyone else's business, which must have contributed to a somewhat claustrophobic atmosphere. Apparently the Sultan's greatest pleasure was to observe foreigners from his palace window using a very large telescope – a sort of majestic peeping Tom. As a result, according to Thomson, 'he had more than once revealed knowledge of a kind and extent which has rather unpleasantly taken some Europeans by surprise'.[47]

Shortly after their arrival, Keith and Thomson were required to make the customary formal call on the Sultan. While Kirk dressed in his consular uniform, complete with sword, the explorers borrowed the obligatory evening dress, and dripped with perspiration while awaiting their delayed summons. Walking through the streets lined in their honour with the Sultan's Baluchi guard, Thomson noted their antique sidearms and disreputable appearance, before they encountered a much smarter African guard nearer to the palace. A band played 'God save the Queen' and the party were ushered up the palace steps into a corridor crowded with Arabs in most brilliant colours, wearing expensive gold-hilted swords and knives. The reception room was adorned with floor-to-ceiling mirrors throughout, with the many different clocks and telescopes which the Sultan prized, and with rich oriental carpets on the marble floor. From the ceiling hung crystal candelabra, while around the room were placed ivory-inlaid chairs with crimson-covered seats. (The palace had been built on several floors to accommodate the previous Sultan's several wives, children and grandchildren, and no fewer than 75 concubines.)[48] The Sultan received the explorers warmly, politely enquiring about their health and the purposes of the expedition, before the traditional dark coffee and sherbet was served in crystal cups.[49]

Life for the European community was greatly eased by the availability of servants. Writing to his mother, and considering her probable interest in his domestic arrangements on the island, Keith said:

> With Mrs. Kirk's aid, we have begun housekeeping here, and are getting along famously. Noho, the late Captain Elton's 'boy' is steward and valet; Lituala, formerly cook at the English Mission does up our steaks and banana fritters, and with Abdulla, a sweeping boy, our domestic establishment is complete. Cook goes to market every morning with his basket, forages for us, and then brings his gatherings for inspection ...the air, is indeed, somehow hothouse like and steamy but it seems to agree with us remarkably well.

(Thomson, who had little time for missionaries, was later to ascribe the cook's impudence and acquisition of a considerable stock of pious words to his mission upbringing.) An insight into the rough and ready medical treatment is indicated in Keith's response to Noho's fever when he administered 'one pill out of each of the bottles in the medicine chest and half a pint of castor oil to follow'.[50] Early in their stay both explorers had 'fever' – almost certainly malaria – and Keith suffered from painful headaches, which he treated with bromide, potassium and mustard plaster.

A quite detailed indication of the routine of daily life in Zanzibar is given in Keith's diary for this time. Most days, Keith would be working for a time on Stanford's *Compendium of Geography*, and there are cryptic references to the various countries involved, the work eventually being published posthumously in 1880. Grace claimed that this alone would have brought him fame, the *Athenaeum* commenting that it was 'a work of much thought, wide research, and no inconsiderable literary skill'. From his many conversations with other travellers, missionaries and others, Keith also collated any relevant information on the geography of Africa, as he had done most of his professional life, and compiled these in the form of an up-to-date map which he sent back to the RGS,[51] in addition to the progress reports sent back regularly to the Society. There were regular Kiswahili lessons, often under the tutelage of Bishop Steere, and with Mrs Kirk participating – she was verbally fluent in the language, but wanted to improve her grammatical background.[52] Sometimes, these lessons would take the form of an outing to Mbweni, a few miles along the coast from Stonetown, where the Kirks were building their country retreat, and where John Kirk assiduously cultivated his garden, planting many native and exotic species from all over the world, a welcome retreat from the considerable stresses of consular life. The party would sometimes travel by boat down the coast, and in fine weather share a picnic on the beach after lessons under the shade of the spreading mango trees, where the bishop would examine them on what they were supposed to have learnt during the week.

Something of the flavour of these relaxed occasions is given in a letter from Mrs Kirk to one of Keith's sisters:

> Your brother used to like coming here with us and sitting under the trees. Sometimes during the day he would pull the Swahili exercise book out of his pocket and say 'Time for lessons' and we would set to work. I was writing the exercises too and Mr. Thomson, and we would take it in turn to question each other and sometimes John would come and catechise us all. I used to have great laughs over it – you would know the way he had of throwing his head back and laughing when anything tickled him.[53]

On these occasions, Keith would take the opportunity to sketch and photograph anything of interest, although he noted how frequently the photographs failed in the developing process – a few of his African photographs still exist.

Kirk's interest in botany and scientific gardening based on Mbweni (where the Sultan with whom Kirk established very cordial relations had granted him some land) was to lead to the revitalisation of the island's economy with the end of the slave trade. While on the mainland, Kirk had noticed a boy playing with a ball made of elastic substance and discovered that the material had come from the latex-bearing *Randolphla* tree which grew abundantly in the interior. With the support of the Sultan and other Zanzibaris, he helped to establish the very successful rubber trade which more than made up for the loss of income from the slave trade – perhaps, after the part he had played in the cessation of that trade, his single most important contribution to the island.[54] Near to Kirk's house and garden at Mbweni, the Universities Mission had established a school for freed slave girls – Keith recalls listening to their singing on one of his visits. This was administered by the redoubtable Caroline Thackeray, a cousin of the famous novelist, who was to become a much loved figure over her 30 years training the girls as teachers, and who resided in Kirk's Mbweni house after his departure. She was always present at the church services which the Kirks and Keith attended regularly. Keith made acute comments on the various preachers and the quality of the singing in his diary.

Chuma and the caravan

> Yesterday good Bishop Steere called, and brought with him Chuma, one of Livingstone's men, whose portrait is the frontispiece of the book on 'Africa' that

I edited. Bishop Steere thought he would be a good man to take with me, and indeed he is the very best man I could possibly have, thoroughly trustworthy, experienced and acquainted with all the languages we are likely to meet with in the line of route, besides having a good knowledge of English.

So wrote Keith to his mother on 7 January 1879 (Steere had taken Chuma on his overland journey to Lake Nyassa in 1875). The success of any African expedition was dependent to a large extent on the character and leadership of the African caravan leader, and the headmen he was usually responsible for appointing. Keith was particularly fortunate in being able to recruit, on Kirk's recommendation, one of the most notable and experienced caravan leaders in the person of Chuma. He would have the responsibility for the good order and conduct of approximately 150 men and pack animals, reporting directly to the expedition leader. He would oversee the packing of all the stores, the allocation of loads, as well as recommending the most appropriate trade goods, and would act as interpreter and negotiator with often suspicious tribal chiefs.

Chuma and another retainer, Abdulla Suzi, together with others, had gained undying fame for bringing Livingstone's body back to the coast following the missionary's death in the interior in 1873, a distance of well over 1,000 miles. At his death it was said that they 'acted with a calm decisiveness that no European could have bettered'.[55] Another Scottish industrialist and classmate of Livingstone, James 'Paraffin' Young, financed their journey back to England, where they were lionised as the faithful servants of Livingstone's last journeys. Chuma had been captured as a slave, but freed by Livingstone in 1861, and had been taken with others to the Free Church of Scotland Mission in Bombay, where he acquired fluent English. He is known to have spoken a number of African dialects, although he did not know the language of the Wahehe, the warlike tribe whom Johnston most wished to win over. (Keith had good reason to be wary of this tribe, which later, under its martial Chief Mkwawa, inflicted at least one serious defeat of well-armed German military expedition in 1891. In the following year, his tribesmen wiped out the German garrison in the Kilosa fort which still bore the scars 70 years later when I used it as the base for forest exploration.) By the time the explorers arrived in Zanzibar, Chuma's old companion Suzi had apparently become a drunkard and was not recruited, despite his desire to accompany the expedition.[56] (Suzi was, however, taken on by Stanley not long afterwards to head his own expedition to the Congo and apparently proved reliable and loyal.)

Thomson thought that there was no one among the caravan leaders to equal Chuma, who apparently picked up on Europeans' meaning very quickly. He was full of anecdote, fun and jollity, a great favourite with the men, but was always capable of preserving his authority.[57] He was especially noted for his unrivalled eloquence in speech making, and Thomson knew that he would have far greater effect on the men than himself, commenting that it was quite a treat to watch his animated manner and gestures. He was something of a character, a firm disciplinarian, who was quite capable of delivering a physical lashing to miscreants when required. Above all, he had those leadership qualities which maintained morale when the going got tough.

Chuma had his faults: he was inclined to tell Europeans what he thought they wished to hear – as Thomson said, 'lies came naturally to him not premeditated or for profit but always because they seemed to be nearer his tongue than the truth'. However, on one occasion this habit came in useful when he claimed that the nubile young ladies in photographs being shown by Thomson to a chief were all Thomson's wives, greatly enhancing the explorer's prestige. He was always fond of acting the big man, and to maintain his status would be lavish in handing out gifts, so that he could not be trusted to keep expenditure within bounds. This was particularly the case where he wanted to impress women, and on one occasion Thomson complained that he had been left with the cheapest cloths, while Chuma had expended the finest on native beauties. At the end of it all, Thomson paid handsome tribute to Chuma as 'a treasure that cannot be valued too highly…ever at my elbow, with his ready tact and vast stores of information, ever ready to guide and direct me'. At the same time, Thomson's boyish exuberance might have appealed to Chuma's extrovert personality, perhaps rather more than to Keith's much more reserved and distant attitude – both Thomson and Chuma shared a certain *coloratura* approach, which stood both of them in good stead with the African porters and headmen, who tended to have an admiration for 'larger than life' characters.[58]

Chuma recruited Makatubu as chief headman. Although very intelligent, and very full of life and energy, apparently he could not maintain any semblance of discipline.[59] Headman Nasibu, on the other hand, was tall, rather Arabian in appearance, and immensely strong, but had a huge capacity for strong drink. His function appeared simply to be a companion to Chuma, while Asikiri, as a former slave to the Sultan, was quite unused to camp life and seems to have been something of a dandy, who with his gorgeous turban, white robe, and carrying enormous shield and spear, was more of an adornment than anything else.[60] Among the most flamboyant of the company were the *Kiringosis* or lead guides, ten of whom accompanied Keith's expedition. Dressed in crimson robes, with tall feathered headdresses, and flaunting spears and shields like the warriors they attempted to portray, they would be the bearers of the Union Jack flag at the head of the expedition and would intimate the arrival of the expedition in a village by sounding their drums and blowing on their kudu horns, dancing all the while.[61]

The porters themselves were a mixed bag of Zanzibaris and Unyamwezi, the traditional porterage tribe. Among them were a number of slaves under contract to their masters, though Keith records having to return at least one who attempted to join the expedition without his master's permission, and was put in chains. There was no difficulty in finding volunteers, a number of whom were anxious to avoid conscription in the Sultan's new army and had to be weeded out.[62] (Keith also apparently had a numbered list of porters who had served on a previous expedition with Stanley.) Apart from the guaranteed pay and rations, there was considerable prestige attached to serving on such an expedition. It gave the men something of an heroic status among their peers, which they played up to, not least to impress the women. Some of them may well have come from the ranks of the Zanzibar harbour porters – at the time of the expedition, there were over 400 porters working at the harbour, who were, according to Kirk, generally well treated.[63]

In his diary, Keith records in considerable detail the process of selecting his men, and agreeing the terms of their contract with the help of Kirk and his most trusted African assistants.[64] Keith's documentation of the expedition was unique in listing every essential detail of each of the porters, from their name and tribe to their rate of pay, who had recommended them, and their previous expedition experience. The average rate of pay, in addition to free rations while on the march, was 5 dollars per month, the currency being Maria Theresa dollars, each worth slightly more than 4 British shillings.[65] In order to buy personal essentials, the porters were given advances on their wages, which Keith tried to restrict, but he records a show-down with them when they insisted on receiving their agreed 4 dollars a month for four months, no doubt supported by the *Kiringosis,* who formed a sort of caravan trades union. Keith selected the most trustworthy of his men for firearms training with the Sniders and Lee Enfields supplied by the War Office, but despite the efforts of Lieutenant Mathews, the Sultan demurred at the use of his Swahili sergeants for this purpose, suggesting that the Arabs might seduce these instructors for their own service – and presumably could then pose a possible threat to the Sultan's authority.

The explorers were completely dependent on their men, especially the caravan leaders, and not infrequently Arab slave traders, for their knowledge of routes, local languages, the customs of tribes and the idiosyncrasies of native chiefs. To an extent which few explorers admitted, they themselves were largely controlled by their African support (although Thomson was unusually gracious in his acknowledgements) and were exploited by most of those with whom they came into contact. The so-called 'discoveries' which the explorers made, albeit that they set these in context and disseminated them in written form, were often simply what Africans and Arabs already knew.[66] An earlier description of the business of negotiating for caravan equipment and trade goods suggests that this was a stomach-turning business, when the captain of the *London,* visiting one of the largest stores, French Charlie's, stated:

> situated in one of the narrowest and dirtiest streets of that pestilential town where to enter this place requires a strong constitution and a well-scented handkerchief… the first things that attract the eye are great piles of mildewed bags and rusty preserved-meat tins stored against the wall up to the cob-web-covered ceiling… The ground of this shop – it has no flooring – might be taken for the model of a battlefield, or for a plan of Africa with its hills and valleys… but with a far larger

population represented by millions of ants, while the wild beasts are replaced by innumerable spiders and cockroaches.[67,68]

The RGS had clearly stipulated the extent of their budget, which was a very tight one. The Society had been deeply overdrawn by Verney Lovett Cameron's earlier expedition across Africa[69] and his cavalier attitude towards money – they were not going to make the same mistake again. Kirk appears to have acted as the purser on behalf of the RGS for their sponsored expeditions, but as late as January of the year in which Keith arrived, he complained to Henry Bates that he had received no instructions to draw on the RGS account for Keith's expedition and there were large bills still outstanding from the Cameron expedition.[70] (Keith's necessary advances had to be paid from Kirk's own private account as late as18 April.)

Thus the expedition had a mere £1,500, of which a third was spent in one afternoon at Essa bin Lila's store on essential trade goods for bartering their way to Lake Nyassa; Keith cut down on Chuma's original list of stores and made a careful check on prices.[71] These items of cloth, beads and wire were batched in cylindrical bales of about three and a half feet by one foot, with each item in each mixed bale recorded for quick reference, and to avoid opening more bales than was required.[72] The total amounted to 71 bales of cloth, 2 loads of wire, and 10 of beads. The values of each bale were carefully calculated and a list sent back to the RGS in Keith's punctilious way.[73]

The sorting and packing of these goods for an extended expedition, combined with their careful wrapping to make them as waterproof as possible, was a long drawn-out business. Fortunately, the old consulate where Keith and Thomson had their residence had a large enough room for this bulk storage, but Kirk did advise the posting of a guard to deter thieves. One slightly unusual item of equipment was a folding wooden boat, the invention of a certain Admiral Macdonald. This was in sections, built of mahogany, 16 feet long by 4 feet wide, weighing 150 pounds and capable of carrying twelve people.[74] Keith tried this out on a visit to Mbweni saying that 'she does very well but spins around like a tee-totem'. It seems only to have been used in earnest after Keith's death, when Thomson christened it 'Agnes' after his mother.

The one event at Zanzibar which was most eagerly looked forward to was the arrival of the mailboat, with its news from Britain and elsewhere. (In early February 1879, by a curious historical transposition, there was the news from Bombay of heavy fighting in Afghanistan, involving British troops, and of a mob being fired on in Belfast.) While the mailboat was in harbour, everything else stopped while the expatriate community read their letters and hurriedly composed their replies before the next sailing, Keith among them. Apart from the mail, the boat also brought passengers either to take up post in Zanzibar or the mainland, or to travel onwards to South Africa. Keith records a number of personalities who were invited to dine with him at the Kirk's official residence, including Lord Beresford[75] *en route* to the Cape accompanied by the famous war correspondent, Archibald Forbes, whom Keith did not take to.[76] Later Keith tells the story of how a lady UMCA missionary, Lucy Amy Bashford, stated that all soldiers are hired cut-throats and that the Zulus should be treated with kindness, to which the blimpish Lord Beresford responded: 'To think that I should have lived to see the day when I would be called a hired cut-throat!' Miss Bashford had recently arrived with the new UMCA preacher, a Mr Sayres, who obviously upset his European congregation with his evangelical views and over-zealous approach – he was invalided home in the following year.[77]

One of Keith's diary entries (3 February 1879) states: 'Morning eagerly looking out for the mail steamer. Now Mrs. Kirk in to say that the vessel in sight was *not* the mail, only a despicable Portuguese war vessel…' The adjective is interesting – the Portuguese in East Africa appeared to be universally loathed – or at least by the British. The attempt to forge a way to the Central Lakes from the east coast was in part a response to the intransigence of the Portuguese about allowing access up the Zambezi, while there was resentment about the imposition of high customs duties by the Portuguese on goods transported to the interior: the subsequent opening up of this route led to the alignment of the Central Africa territories along this axis rather than from Tanganyika. On this occasion, the Zanzibar community heard of the major defeat of the British, at the Battle of Isandhlwana at the hands of the great Zulu warrior Cetawayo, which stunned the public at home. Keith records Kirk's comment that it would have a bad effect all along the coast – presumably referring to the loss of British prestige and possible local rebellion.[78]

A dry run

Because of the continuing late rains, the explorers had time on their hands before they could begin the main expedition, and Thomson was delighted when Keith suggested a trial trip to the Usambaras, in north-east Tanganyika. It would be 'a gentle introduction to the difficulties of managing a caravan'.[79] The Usambaras form a mountainous district noted for its lush scenery and dramatic landscapes, sometimes dubbed the 'Switzerland of Africa'. The area was well-known for the mission station which had been established there for some time, the explorers had already met some of the missionaries in Zanzibar, and the climate was temperate. They took with them Chuma and nine porters plus an assortment of cloths, some hoes, and several kegs of gunpowder as presents. Some indication of the fitness of both explorers is indicated by the fact that, to reach their departure point on Zanzibar, they walked no less than 30 miles between daybreak and sunset on the first day to the north end of the island for their boat departure.

Both Keith and Thomson published accounts of their trip in very different styles, in part reflecting their audiences, in the RGS[80] and a popular journal respectively.[81] In the main, Keith provides a comprehensive, factual description of the country, replete with topographical and ethnological detail, while Thomson, in somewhat florid and colourful prose, concentrates on incidents and encounters.[82] Even before leaving Zanzibar, at the end of their first day's walk, Thomson lets his readers know that despite the prevalence of sharks they plunged into the sea for a refreshing bath.[83] It is interesting to compare the previous description by Thomson of the leopard carrying off a nearby dog, 'within a few feet of where I lay', with Keith's prosaic one-sentence account: 'Our rest was interrupted by the wailing of one of the village dogs, as it was carried off into the jungle, no doubt by a leopard.'[84]

Keith was not indifferent to the beauty of their forest surroundings, however, and, no doubt with an eye to his mother's botanical interests, he wrote home:

> I could not have believed such trees as these of the forest we passed through existed in Africa – great buttressed trunks, rising 70 or 80 feet without a branch, and then spreading out in leafy tips that interlaced and shut out the sun, making everything below dim and cool. The ferns too are very abundant in the woods, but all, or mostly all, of the commonest kinds known in Britain. Some few, tree-growing ferns were in clefts in the branches far too high up to reach by any available means.

Meanwhile Thomson waxed lyrical about the countryside, claiming that it would be impossible to speak too enthusiastically about it and that he was at a loss for words to describe it. At one point he became euphoric when 'we were suddenly ushered into one of the most romantic little villages that can well be imagined'.[85] Thomson's super-abundant energy led him to blunder into swamp forest whose thorns ruined two of his suits. He was usually well ahead of the rest of the party – on one occasion encountering a group of local women whose hearts he claimed to have won immediately by opening his black umbrella. His attempt to repeat this success with another group saw him immediately threatened by bows and arrows.[86] Keith's remarks on tribal customs are strictly factual and entirely eschew Thomson's salacious details of the scantiness of the dress of the local women. Thomson was also unable to refrain from criticising the absurdity of the dress and ritual of the UMCA missionaries at Magila.

Both explorers claimed that, at the end of a quite arduous trip, involving a good deal of steep climbing up slippery mountain paths, and various encounters with local people and wildlife, it had given them at least a taste of the real thing. However, it would be possible to read into Keith's ambivalent remark that it 'was a most enjoyable one in almost every way' that perhaps he had had a little too much of his boyishly exuberant companion. For his part, Thomson became so ill on arrival back at Zanzibar that he could barely walk into the town. His remark is typical: 'These troubles by no means alarmed or discouraged us. They were not unexpected, and they formed a seasonable discipline. We had thus, then, in a sense, completed our apprenticeship as African travellers.'

Stanley again

Following their trip to the Usambaras, Keith was made very uneasy by the quite un-expected arrival of the renowned explorer, Henry Morton Stanley, forever remembered for his meeting with Livingstone and his alleged greeting. Keith's diary for 14 March records the impending arrival of the explorer in the steamship *Albion*, which astonished the Zanzibar community, especially when, later, four Indian elephants[87] also arrived to accompany the expedition of the African International Association, with which Stanley was connected. Keith records: 'Mr. Stanley's steamer *Albion* arrived from Aden. What has he come for? He puts up with the American consul who went off to meet him arrayed in a black tie, his clerk wearing evening dress and white necktie and wouldn't that touch the explorer's heart!'[88]

Stanley refused to disclose his reason for being in East Africa, but had come to organise and obtain porters for his expedition to the Lower Congo (later to be incongruously named the Congo Free State) at the behest of Leopold II of the Belgians, and had actually left Brussels in disguise and under an assumed name. In a letter to Bates, Kirk remarks 'the whole thing since Stanley came has been made a mystery and the result is no one can help them… Stanley has done them as much harm as possible while here – I suppose he did not mean it.[89]

Keith's diary for March 1897 states: 'Mr Stanley remains to introduce the Belgian officer he has brought with him, M. Dutalis, to the Sultan tomorrow. The King of the Belgians has sent Dr. Kirk a fine gold snuff box with his chiffre done in diamonds and blue enamel on the lid, along with a complimentary letter in very good taste.'[90] This expensive gift was to honour Kirk for his efforts to end the slave trade. Later he was to comment that Oswald Charles Dutalis did not know exactly where he was going but appeared to be much more used to court than camp life. The general view of the Belgian organisation and staff was that they were incompetent. Arthur Dodgshun, of the London Missionary Society, who had had to bury Dutalis's countryman Wautier on the road to Ujiji, confirmed this:

> Wautier's expedition is practically dead…his personnel was defective from the first, consisting as it did from rivals, without any further interest in their work than the hope of promotion in rank or decoration as soon as they should be fortunate enough to return to Europe. They seem to have no settled plans and no idea of brotherly cooperation.

Keith was later visited by Stanley and US Consul Haythorne: 'S. states he is not going to do any exploration but only going to shoot hippo on the Wami River. Mr S. in going away wishes us a prosperous journey and says "If you meet anyone like me in your travels, please give him my best respects." To Captain Earle he said "They (referring to us) will do good work, very good work if (with a chuckle) no one is there before them." '

At the end of that month Chuma called to say that five men had gone into Stanley's service, obliging Keith to write to Stanley informing him of this and asking his help in recovering their contracts. Writing home, Keith expressed his unease about Stanley's presence and objectives:

> We were all very much surprised when Mr Stanley appeared about a fortnight ago in a small steamer that he has charted. What his object in coming is does not transpire, but is kept a close secret. He brought with him a M. Dutalis to join the unfortunate Belgian Expedition, but, like the rest, this is much more a French-Brussels courtier and man-about-town than one likely to stand the rudeness of African travel.

Later, he states: 'The great Stanley has gone to explore the lower Lufiji again in his boat, and after that he is going north in his boat to the Juba. I suppose he is passing his time till the rest of the Belgian Expedition comes out, but his whole proceedings are still kept as dark as possible.'

Undoubtedly, Keith would have discussed Stanley with Kirk, and may well have been influenced by Kirk's views. Both came from that stratum in British society which regarded Stanley as a vulgar upstart, a view held by a high proportion of the members of the RGS. Perhaps more significantly, Stanley had previously attacked Kirk for his failure to get supplies to Livingstone on his last journey, and had attempted in various ways to undermine his reputation – some said to enhance Stanley's own status.[91] Livingstone himself appeared to go along with this castigation for a time, perhaps under Stanley's influence, but also from his inclination to blame others for shirking their duty. This had created something of a scandal, which almost ended Kirk's career. He was completely exonerated by a special commission of enquiry under Sir Bartle Frere in 1874, but the whole unsavoury episode would not have endeared him to Stanley.[92] Subsequently, Kirk had refused to meet Stanley when he stopped at Zanzibar, because of the explorer's reputed behaviour in the Congo: Kirk felt that his irresponsible, if not immoral, attitude had jeopardised European development in that region. Other observers claimed that Kirk depended too much on hearsay in the matter. Stanley's arrival in Zanzibar in 1879 would have been fraught with the conflicts between Kirk's distaste for the explorer and the requirements of consular courtesy.

Keith was at this time more than usually uncommunicative, apparently suffering from depression, which his confidante Mrs Kirk considered was due in part to Stanley's unheralded arrival:

> I think for one thing Stanley being in Zanzibar worried him. No one knew what he was going to do, and he used to make mysterious speeches as 'perhaps someone would be at Nyassa before these Johnny Englishmen' and so on. Of course no one ever believed anything Stanley says, while it used to bother Keith. In one of his notes to me when he was not well he said 'Stanley has been troubling all my

fevered dreams – I get close to the Lake and at the last…he appears, takes off his hat and says. "Mr. Johnston I presume" gives a malignant chuckle and disappears. And somehow it became known to me that the title of his next book was to be *How I did the RGS again!*'

Stanley would have known about Keith's close association with the RGS before the expedition: Keith was the secretary of the Geographical Section of the infamous British Association meeting at Brighton in 16 August 1872 and the subsequent RGS meeting two days later, when every attempt was made by several eminent members of the Society's establishment to humiliate Stanley, so that his attitude towards Keith is understandable.

Mrs Kirk then gave vent to her own feelings about Stanley, no doubt impassioned by his treatment of her husband:

To anyone knowing, as we had reason to do, Stanley's methods and manners, there will not appear to be anything in this fevered dream inconsistent with his nature. A braggart and a bully, absolutely without conscience or regard for the feelings of others, he fought his way through seas of blood, and it must ever remain a mystery how he came to be the rescuer of Livingstone, gentlest, humblest, and most humane of men.[93]

Preparing for the expedition

Keith had the good fortune, in late January, to meet up with the Rev. Thomas Wakefield when he was in Zanzibar, whose paper on native routes in East Africa Keith had presented to the RGS. He spent what must have been a very useful day discussing the various options with Wakefield, poring over his sketches and maps, and cross-examining him on the conditions of terrain and tribes to be encountered.[94] Keith talked with anyone who had been to the interior so that he could glean and assess any information on trade goods preferences, availability of food, topography, etc. Subsequently, Keith spent much time revising his maps of the possible routes the expedition might take and, consulting a dhow captain, made very careful calculations of the journey stages between Kilwa and Ubena. Kilwa was an important starting point for trade caravans, on the mainland coast, but in mid-February Chuma called on Keith to say that he had failed to get men who knew the route from this point.[95]

Keith was disappointed, on reading a book by Captain Elton about his travels to Lake Nyassa, at his scanty diary notes.[96] This would have been important to him, as the purpose of his own expedition was in effect to complete Elton's work in attempting to find a feasible route between the Indian Ocean and the Central Lakes.[97] Keith was obliged to report to the RGS that he had decided to modify the original route, since there was so much uninhabited country on the original one, with grain apparently very scarce in the districts concerned. So, instead of following a line south-west from

Kola at the then terminus of the Mackinnon–Buxton Road, he would strike more or less directly south-west from Dar-es-Salaam, following the route to Berobero (*sic*). Even so, he would have to recruit additional porters to carry food for the first 10–14 days.

On 22 April, Keith sailed for Dar-es-Salaam on the mainland coast to carry out a reconnaissance of the first part of the proposed expedition route and to gather any further information on the country ahead. The winds were so contrary that, by nightfall, he had only reached Mbweni, about 4 miles down the Zanzibar coast: it took almost two full days to reach Dar-es-Salaam, a journey which now takes a few hours. Here he met up again with William Beardall, the lay missionary who was constructing the so-called Mackinnon–Buxton Road, financed by Sir Fowell Buxton, an English philanthropist and Sir William Mackinnon, the Scottish shipowner.[98] The proposed road into the interior had been plagued by problems of previous poor supervision under a Sergeant Myers of the Royal Engineers. By midsummer 1877 it was reported that 6 miles of good road had been completed and as many as a 100 natives a day were using it to bring their goods to the coast – four years later it was 73 miles long and well constructed, but the presence of tsetse fly after the first 40 miles made it hopeless to use bullocks or horses. Keith also met up with a coastal Swahili man, Bwana Muji, who traded independently in this area, and travelled each year into the interior. From his detailed conversations with the trader, and with the assistance of Beardall, Keith obtained a good deal of information on possible routes, which he set out comprehensively in his diary.[99]

Apart from the various routes, Keith made detailed notes on the names of the chiefs, their attitudes, the availability of food, the location of possible stopping points at villages, and the nature of the terrain, including the rivers to be crossed, all of which were assiduously set out in a paper published by the RGS that year.[100] He found that, with the rains still continuing, the two most frequented paths were too wet, while the other option had already been explored. Keith opted for a third possibility which he thought would be higher, less liable to flooding, and 'healthier'. The unusually long rains that year had already seriously delayed their departure and compromised their earlier proposed routes. It had also halted work on the road which Beardall was constructing. Keith relayed the essence of this research to the RGS. It was published, and in it he refers to the problem of encountering the Wahehe and Mativiti tribes who had fearsome reputations as warriors. Keith spent four days prospecting the first part of his route, and had a pretty miserable time from incessant rain, leaky huts, recalcitrant guides and plentiful mosquitoes. It did not augur well.

Neither were things going smoothly in his relationships with his deputy. Keith's diary for 4 April refers tersely to writing to Bates at the RGS about Thomson (always referred to simply as 'T'), without giving any details of the substance of this, but on the following day it mentions that he has spoken to Thomson – again without any detail. There is virtually no other reference to Thomson in this diary, so it can be

Dar-es-Salaam harbour some time between 1866 and 1874 (Source: John Kirk Archive, Trustees of the National Library of Scotland)

Mbweni beach scene near Zanzibar Town

assumed that this must have been a matter of some importance. It was apparent that, in the two months following the Usamabara trip, Keith had seemed very much out of sorts, even although he went about his expedition preparations doggedly. His morose reserve alarmed Thomson, who knew that something was wrong, but could do nothing about it since Keith was so entirely uncommunicative,[101] except, as will be seen later, with Mrs Kirk – his diary for 18 April refers to speaking with her about 'T'.[102]

Kirk himself was to remark privately that Thomson had 'an awkward uncouth manner and had certainly seen little society but he was a man anything could be made of and who in time would get the awkward corners rubbed off him, but that Keith couldn't stand the friction in the process'.[103] However, the diary entry for 4 April, mentioned above, does indicate that Keith had not only written to the RGS about Thomson, but had also immediately afterwards spoken to his assistant. It is known that, before the start of the expedition, Keith had requested Thomson's recall, and it is difficult to avoid the conclusion that that is what these terse diary entries must refer to – he would have felt obliged, if only as a matter of courtesy, to warn Thomson of his request. It is also likely that the Usambara trip was the break point: in close proximity with Thomson in the field, his worst fears were confirmed – he could not stand the company of his ebullient assistant.

A tetchy letter from the RGS to Kirk at this time indicates their anxiety:

> We have had no letter from you by the mail which reached Sat. (26ult.) *In November* there was plenty of written matter from Johnston. The unhappy incompatibility of temperament which has developed between him and his assistant; If this has not by this time become more reconciled and Thomson should be really dismissed, will you kindly pay on our a/c the expenses of his passage home? It is now way past time for advice![104]

(If this does indeed refer to Keith raising the matter of Thomson's personality in November 1878, it would appear that Keith had serious reservations about his deputy from the outset, and possibly even before they had left for East Africa.)

For such an introverted person as Keith, this must have been a special sort of agony, including the period leading up to his decision, which would certainly have explained his continuing depression. For him, the success of this first major expedition, with all its expectations, would have been a total preoccupation; now, even before the start of the journey, he was taking the most serious step of asking for his only European assistant to be sent home. However, none of this concern is relayed in his letter home just before the start of the expedition:

> Just a few lines to bid you goodbye once more before we start finally… I am thankful that none of my men have shown any sign of desertion as yet – all are well and merry, the weather is now lovely, and all the country before us is quiet and undisturbed so that I think we shall have a most easy and prosperous journey…'

Certainly, the expedition left with a very fair wind: Dr Kirk's direct involvement (he actually accompanied Keith to Dar-es-Salaam to help the expedition get started) gave it considerable prestige, and the Africans felt that as a result it was a British Government affair. The Sultan had given a warm farewell, and the *London* had dipped her flag in honour of the departure. Kirk celebrated their departure with a modest show of fireworks. Some of the wives of the porters broke down on being separated from their husbands, with memories of those who had not returned from previous expeditions, notably those of Stanley. Thomson recorded an emotional leave-taking:

> I shook Dr. Kirk's hand and bid him farewell with a quivering lip, yet with a heart full of great hopes and expectations...we were entering a valley of the shadow of death into which many have passed and few have returned. In that great moment vivid pictures floated through my excited brain. I thought of Stanley beleaguered by thousands of bloodthirsty natives, and compelled to slay on every side to save himself. Would we have to do likewise? I pictured Livingstone dying in the swamps of Bangweolo. Might such not be our fate ?[105]

On the eve of departure, Kirk remarked ominously 'Things are as unhappy as ever between Johnston and Thomson, they never speak unless in monosyllables.'[106] Exactly what that unhappiness was all about was only to be revealed after Keith's death.

NOTES

1   According to Arthur Dodgshun (see Bennet 1969, ix–xii) these ships carried no doctor or medicines and had a very bad reputation for sickness.
2   Foreign Office (FO) to Kirk 1879, FO 84/1555.
3   Marsh and Kingsnorth (1972), 17–18.
4   Bridges (2000), 65–113.
5   Miller (1972), 36.
6   Ibid., 37.
7   Sulivan (1873), 429 quoting *Times of India* Oct. 1872.
8   Miller (1972), 38.
9   Packenham (1991), 285.
10 Thomson (1881a), 10.
11 Ibid., 5.
12 The remarkable Bishop Steere made the first Swahili translations of the New Testament and his Handbook of Swahili remained the standard text for many years. He had led the Universities Mission to a new settlement on the shores of Lake Nyassa after Livingstone's death and worked with Bishop Tozer at Magila in the Usambaras which Keith visited. Thomson's remark could equally have been made in relation to Steere's skill as an architect and builder, which he put to good use in the construction of Zanzibar Cathedral.
13 These 'narrow crooked lanes' still survive in present-day Stonetown, which is now a World Heritage Site and attracts considerable numbers of tourists. The author can testify to the challenge of orientation in the maze of backstreets.
14 Many of the descendents of these Arabs were killed or expelled in the violent revolution against the minority coalition parties which ruled in the islands following independence in late 1963. Despite the subsequent inclusion of Zanzibar within the United Republic of Tanzania, Zanzibari politics have remained volatile and the relationship with mainland Tanzania is an uneasy one.
15 Thomson (1881a), 15–18.
16 Drummond (1889), 5. Henry Drummond, a divine with scientific notions, accompanied Archibald Geikie on geological expeditions to the Rocky Mountains. His commission in Africa in 1887 was to make a scientific and especially geological exploration of the Central Lakes and Tanganyika for the African Lakes Company.
17 Miller (1972), 39.
18 Livingstone (1923), 117.
19 Coupland (1939), 75–79.
20 Taylor (1989), 46.
21 Liebowitz (1999), 21.
22 For a comprehensive account of the effects of the slave trade see Hugh Thomas, *The Slave Trade*, New York, 1987.
23 I was able to see for myself, underneath Zanzibar Cathedral, the appallingly cramped airless pens in which the men, women and children were kept, with insufficient room even to stand up, before their display at auction. Outside the cathedral, there is now a very moving series of sculptures of slaves, appropriately set in a sunken pit.
24 Thomson (1881a), 4–5.
25 Livingstone (1923), 119.
26 Miller (1972), 41.

27 Thomson (1881a), 143.
28 Gum copal is a fossilised exudation from the roots of *msandarusi* trees (*Trachylobium verrucosum*) after their death, found only in the red sands near the coast. The underground pits from which it was dug haphazardly by local people proved a hazard on the expedition route. The resin could be found in sizes ranging from small pebbles to 4–5 lb in weight. It was particularly prized for the making of fine varnishes for coachwork. Some 2,000 hundredweight of copal was being exported at this time. Kirk had studied this plant and published an article on it in the *Journal of the Linnaean Society* in 1871.
29 With the decline of recruitment to the Indian services, Holmwood was noted as a promoter of imperialism for the purpose of absorbing the energies of educated middle-class Englishmen and the future employment of the 'sons of gentlemen'.
30 Jeal (1973), 198.
31 Liebowitz (1999), 136, 142.
32 Waller was very closely associated with Livingstone, being entrusted with the completion and publication of his journals. It was largely due to his influence that Kirk was initially appointed as permanent political agent and Vice Consul at Zanzibar.
33 Liebowitz (1999), 125.
34 *Central Africa Monthly Journal of the Universities Mission*, July 1914.
35 McCarthy (2000), 21–3.
36 Thomson (1881a), 13–14.
37 Detailed meteorological observations had been kept over a number of years by the consulate physician, Dr Robb and the Rev. Wakefield.
38 For an up-to-date biography of John Kirk, from which much of this material is drawn, see Liebowitz (1999). The National Library of Scotland, Edinburgh also holds the most comprehensive collection of Kirk papers.
39 Drummond (1889), 76–7.
40 Miller (1972), 43–5.
41 FO/84 1525 1879.
42 This guest was Arthur W. Dodgshun of the London Missionary Society who in 1877 unsuccessfully attempted to take ox-waggons to Ujiji.
43 Bennet (1969), 48.
44 McCarthy (2000), 40.
45 Thomson (1881a), 26.
46 In 2001, I encountered an elderly guide on Zanzibar who recalled playing in the police band below the seaside verandah of the English Club, now sadly dilapidated.
47 Thomson (1881a), 28.
48 Miller (1972), 35.
49 Thomson (1881a), 20–23.
50 McCarthy (2000), 47.
51 Ibid., 48.
52 Swahili was the predominant language of Zanzibar and coast region; elsewhere it was an imperfectly spoken *lingua franca*.
53 Mrs K to one of Johnston's sisters, 10 Dec. 1879.
54 I noted two very old cycads in this garden, which were most likely planted by Kirk.
55 Jeal (1973), 367.
56 McCarthy (2000), 30.
57 Thomson (1881a), 31.
58 Chuma performed the function of a regimental sergeant major: I can recall one such who fitted this description almost exactly.

59 Thomson (1881a), 82.
60 Ibid., 83.
61 Ibid., 87–90.
62 Ibid., 34.
63 National Library of Scotland, Edinburgh: Kirk Archive; Notes by John Kirk.
64 McCarthy (2000), 49.
65 Rotberg (1971), 41.
66 Rotberg (1970), 317.
67 Sulivan (1873), 208–9.
68 The description is given by Capt. G.L. Sulivan R N, an impassioned opponent of slavery, who first brought the *London* to Zanzibar in 1874. His book *Dhow Chasing in Zanzibar Waters* is a gripping, first-hand account of his attempts to suppress this trade throughout East Africa and the Middle East.
69 Keith records Mr Hore of the London Missionary Society sending back a packet of Cameron's letters from Ujiji to Zanzibar. Cameron, sent by the RGS to carry aid to Livingstone, met the party carrying his body back to the coast.
70 Kirk to Bates, 21 Jan 1879, RGS Archives.
71 Thomson (1881a), 4.
72 Ibid., 36.
73 McCarthy (2000), 47.
74 Letter from MacDonald to RGS, 22 Nov. 1880, RGS Archives.
75 Lord Charles William de la Poer was at this time ADC to the Viceroy of India.
76 Forbes was a war correspondent for the *Daily News* and a prolific author on many military campaigns.
77 McCarthy (2000), 50.
78 Ibid., 27.
79 Thomson (1881a), 36.
80 Johnston (1879b), 545–58.
81 *Good Words* (1881), 36–43.
82 Although Keith's expedition diary covers the Usambara trip, much of it is virtually indecipherable. However, its factual style is enlivened from time to time by more lyrical descriptions than he allowed himself in the RGS article. Thomson also wrote an entirely scientific account, to accompany Keith's, of the geology and natural history of the area.
83 Thomson (1881a), 36.
84 McCarthy (2000), 554–5.
85 Thomson (1881a), 37.
86 Ibid., 39.
87 In a short note to the RGS, Keith indicated that he had considered their use for the expedition, but had discounted this partly on the basis of cost, but also because of the risk of their death by disease, inappropriate food, etc.
88 McCarthy (2000), 39.
89 Kirk to Bates, 23 July 1879, RGS Archives.
90 McCarthy (2000), 39.
91 Jeal (1973), 347–8.
92 Liebowitz (1999), 157–63.
93 Mrs Kirk to one of Johnston's sisters, 10 Dec. 1879, Bartholomew Archive, NLS.
94 McCarthy (2000), 23.
95 Ibid., 32–3.

96   Ibid., 61.
97   Captain James Frederick Elton had been appointed political agent and Vice Consul at Zanzibar in 1873 to assist Kirk in suppressing the slave trade, and was subsequently Consul at Mozambique. In 1877 he headed an expedition to Lake Nyassa but died on the return journey.
98   It was Sulivan (see note 68) who in 1873 first proposed a road to Lake Tanganyika to be constructed by freed slaves from Bombay and Aden, with villages to be established at intervals along its length – see Sulivan (1873), 287.
99   McCarthy (2000), 52–6.
100 Johnston (1879a), 417–22.
101 Thomson, J. B. (1896), 53.
102 McCarthy (2000), 50.
103 Kirk to Bates, 23 July 1879, RGS Archives.
104 RGS to Kirk, 2 May 1879, RGS Archives.
105 Thomson (1881a), 87–90.
106 Kirk Archive, Acc 9942, fo. 19, 18.

9

The Road to Behobeho

———

With the scarlet-cloaked *Kiringosis* dancing in front, beating their drums, blowing their kudu horns, and waving the Union Jack, the expedition departed from Dar-es-Salaam at noon on 19 May 1879. The explorers left amidst cheers, good wishes, the rousing chants of the porters, and the firing of muskets – a noisy cavalcade stretching for more than a quarter of a mile. Kirk and William Beardall also bade farewell to the expedition from the *Star* which had sailed up the creek ahead of their departure. Despite suffering from fever and bad earache, Keith was glad to be starting at last, particularly since their leave-taking had been delayed for three hours by a guide who was missing. There had been the usual chaos of porters fighting and arguing over which loads should be assigned to them, but here Chuma proved his worth right at the start, where necessary 'seizing them by the ear and throat' to assert his authority.[1] Perhaps due to a sense of *amour propre*, Keith started the journey on the back of a donkey, whose saddle kept slipping, while Thomson was to claim, probably truthfully, that he marched on his own feet every inch of the way, even if he dropped to the ground with exhaustion at the end of some days. It appears that Thomson was up with the leaders, while Keith brought up the rear.

For the first few days, their route would take them through undistinguished grassland and woodland, but with frequent villages and cultivation. The villages were much alike: usually a clump of mango trees, a few banana plants, and sometimes one or two coco palms, with a number of small scattered huts thatched with palmetto leaves in the middle. William Beardall, journeying up the Rufiji River 18 months later, described[2] a variety of crops being raised. Rice was the staple crop, but maize, sweet potatoes, bananas, cassava, pumpkins and sugar cane were also grown – all of these depended on the reliability of the rains; because of the lack of rain in the previous wet season, there was widespread famine and deaths from starvation during his journey. Keith's caravan suffered from the converse: it was plagued by continuing rain, virtually every day, and in the lower-lying stretches of their route, the men were often up to their waists in water and sometimes up to their armpits. Drier wooded areas were interspersed with extensive marshland, or *mbugas,* which impeded their progress, with the porters slithering and slipping under their considerable loads. Even in the stretches that were relatively drier, the passage of 150 men and five donkeys created a quagmire for those at the rear of the caravan.

The donkeys proved more bother than they were worth, baulking at every river crossing, where they had to be unloaded and driven forcibly into the rivers. The first one was usually flung headlong into the water *pour encourager les autres*, while the others were dragged across by ropes, protesting loudly, before being reloaded.[3] (Thomson was later to comment: 'It was with a genuine feeling of relief we saw these weak creatures die off by some mysterious malady.'[4]) Keith recorded one such crossing, which took over two hours, with the men forming a double line facing one another to pass the long bales from one to the other. On one occasion, he himself, with great chants and cheering from the men, was passed across a river over their shoulders like a bundle of trade goods.[5] Thomson adopted his characteristic method of approaching obstacles: 'We had capital fun in crossing...I was in front, and wanting to show the men I was no milksop, though I might be a greenhorn, I marched bravely into the stream. A few seconds after, I was hauled out, spluttering and half drowned.'[6] If the trade goods got thoroughly wet, it was a serious matter, as this caused delay while they were being dried out – provided there was some sunshine. It was not unusual for the explorers to go to bed wet in their miserable little tents – because of the size of these, they would, whatever the weather, have to do any undressing outside. Before the end of their first week out from Dar-es-Salaam, at the village of Liwela, the tents were completely flooded. It is hardly surprising that, in the first weeks, Keith was complaining about what he described as bad rheumatism affecting his back.

Despite these privations, and no doubt anxious not to worry those at home, when they were in Liwela, some 44 miles from Dar-es-Salaam, Keith wrote what was to be his last letter – in a very positive vein – to his mother on Sunday 25 May:

> I have a chance to send you a little hurried line by a man who is returning to Dar-es-Salaam, after following us thus far with his brother. We have made, I think, a most promising and fortunate start, and have not had the least trouble of any sort with the men, indeed with anything for these first few days of marching, and the starting time is always the most critical. The men are an excellent set of fellows, and Chuma is invaluable. The only little bother in getting along has been with the donkeys. The streams and marshes have been very numerous and getting the donkeys across these has been tedious, but that is all; everything is going well, and I am most thankful and jolly and in capital condition, fit for anything. The country we have been passing through this past week has been very uninteresting – almost continuous jungle of tall grass and small trees without a single bit of open view, but that will soon improve as we get past the coast plains. I hope to get the letters from next mail before we reach the Ruaha River which will be in about 3 weeks at the present rate of progress, but I will be able to send you news before that, as some of my men have been engaged for a short distance only, and will be coming back. I am anxious to know your plans for the summer... Best love for you and Gracie and Joey. Please give my love to Belle and Berta too.

Camp would be made in the vicinity of a village wherever possible, in order to secure food. Initially, payment would be in the local currency of Maria Theresa dollars, but after a few days into the interior, only trade goods were acceptable and the men would be given a ration of cloth to barter for food. (Keith was meticulous in keeping a note of the local exchange rate for various food items and how much was spent in cloth each day.) With minimum fuss, the men would form themselves into groups to quickly construct their own huts built with forked sticks, grass sides and palmetto leaves for a roof, while others gathered firewood, and organised their meals, each man assuming a particular task. Any sick men would be doctored, sometimes by such native treatments as walking on the body of someone with stomach ache. Thomson often took the opportunity before nightfall to collect insects or hunt for other fauna, while Keith cross-examined anyone with knowledge on the conditions of the route ahead.[7] At sunset the British flag and the red flag of Zanzibar would be ceremonially hauled down.[8]

*Thomson's own photograph: a Makua woman showing the lip ornament or **pelele**
(Source: Random House Archive)*

Thomson's own photograph: 'Staring at white man' (Source: Random House Archive)

While in camp, the curiosity of the villagers was insatiable – some had not seen a white man before. Sometimes a group of gesticulating locals would sit as close as they dared to the explorers' tents, noting and commenting on every aspect of their behaviour, like animals in a zoo, before running off in terror if Keith or Thomson approached them. This was the usual reaction of individual local people encountered on the march who, far from being hostile, were remarkably peaceable in the Uzaramo country.[9] If any one of the villagers had been in contact with Europeans before, he would adopt the pose of informed expert and interpret their every move. Like others travellers before them, perhaps initially responding to this curiosity, the explorers would soon tire of being such objects of close scrutiny and would wish for nothing more than their privacy. Then a caravan headman would be called and, with imprecations, the crowd would be at least temporarily dispersed. Once a local witch doctor appeared with a fetish: a roughly carved representation of the upper half of a woman, decorated with beads for hair, and bracelets, necklace, and a flap covering her stomach. It might have been a fertility symbol, and the Zanzibaris laughed gleefully at it, no doubt considering themselves above such primitive superstition.[10]

Later, if the chief was in hospitable mood as at Mkamba, a dance might be arranged. The participants would be well provided with *pombe*, the local beer, and would use every local instrument they could lay their hands on, from the *zomiri* or flute, which wailed somewhat like a bagpipe (according to Thomson), stringed instruments, and the inevitable drums. Keith said they made 'a horrible din...the piper with cheeks distended...a man thwacked main drums suspended on four posts, two cylinder drums, with one or two drummers on the ground...a circle of people moved around with a sort of wriggle carrying spears, while one woman held a long knife which she turns at each step'.[11] Thomson gives a vivid description of such an occasion in which 'we could almost imagine ourselves in the infernal regions and witnessing a witch's carnival'. Apart from the *zomiri* or pipe, there were twelve drums of different types and sizes, which got the dance off to a quite circumspect start but, before long, this evolved into 'a terrible whirlpool of human beings surging about in the maddest excitement, and punctuated with ear-piercing screams'. This dance went on interminably throughout the night, forcing Keith in desperation to cover his sensitive ears and rush into his tent to cower under a blanket. Even at a distance of a mile, the entertainment apparently produced nightmares and awful dreams.[12] Later, Thomson was to observe that men who at the end of a day's march complained of utter exhaustion and demanded rest, would be quite capable of dancing the night way, including the previously halt and lame. Describing a 'bacchanalian exhibition by dark damsels', Thomson declared that above all else he abhorred a dance 'by almost nude savages', and on one occasion was obliged to rush into his tent to fetch cloth as a bribe to oblige them to go away.[13]

There were obviously other distractions for the men, as Thomson later records: 'The women make no scruple of deserting the village *en masse* with my porters, whose actions in this respect I had no power to prevent.'[14] Perhaps these actions were stimulated by the fact that, according to Thomson, the 'clothing here is diminishing in a rather alarming manner' – although it is doubtful how much 'alarm' this actually caused.[15]

Normally, the camp would be astir by 5am, woken by a reveille on the drums, but it would be more difficult to rouse the men if the night had been uncomfortable because of rain. There would be a muster and a roll call to check on any desertions. Usually within an hour the bales would be loaded (not without much cursing and swearing at the recalcitrant donkeys) and, unless delayed by morning rain, the main caravan would be on its way, led by the *Kiringosis*. Keith would make certain that he travelled close to his precious box of surveying instruments, anxious to obtain a fix on the sun by sextant whenever the opportunity arose – which in this damp hazy weather was rare. Whatever the weather, he would be timing the rate of travel at intervals as close as 15 minutes and recording each significant change in compass bearing in order to construct his route maps – much of the expedition diary consists of these details carefully recorded throughout each day's march, together with observations on the terrain and vegetation. (There is no evidence that Thomson participated in this route survey until Keith became incapable.) Both Keith and Thomson, having experienced

191

the tropical grandeur of the mountain forests of the Usambaras, were considerably disappointed by the monotony of the undulating plains with small scattered trees, broken only by even more tedious tall grass swamps which reduced their progress to a crawl. They immediately recorded any more attractive scenery where this occurred. Between Liwela and Kidonga, Keith calculated their speed at only 2 miles per hour and, partly because of the ground conditions and delays involved in securing food, their average daily rate in the first eleven days of the journey was a mere 6 miles – a rate comparable to that recorded by other African explorers.

The question of food for a large caravan was a major problem. A small village would normally grow little more than required for its own subsistence, unless there were opportunities for regular trade, which was often inhibited by inter-tribal warfare and slaving. (Despite the prohibition of the slave trade at this time, even 18 months later, William Beardall was made aware of a nearby caravan of 50 slaves on his journey up the Rufiji, not far from the expedition route.[16]) While the larger settlements might have some surplus, the local people knew that, in this situation, they were in a seller's market so they could charge quite extortionate prices in terms of amerikani, kaniki, beads or whatever. And the chief might refuse to allow food bartering until he himself had received a handsome present. Reaching Msangapwani on 4 June Keith knew that he had to obtain enough food to carry his caravan over several days of deserted country without local food supplies. He was forced to send his men out far and wide to scour the area to locate additional supplies – he had taken the precaution of sending messengers ahead to this village to order food. Unfortunately he then had to recruit additional porters to carry the food – leading to a vicious circle which was not helped when one of the guides, promising a good supply of food, took Keith's money and promptly disappeared. The guide was in league with none other than Bwana Muji, who had advised Keith on routes during his first exploratory visit to Dar-es-Salaam.

When the uncleaned rice did arrive to feed the hungry men who had gone for some time without rations, it had to be dehusked by laborious pounding and winnowing.[17] (If the guide had returned, Keith had resolved to dismiss him and to give him a good flogging, which implies that he would have carried this out himself. In fact such punishments were meted out by Chuma, apparently to the enjoyment of the Africans. This disgusted Thomson, but he admitted that the miscreant would bear no ill-will to those who had held him down and taunted him.) At about the same time, another man disappeared, but reappeared three days later, having travelled 120 miles on foot to see his dying wife. This impressed the explorers, although Keith gave him a 'good jawing' for not indicating his intentions. Keith would by now be familiar with the un-western ways of African porters.

There is no record of any systematic shooting for the pot, probably because game seems to have been conspicuous by its absence in this relatively well-populated country, but on 30 May Keith described in some detail an abortive hippo hunt, which saw both the explorers floundering around in the mud by the margins of an extensive reedbed, eventually up to their armpits. Keith noted his colleague arriving 'full of energy, plunging in at two or three places, only to come back' – all sounding very much like Thomson's impetuous charge into the Usambara swamps. But Thomson was obviously capable of laughing at himself: 'I dashing in got a fine ducking, by tripping over a root in my haste to show that I could rough it with impunity. I however, only laughed, and declared it to be the very best of fun.' They returned to their camp soaked to the skin, with Keith chilled and shivering, accompanied by a disappointed mob of villagers and porters. Thomson was in no doubt that it was this shooting excursion which resulted in Keith's subsequent attack of dysentery.[18]

As to the explorers' diet, there was a certain monotony according to Thomson:[19]

> we rejoice in a wonderful sameness in our food. Fowls and rice greet us morning, noon, and night, with sometimes an egg or two for variety…if you could look into my pocket on the march, you would probably there find a cob of Indian corn, to allay the pangs of the inner man while pushing along…We have also got a remarkable boy who attends on us, and glories in such vagaries as cleaning the plates with the skirt of his *kanzu* (the shirt-like dress of the Zanzibari). When that *kanzu* was cleaned, we have resolved never to enquire, as the knowledge might be disastrous to our appetites…the knives and spoons he wipes clean (!) when not observed, with his fingers.

Combined with the shortage of drinking water which they encountered later, that unsanitary description indicates an almost certain recipe for the lethal dysentery that was to afflict Keith before long. He recorded his first experience of diarrhoea at Msanganwapi on 5 June where they arrived with not a single item of dry clothing, and where 'the close steaming air was impregnated with malaria'. However, Thomson's attitude verges on the masochistic: 'Ridiculous as it may seem, we thought ourselves entirely unworthy of the honourable title of African travellers until we should have undergone such an apprenticeship of endurance and physical discipline. Distance and bad food had not then broken our spirits and undermined our constitutions.'[20]

The nights of 8–11 June were spent in jungle camps, away from villages, with Keith's illness steadily getting worse, although he was still doggedly making and recording detailed observations as before, noting small pools and land crabs and every physical feature of note. However, even Thomson admitted that by 8 June the explorers, through dysentery and fever respectively, presented a miserable appearance. 'I could hardly hold my head erect and Johnston was looking the agonies he would not express in words… I was in front, like a drunken man, to assume some dignity of appearance…Johnston was in the rear in an even worse condition.'[21] In late morning of 8 June Keith had to lie down suddenly and did not resume the march until early afternoon, referring to dysentery for the first time. At the end of that day, he simply sank to the ground with a groan,[22] while Thomson too was suffering from fever. Keith's diary for 10 June has the ominous words '*Unable to go on.*'

*Expedition arriving at campsite in rain (Source: H. M. Stanley, **In Darkest Africa**)*

Keith was prostrated throughout the following three days, plagued not only by dysentery, but by incessant rain. Because of the delay, he had been obliged to send some men back to Msangapwani – the village they had left three days previously – with cloth to procure more food. On 12 June Keith recorded

> Still very unwell...was carried out of the *boma*[23] by Chuma and Sululu on hammock at 7.30...all this morning's march was made in hammock, Mabub and Maribu, Mabouko, etc. relieving one another in carrying me painfully along at a sort of jog which must resemble a camel trot and which frequently gave great pain, so much so that I turned out more dead than alive.

The many unseen gum copal pits presented a treacherous hazard and threatened to throw Keith out of his hammock. For the first time, he allowed Thomson to take and record the bearings along the line of march.[24]

They reached Kimkumbi on the banks of the great Rufiji, but Keith was half dead by the time they reached village and quite unable to eat anything. The thorny bushes on the way 'thro a weary desert utterly devoid of all interest' cut the legs and feet of the porters and made a number lame. Here the Rufiji appeared more of a swamp than a river, with many sandy islands and prolific animal life, notably hippo and crocodiles, but also a wide range of water birds, including kingfisher, heron, stork, ibis, duck, and geese. Thomson had by now appreciated that much of the country they had passed through was effectively submerged by this river system in the wet season, but became almost a desert in the dry months.[25,26] Unfortunately there was no running water to be had and the explorers had to be content with the slimy water in pits or small ponds, befouled by rotting vegetation.[27] On 12 June, Keith recorded; 'still very ill, no rest at night'. There are no further diary entries until Saturday 14 June, when above the date in the diary there appears simply 'Expect mail.' – Keith's last written words.[28]

Despite his condition, Keith was determined to reach the next major village of Behobeho and insisted on being carried there. Thomson recorded 'he determined in spite of his illness, to set out once more. This was an unfortunate decision. He was improving rapidly, and a few more days rest would have given him a fair chance of throwing off the dysentery.'[29] In fact, it was not until almost two weeks after the onset of his dysentery that they arrived on 19 June at the cluster of villages. Around Behobeho, the expedition came into hill country which reminded Thomson of Scotland – it was green and well cultivated, with clear streams, colossal trees (including many palms), and shady green foliage. It was comparable to the Usambaras, and was a relief after the country they had come through. On the day after the arrival of the expedition at this settlement, a hut was constructed for Keith so that he could be more comfortable. He was obviously sinking fast, taking little or no food, and had developed a continuous convulsive cough.[30,31] Thomson felt desperately his lack of knowledge of how to deal with this situation, having no experience of illness of any kind.[32] Being unable to help constructively, Thomson climbed the highest nearby mountain, Hatambulo and, despite not reaching the summit due to fever, provided a good description of its geology. He named the mountain after his leader, considering the native name 'uncouth'.[33]

Behobeho village: sketch by William Beardall
*(Source: **Illustrated London News**, 27 March 1880)*

The story is taken up by Thomson in a letter to Kirk on 21st June:

Mr Johnston being too ill with dysentery, desires me to write to you and inform you of our safe arrival at the above place in capital order…up to the 16th we were hardly ever out of marshes with water varying from ankle to waist deep. It is surprising that we kept our health as well as we did up to the 1st of June, when Mr Keith Johnston got dysentery. On the 9th he became too ill to move on. We had to encamp two days in a forest and then we moved on with Mr. Johnston carried on a stretcher. He has suffered dreadfully and if it lasts much longer, it will become rather serious as indeed it is at present.[34]

Later he was to write sorrowfully to Kirk:

On 21st I wrote to you stating Mr Johnston's extreme prostration from dysentery. From that date on he became gradually weaker and weaker, unable even to stand without fainting. On the night of the 27th he suffered dreadful pain and passed into an insensible condition in which he remained all day of the 28th. At 4.15 of that date he, to my inexpressible sorrow and dismay, died.[35]

Thomson gave orders for a basket coffin to be made and for Keith Johnson's initials and the date to be carved in the large creeper-clad tree under which Keith was buried.

His published account of Keith's deterioration and death in the RGS proceedings indicates that, whether in retrospect or not, Thomson felt that Keith should not have proceeded:

In the meantime Mr. Johnston had contracted the disease which afterwards proved fatal to him, but which, I think, might have been cured if rest had been taken in time. However, as he was only too anxious to proceed, there could be no rest for him. His mind was set upon reaching Behobeho, where he would halt, and, as he hoped, get better; and thus for a fortnight we carried him through swamps, and along great stretches of scrubby desert, in horrible pain from the disease, the jolting of the porters, and the intense heat of the tropical sun...from the day we reached the village, he gradually became worse and worse, and only too clearly was death stamped on his face.

Thomson provides a very moving and heartfelt account of his leader's last days:

on the night of the 22 June the camp was thrown into an uproar by the arrival of men from Dar-es-Salaam, bringing our letters. It was a hard struggle for poor Johnston to get through this. To me there is something inexpressibly touching in the idea of a person situated as he was, trying with dazed eyes to read the many pleasant inquiries from friends at home, the hopes of a successful expedition, and that he was enjoying good health, and yet feeling that he was rapidly sinking into the grave, with his great work prematurely closed. He now became frequently insensible, and gradually grew worse, until the 28th, when he finished his career. For the first time in my life I saw death, and I felt myself alone to take upon me the great responsibilities of leading what appeared to be a very forlorn hope…

On the day following our leader's death we laid him in his last resting place, where his grave is now green, as his memory will ever be. He lies at the foot of a large tree festooned with graceful creepers, under an arbour of dense evergreen bushes. His name and the date of his death are carved on the bark of the tree, and the chief of the village has undertaken to keep the place clear – a contract, I have since heard, he is faithfully carrying out.

Johnston's grave: sketch by William Beardall
*(Source: **Illustrated London News**, 27 March 1880)*

The bereaved explorer then goes on to eulogise his leader:

It needs no words of mine to establish the fame of my gallant leader, or to prove his unequalled qualification for the work laid out for him. But this I will say of him, that his whole soul was in his work, that not the slightest opportunity of adding to our exact knowledge of Africa was missed. Night and day he was ever on the alert, even when tortured by disease, and never satisfied except he himself saw everything done.[36]

The final comment above is significant: although it is intended to be complimentary, it tends to confirm that one of Keith's deficiencies was a disinclination to delegate to, or involve, his deputy, even in areas where he was competent. And, as Kirk had indicated, this left the young man at a distinct disadvantage which he acknowledged:

The position into which I was thus thrown was one of peculiar difficulty, and the question arose within me whether I should forward or not. I was myself ill with fever... I was almost totally destitute of the special scientific knowledge of a geographical traveller; in fact, I knew little of anything that was most needful to know; and my age was but twenty-two.[37,38]

Under other circumstances, this might seem to be false modesty, had it not been literally true: Thomson's crucial deficiency was his lack of knowledge in the use of survey instruments, although he had apparently learnt something by watching Keith at work. Kirk himself had considerable doubts on this score, indicating to the RGS that they could not now depend on the previously anticipated accurate geographical results from the expedition.[39] The question referred to was whether Thomson should simply return to the coast as best he could, effectively abandoning the expedition, which under the circumstances would have been entirely understandable. Thomson remarked: 'I was in a very unfit state for travelling having caught a fever through running in and out of Mr. Johnston's hut during the night time.' This indicates his attention to Johnston, even though unwell himself, and belies the later implication by Mrs Johnston that Thomson might not have done all he could for Keith, although Grace somewhat unkindly hints that this is simply an attempt to exculpate himself. In fact, Thomson was so weak on the day of his departure from Behobeho that he collapsed and needed assistance, simply to keep going in a straight line.[40]

Despite the seriousness of Keith's condition, he did not apparently anticipate death, as he left no instructions or messages either for Thomson or anyone in his family. But Thomson did not lack courage and determination, even if these were expressed in somewhat histrionic terms: 'With my foot on the threshold of the unknown, I felt I must go forward, whatever might be my destiny. Was I not the countryman of Bruce, Park, Clapperton, Grant, Livingstone and Cameron?'[41] He was not to know that he would in time also be numbered among Scotland's famed African explorers. In J.M.Barrie's words 'This made a man in an hour of a stripling.'[42]

NOTES

1 Thomson (1881a), 81–2.
2 Beardall (1881), 646.
3 Thomson (1881a), 94.
4 Ibid., 122.
5 McCarthy (2000), 67.
6 Thomson (1881a), 96–7.
7 Thomson (1881a), 108.
8 Ibid., 91.
9 Ibid., 109.
10 McCarthy (2000), 85.
11 Ibid., 75.
12 Thomson (1881a), 106–8.
13 Ibid., 244–5.
14 Ibid., 306.
15 Ibid., 101.
16 Beardall (1881), 656.
17 Johnston to Kirk, 31 May 1879, RGS Archives.
18 *Proc. RGS* (1879), 103. *Notes on the Route taken by the Royal Geographical Society's East African Expedition from Dar-es-Salaam to Uhehe; May 9th to August 29th, 1879.*
19 Thomson, J. in Thomson, J.B. (1897), 57.
20 Thomson (1881a), 115.
21 Ibid., 116–17.
22 Ibid., 118.
23 A circular stockade of thorn around a camp to deter wild animals.
24 McCarthy (2000), 88–9.
25 *Proc. RGS* (1879), 670.
26 The Rufiji, flowing from the mountains of Western Tanzania has the largest catchment of any river in East Africa, but is aptly named 'sand rivers' from the huge reduction in the flow of both the main river and its tributaries during the dry season It traverses the vast Selous Game Reserve, noted for its unique concentrations of wildlife.
27 Thomson (1881a), 127.
28 McCarthy (2000), 89.
29 Thomson (1881a), 119.
30 Keith had probably earlier become infected with salmonella bacteria which could have caused dysentery and he would have become increasingly debilitated and dehydrated – his cough could have been secondary pneumonia while the malaria would have made its own contribution, according to Liebowitz (1999).
31 Rotberg (1971), 52.
32 Thomson (1881a), 147.
33 Ibid., 148.
34 Thomson to Kirk, 21 June 1879, enclosed in FO 84/1548 Kirk to Salisbury 21 July 1879.
35 *Proc. RGS* (1879), 761, Letter to Dr Kirk.
36 Thomson (1881a), 149–51.
37 Ibid., 150.

38 In his published note of the expedition, Thomson claims he was only twenty-one, which is correct, since he was born on 14 February 1858.
39 *Proc. RGS* (1879), I, 673, letter from Kirk to Bates.
40 Thomson (1881a), 152.
41 Ibid., 150.
42 Barrie (1926), 102.

10

Post Mortem:
the Trouble with Joseph Thomson

A family's anguish

The news of Keith's death came as a devastating blow to his family. Grace, while in Brunnen in Switzerland, recorded a letter from her mother: 'I send you the saddest news that could ever befall us. A telegram came late last night telling of our beloved Keith's death at Behobeho....may God help us in our distress.' (Only five days before her son's death, Margaret had been greatly moved by the death, in battle in South Africa, of the Prince Imperial, son of the ex-Empress of the French: 'I do grieve for her and the end of all her hopes.')

Keith's mother was quite crushed by his death and never recovered from the tragedy, even up to her own demise 14 years later. Given the early loss of her other sons, and her husband's death, the 'mother who had lost so many sons and clung to this one with pathetic love' must have felt that her surviving son's death at the age of 34 was the bitterest blow of all. She withdrew from the world almost entirely in the years immediately following the news and did not wish anyone to be near her, preferring to bear her sorrow alone, pacing her room for many nights, with 'all the pride and hope of her life quenched'. She could not speak about Keith or the tragedy, walling herself in at home in silence and not receiving visitors. (Fortunately she was not to know that one of her grandsons would also fall prey to what Keith called 'that Black Witch, Africa'.) One sister made the revealing remark that Margaret must have let Keith go on his journey...in glad anticipation of all the honour he was to win...' for clearly Keith did not embark on his enterprise for material gain, and of course the family would share in the pride of his achievements. This is clearly reflected in Tennyson's poem which Grace felt was a most apposite epitaph:

> A soul that, watched from earliest youth,
> And on, through many a lengthening year
> Had never swerved for craft or fear
> By one side path, from simple truth.
>
> Who might have chased and clasped Renown,
> And caught her chaplet here – and there,
> In haunts of jungle-poisoned air,
> The flame of life went wavering down.

'None can ever know the magnitude of the loss his going from us was to his own nearest and dearest...the reasons for such a black end to such high hopes and aspirations is, and must remain, an inexplicable mystery.'

Although the hazards of African travel were well known, not least disease, many of Keith's obituaries expressed surprise that such an apparently robust and athletic young man, commanding what, according to Kirk, was the best organised caravan that ever entered the interior of Africa, should succumb at such an early stage in his expedition. This in itself betrays the misunderstanding that fitness *per se* provided a defence against tropical scourges such as malaria and dysentery. There can be little doubt that, whether it would have altered the eventual outcome, Keith's own attitude in insisting in continuing, even while being roughly tossed about in a litter, would have exacerbated his condition. Certainly, nowadays, total rest and rehydration would have been prescribed from the outset. Thomson, himself a 'gung-ho' individual who claimed that 'manly exertion' was the best way to combat afflictions, admitted that Keith's decision to proceed worsened his condition and hastened his death.[1]

The news of Keith's death was brought to his mother by Foreign Office telegram, which would have done nothing to ease her pain. In a letter of 20 July 1879 from Mrs Kirk in Zanzibar to Keith's mother, Mrs Kirk explained the circumstances of this and apologised to her, while writing in the most sympathetic and caring terms. (She was at particular pains to describe how she had dealt scrupulously with Keith's belongings and papers left at Zanzibar, tying up the letters from Miss Chinnery in a separate package, and arranging for the disposal of his worn clothes to servants.) She stated her belief that Keith could not have known how ill he was, otherwise he would have tried to leave some word about his condition.[2] This developed into a warm correspondence over a number of years, although none of Mrs Johnston's letters have been found. However, the depth of Mrs Kirk's feelings for Keith are clearly revealed in her continuing concern for Keith's mother and her family. In that first letter of condolence she indicates this:

> ...this is such a shock to me – I have felt quite upset since I got the news. I liked him so very, *very* much...he was so much with us...and I saw more of him than anybody. We had so many pleasant walks and talks together. No brother could have been nicer and kinder and more thoughtful to one than he was to me and I shall never forget him. It was with a very heavy heart that I saw him start on this journey, I always had a feeling we should not see him again, though I tried to drive it away – and he was so down himself just at the last. I tried all I could to keep up his spirits and make light of the long journey and to think only of the happy return. I never though he was really quite well after the trip to Usambara, he had a little fever after it and suffered now and then with headaches, and was so troubled just before starting.[3]

Their closeness was clearly indicated later in the same letter:

Indeed I did all I could to take care of him while he was here, and to make his stay in Zanzibar happy for him, and I think he really did like to be with us. I remember so well when he came back from his first trip to the coast telling him how I quite missed him and how glad I was to see him back; and he said so pleasantly 'It seems like coming home!' And you know a few words of his meant more than a great deal of talk of most people. I so often think of a little talk we had one Sunday evening after a service of Bishop Steere's about 'Rest in Heaven'. We both agreed we hoped there would be work there of some kind...we were out on our terrace looking at the stars, and I remember so well saying; 'perhaps God will have some exploring work for you in some of his other Worlds, Mr. Johnston'...and he smiled brightly as if he would be quite ready whatever it was.

Mrs Kirk ends by saying that she doesn't think there is a chance of hearing again from Thomson for a long time. In another letter on the following day, she writes to Grace:

I can truly say that I have not felt anyone's death since my own dear brother years ago. I think I first liked your brother so much because there was something about him that reminded me of mine. Brother had the same gentle, quiet manner and much the same tastes, and my brother like yours died in Africa.[4]

Mrs Kirk then goes on to an intimate revelation, which is an indication of the depth of her feelings for Keith and her sympathy for the grieving sister who was so close to him:

Will you think me a very foolish fanciful person if I tell you a dream I had about your brother a few nights after I heard of his death? I feel I want to tell you so much you were in it and it was a pleasant dream ... I had gone to sleep thinking and grieving about him and wishing there was a way of telling him how sorry I was and longing to know how it was with him as one always does long to know about anyone we have cared for at all who would have 'gone before' and I dreamt I was in the same room with him, your mother and you were at the piano playing one of Mendelssohn's *lieder* – which changed into a song as things do change in dreams you know. He was looking so wonderfully happy and I went and sat by him and he smiled that kind bright smile of his – and I said 'I like that song so much and I haven't heard it in a long time' It was a song of Mozart's called 'L'Addio'. I have not sung it or heard it for years but I know it finishes with 'vivi pui felice, e scordati di me – addio' etc.' The air seemed so clear in my ears as I woke and I felt I wanted to tell you, because it was *you* who were singing it...

(The translation of the Italian – 'Live more happily, and forget me, Farewell!' has a particular poignancy under the circumstances.) She is also sensitive to what would be a distracting and suitably flattering comfort to Grace when she says:

He was so pleased one day I told him of a favourable review of one of your books I had found in some papers. He told me of your writing one evening when I was saying how proud I should be if any one of my daughters should even take to writing. He used to laugh at me sometimes about my early anxieties about my children's future. My little Jack, a baby boy of 10 months was so fond of him.

She then refers to Miss Chinnery, wondering how she will bear her fiancé's death, saying she will write and return to her his ring and a locket. In a later letter to another of Keith's sisters, she reveals how Keith had indicated, in his very shy and reticent way, that he was engaged. She requests from Grace a 'nice likeness' of Keith; the one she has shows Keith with a 'troubled, worried look in it as if he was either ill – or if someone was bothering him when he wanted to be left alone'. On the last remark, she states:

I used to wish he would speak out more of what he was thinking – I think it would have been better for him...I never knew anyone of such a reticent nature...he was such a perfect companion when he opened his mouth...I always knew when he didn't want to talk or be talked to... I am only glad he was able to give me so much of his confidence as he did – he knew I liked him thoroughly and he could speak or not as he liked to me.

Grace recognised Mrs Kirk's understanding of her brother's traits:

We owed Dr. and especially Mrs. Kirk a debt that could never be repaid for all she was to him. Her own letters...show that the attraction was mutual. She was quick in her sympathetic way, to recognize the nobility of nature that lay behind his extremely reticent manner... Sensitive, proud, fastidious to a degree he only showed his real self to those who understood him, but with them his fine face would light up and he would become quite talkative and merry. We all remember the little outbursts of fun and nonsense that so charmingly broke in on his usual silence. Perhaps his critical fastidiousness – I had almost said his ultra-refinement of feeling, which seems in some degree to be a characteristic of his Johnston ancestors...did not make for happiness. Like all whose standard is high, he suffered in a world not created for sensitive souls, and it was the harder for him, may be that he could only suffer in silence.

The fiancee

Grace in her *Recollections* also refers to Ida Chinnery, Keith's fiancée, confirming that there was regular correspondence between them during Keith's absence. She gives her opinion of Ida in a series of deprecatory comments. Although some of this may be ascribed to the jealousy of a sorrowing sister who was clearly very close to Keith, Ida's behaviour after his death greatly offended the family, not least Mrs Johnston, especially after the considerable welcome and hospitality which had been given to her in Edinburgh.

Ida had come to Edinburgh on 3 December 1878 on what was expected to be a long stay, and as Grace wrote to Keith in Zanzibar:

> as she will likely travel by day you may think of her on Friday evening about 7.30, when I shall be rushing along the platform, looking out for a slight black figure with a big dog. She is to have the front bedroom…and there we will pop her very soon, with a big fire…In the morning, mother and she will lay their heads together over crewel work: after lunch we shall trot off with 'Scot' to guard us, sightseeing, shopping, etc., and in the evening, when no one asks us out, you may imagine us reading aloud, with music as variety…when you are turning in, you can send a thought to two people in dressing gowns, sitting over a fire, and talking, talking, always of the same person…I can only end up with the old promise: we shall do all we can to make Ida happy and to comfort her, and I am sure that long before you come back to claim her, she will be quite one of ourselves.

In a letter from Zanzibar, Keith had written: 'Ida has been telling me…how good you have all been to her, and I am just as grateful as I can be.'

Grace described her as 'a girl of refined and gentle manner, with a sweet, low voice, but intellectually she could never have entered into Keith's tastes or pursuits – an amiable and well-intentioned girl when under good influence, but weak and easily led', claiming that she 'was helped to be her best and brightest' while she was engaged to Keith, rather indicating that the family had managed to make something of a silk purse out of a sow's ear. (Something of the same sense of assumed superiority of the Johnstons is evident here as was used to judge Joseph Thomson.) Grace continued: 'I hope I do her no wrong in saying that she could never respond to the deep and abiding love he gave her, the love that contributed to his death.' This is a strange statement – not only in the use of the word 'abiding' for a relationship which hardly had time to justify this, but even more so, in the reference to it contributing to his death, which is enigmatic to say the least. Even more extraordinary is her comment: 'we had wondered whether our boy, with his sensitive, reticent, tender nature and his fastidiously high standard, was not happier in passing away with love untarnished, than in living to see a dream dissipated'. The romantic sentimentality of this is perhaps typical of the age, but it also indicates a possessiveness about the son and brother which might have jeopardised any marriage from the start. Nor is it easy to equate Grace's portrait of Keith with the conventional image of tough outgoing explorers.

Within two years of Keith's death, Ida was again engaged to be married, but from Grace's cryptic comment about 'her extraordinary conduct' there was obviously in her announcement of her plans something offensive to the family, which was ascribed to 'evil domination' by her relatives. This was partly because the engagement was announced while the family were still deep in the conventional Victorian mourning, indicating her 'impatience with sorrow'. All this was very hurtful to Keith's mother, who had clearly treated her as a daughter, and given her many mementoes of Keith, none of which were returned, despite pleas. She subsequently wrote: 'I am exceedingly sorry for the painful end of what promised to be a true friendship, but see no possibility of any further acquaintance. It is much to be lamented for our Beloved's sake.' The second engagement was terminated (apparently one of several unfulfilled engagements) and Ida subsequently went to India where she became the matron of a hospital. However, when a memorial stained glass window to honour Keith was placed in Zanzibar Cathedral, initially at the suggestion of Mrs (now Lady) Kirk, it was Ida who made the first significant donation. In 1883, Grace wrote:

> Surely there can be no other Cathedral church in England's outlying possessions of such pathetic interest as this of Zanzibar. Built upon the Slave Market, the High Altar now covers the place of cruellest executions where devil worship was rampant, and innumerable horrors were of daily occurrence. There were nine available windows, and it was proposed to dedicate these to the memory of Explorers, Missionaries, Officers and Men of the Royal Navy and of the Consular Service. This scheme has, I believe, been more or less fully carried out, and for all time, the church on the far East African coast stands for a memorial of those representatives of England's manhood who gave their lives for African civilization. Livingstone's imperishable name will be found present in that gallant company, and among the missionaries, the good Bishop Steere. So the generous wish of Lady Kirk, so eagerly talked over in the fields of Arrandene one summer day, she lived to see fulfilled.

'The prowess of a Wallace'

From the correspondence between Mrs Kirk and Mrs Johnston, it is clear that Keith's mother held Thomson at least partially to account for Keith's death. Some of this casting about for culpability is understandable in the light of the circumstances of his death and the family's grief. This grief, at least in Grace's case, became bitter: she could not completely hide her sense of injustice at Thomson's survival and subsequent fame, while her beloved brother's early death relegated him to less than a footnote in the history of African exploration. Even Thomson's later remark of his catching a feverish cold from running in and out of Keith's tent during his last hours was seen as a *post hoc* justification for his action. In all this, what seems to have been overlooked was Thomson's extreme youth and lack of experience, not to mention the considerable stress he would have been under, accompanying his dying leader for weeks, and effectively having to take charge of the expedition even before Keith's demise. He would almost certainly have been in a state of shock in the days following Keith's death. What is perhaps less excusable is that there is no evidence that Thomson then or subsequently made any attempt to contact Keith's family. In Grace's words:

> That young and inexperienced as he was, he succeeded in the objects of the expedition is to his credit, and perhaps in his own later years of hardship and

suffering he learned the sympathy that failed him when he saw his chief die and sent not one word to the kindred at home.

She goes on to say that Thomson's subsequent triumphs and public acclamation only served to twist the knife and reopen the wounds. Her mother was not apparently impressed by Thomson's narrative of the expedition:

> He speaks as if he helped more than he did…as I read on, his egotism so increases and his criticism of all former travellers and his giving of advice – he would need to grow humbler, for he has the prowess of a Wallace, and the skill of long-tried explorers in his own eyes… he is young in all respects, and surely will gain wisdom. The first volume gives details sadder than can easily be conceived, and deepens the bitter regret. But T. admits Keith's perfect arrangements in every way, and the men were so chosen to make *his* success!

Mrs Kirk thought Thomson wrote 'very easily and amusingly', which most readers would agree with.[5] Thomson was to be criticised for making light of the dangers of African travel, he himself suggesting that he was at more risk in crossing Piccadilly. In fact his narratives are quite cleverly designed to make sure that the reader's hair stands on end from time to time, while giving the impression that he dealt with these incidents with boyish insouciance, which in all probability was true. He was a genuine *ingénue*. Later Keith's mother stated that she was glad she never met Thomson, and salt must have been rubbed in the wound when, in a letter of 1 June 1881, Mrs Kirk unknowingly said she was glad that Miss Chinnery had seen Mr Thomson and 'was pleased with him'.

Almost any complaint which could be laid at Thomson's feet was made by Grace, even if these were pure conjecture. She could not have been aware of the problems of African travel and security of belongings when she recorded:

> To his youth and his ignorance, may be attributed the fact that none of Keith's personal belongings ever came back to us, with the exception of the ring and the locket already mentioned (given him by Ida) and his Bible and Prayerbook and the latter were only returned at Mrs. K's request. This was an additional wound to us since the greater part of his outfit was the gift of friends who loved him. One cousin, famous for her fine needlework, stitched his shirts with her own hands, another had a woollen plaid specially woven for him, his guns, his fine instruments were presents. Not a personal want that thought could supply was missing, and all of these with the little comforts Mother and sisters had added, were bartered with the natives – or perhaps used by T personally… Is it too much to wonder whether, if he had had a different companion, he might not have been with us even now? Yet it was by his wish that he was carried to Beho-beho… At home we were to know nothing of the shattering of all our hopes until Keith had lain in his quiet forest grave for nearly seven weeks…

Thomson, with Chuma on his right, and Makatabu
*(Source: J. Thomson, **Through Masailand**, Trustees of the National Library of Scotland)*

It is Mrs Kirk's letters to Keith's mother which most clearly expose the contrasting personalities of Keith and his young deputy, which for Keith created a serious psychological crisis even before their departure from Zanzibar. A hint of these differences was revealed in the trip to the Usambaras, where the exuberant Thomson at one point dashed headlong into a dense mangrove swamp, only to quickly exhaust himself and ruin a suit of clothes – something the much more cautious Johnston would not have considered. But, in fact, differences between the two men had been exposed much earlier when, at Aden, Thomson went gaily off on his trip to Berbera, much to Keith's annoyance and anxiety. The playwright James Barrie, later a close friend of Thomson, said: 'though there is an abundance of Scotch caution about him, he naturally is an impulsive man, more inclined personally to march straight on than to reach his destination by a safer if more circuitous route. Where only his own life is concerned he gives you the impression of one who might be rash, but his prudence at the head of a caravan is at the bottom of the faith that is placed in him.'

A clash of personalities

African travel, even in the mid-nineteenth century, was known to have more than its fair share of hazards and stresses, as indicated previously. The combination of climate, fever, often rebellious porters, grasping chiefs, and the frustrations of delays caused by physical conditions made unusual demands on the character and attitudes of explorers. Where Europeans were put together on expeditions, it was natural, through language and culture, that they would look to each other for moral support and companionship in what was perceived as a hostile environment. With expeditions which might be expected to last years rather than months, the acute proximity of the explorers, from which there was no escape, demanded a high degree of tolerance.

For all of these reasons, and the critical nature of the relationship between European colleagues on such expeditions, it now seems astonishing that, while serious consideration was given to expedition members' professional qualifications and experience, no thought was apparently given to their compatibility in terms of background and personality, despite the history of journeys seriously threatened by personal antagonisms and petty animosities, not least in the annals of African exploration. Sometimes the interpersonal reactions could descend to the farcical – Keith commented on Thomson's appetite, complaining of his 'eating like a horse': Thomson was notoriously energetic and probably required substantial refuelling. There was no indication that Keith or his colleague were given any systematic training in tropical medicine or first aid, although the RGS *Hints for Travellers* attempted this in a superficial way.

There is clear evidence that immediately before the departure of the main expedition, Keith felt sufficiently strongly about Thomson to formally request RGS for his recall. This is quite remarkable on a number of counts. First was the sheer logistical difficulty of replacing his deputy at this very late stage. Second, Keith must have known that any such recall would not only have serious consequences for Thomson's career, but that it could not be disguised as anything other than a breakdown in relationships between himself and Thomson and would inevitably become public and redounding to no one's credit, including his own. Finally it is difficult to understand on what basis Keith would have justified this recall: although Thomson was inexperienced, and lacked knowledge of the use of survey instruments, this would have been known before their departure from England, if not even earlier. There is nothing to suggest that Thomson was other than competent as a naturalist, or that there was any question of his enthusiasm or fitness for the work in hand. Nevertheless, despite their reservations, the RGS Africa Fund Expedition Committee acceded to Keith's request, but this confirmation did not arrive before the expedition set off, with some suspicion that Kirk simply delayed forwarding it.[6]

Some indication of Keith's view of Thomson is given in a letter from the Consul John Kirk to Henry Bates dated 17 May 1879 (i.e. while the expedition was in Dar-es-Salaam and just about to depart for the interior). There his young assistant is described as 'terribly vulgar, provincial and selfish, he is a gross eater...clumsy and uncouth in all he does'. Kirk said that there is no friendly intercourse between the explorers 'so that how they are to arrange matters up country I can hardly see. It is an awkward business and may be the first of another squabble as we have had too much of already in Africa'. Kirk had recognised that as an official RGS expedition, and thus supported by the British Government whose agent he was, he had personally invested much energy and time in ensuring that it got off to the best possible start, and must have therefore felt some personal responsibility for its conduct. He would also be aware that any public 'squabble' would have done harm to the reputation of the British in East Africa, at a time when other nations were beginning to jockey for position in this part of the world and when questions were being asked as to what exactly Britain's role and intentions were there.

Keith's mother had obviously heard of the differences between the two men, for on 11 November 1879 Mrs Kirk wrote:

> I am so sorry you know of the uncongeniality between them. I half hoped you never might but these things always do come out ...he never spoke of it to a creature here except myself, not even to my husband for which I was sorry. I used to think that if he could have had a talk with him about it it might do some good – you know how very reserved he was. Even to me he never spoke very much and I was afraid to say much to him for fear of making things worse and I did not think there was the least chance of the Society recalling Mr. Thomson.[7]

From his comments to Bates, Kirk obviously knew of the difficulties between the two men, so presumably if, as Mrs Kirk implies, Keith had not raised the issue with Kirk, his wife must have done so. Mrs Kirk then tried to assuage Keith's mother's feelings about Thomson, who obviously had talked to her about his difficult relationship with Keith; it is interesting that, rather than the Consul himself acting in this capacity, it was his wife who had become the respective explorers' confidante.

> When they came first, I can assure you that Mr. Thomson liked and admired your son beyond Everything. I was never weary of talking of him, and though he knew before leaving Zanzibar that Mr. Johnston had written asking him to be recalled, he did not seem to resent it at all, and one of the last things he said to me is that he hoped they would get on better when really away, and that Mr. Johnston would like him better…I think you will feel happier about it if you do not think badly about Mr. Thomson…two more unfortunate people to go together could not have been picked out, of all people.

Mrs Kirk then came to the nub of the problem:

> …your Keith was the one who ought to have had a companion he thoroughly liked and knew. Mr. Thomson, though good hearted and well meaning, I do believe was tough and utterly without tact, a person who grated on one, if you know what I mean! I do hope he [i.e. Keith] did not think me unsympathetic about it – I sympathized so thoroughly with him about it in my heart. I felt as if I could not be quite unprejudiced …and I wanted him to make the best of Mr. T. as he had got him. I am certain Mr. Thomson would do all he possibly could for him in his illness.

The last remark, reading between the lines, does indicate that Keith's mother still felt that, in some way, Thomson had been negligent in caring for Keith, though there is no evidence for this – the description of Johnston's condition over a period of time, exacerbated by the rough travel in a makeshift stretcher, suggests that he was beyond aid, even if Thomson had known what to do.[8] However, Keith's mother must have again referred to this issue, for as late as March of the following year, Mrs Kirk was still trying to reassure her, having received a letter from Thomson describing the circumstances of the explorer's death:

> I hope you will believe that Mr. Thomson really did all he could for him – I wonder if you would like to see him when he gets home

Referring to Thomson's anticipated return, she says:

> …I can't help feeling if it was only him that was coming back in May, how different I would be feeling about it…it will seem so hard to see Mr. Thomson come back without him…I don't feel that I can get up any great interest in the Expedition

Mrs Kirk then made a remark which was almost certainly deeply felt and derived from her experience of seeing off many travellers from Zanzibar who never returned:

...I am beginning to doubt whether African exploration is *worth* the good valuable lives it has cost – and what is the use of it – when one man goes and says he has discovered something. The someone else goes and says 'No such thing' and then some other body after him saying he's all wrong too and there seems no end of it. I think if Solomon had lived in these exploring days he would have pronounced it 'vanity and vexation of spirit' like other things.[9]

Towards the end of the year, Mrs Kirk felt able to go into more detail on Thomson in a letter to Grace:[10]

I think it was Mr. T.'s utter tactlessness that worried poor Keith more than anything – I know it did me – they were so totally different in every way... I remember finishing up a talk about it with 'I suppose he can't help being what he is, and you can't not keep being yourself, so you must try to make the best of it' and he laughed and said 'I dare say we shall rub along when finally started', but it was a dreadful disappointment to him.

The expedition, because of the late rains, had been forced to delay in Zanzibar for several months, and the lack of action over this time, possibly combined with the embarrassment of Thomson's behaviour in that mannered society, would have been a source of frustration to Keith. Mrs Kirk continued:

I feel so savage when I remember how many pleasant walks he spoiled. He had a way of trotting after your brother wherever he went. Now you know generally speaking 'Two's company and three's none' and it was specially so with your dear brother, reserved as you know he was. I never got a comfortable talk with him unless I got him quite to myself, and if he was in the humour, he would talk so delightfully very often about his journeyings in South America.

She then describes how tiresome it was to see Mr Thomson in the distance:

bearing upon us at the rate of ten miles an hour as he so constantly did, joining us with a beaming smile, never for a moment even doubting his society was a charming addition. The effect was that your brother subsided into silence for the rest of the walk, and Mr. T. did all the talking, with I fear, the occasional snub from me...[11]

While it is possible to sympathise with Keith's embarrassment over the gauche behaviour of his colleague (who comes over as a friendly, lolloping, but untrained hyperactive puppy), Thomson may well have been only too glad to have some company if, as it appears, he was excluded from much social intercourse on the island. It would be fascinating to know the terms of Keith's request for recall – a request which not surprisingly was resisted by both Kirk and, initially, by the RGS.

It is likely that Keith's judgement was quite significantly affected by depression, brought about at least partially by several bouts of illness, the last on the point of departure of the main expedition. Thomson was made aware of this threatened recall, although it is not clear that Keith spoke directly about this to him. There is no evidence that he objected to or resented this, although it is difficult to believe that he did not consider it unjust, unless he was unusually thick-skinned. From Thomson, there were only the very occasional hints that his relationship with his leader was not a cordial one. Given Thomson's age – he was only 21 – it could be said that the onus for providing understanding and encouragement should have rested with the more mature expedition leader.

In a long letter of 23 July from Kirk to Bates at the RGS, the Consul expressed some sympathy for Thomson in the matter of his induction. After stating his belief that Thomson would be in the unfortunate position of knowing nothing of the financial arrangements of the expedition when he decided to press forward, he then made some revealing remarks about Keith:

> We had known him here long enough to understand his steady good qualities and to like him personally. He was one you required to know well, and to those he did not sympathise with, he was distant and uncommunicative. The unfortunate dislike he took to Thomson no doubt depressed him at setting out, and he had not the power to adopt an artificial friendly relation with anyone he did not heartily like. This again put Thomson at a disadvantage, as he had no opportunity of making himself acquainted with the use of instruments or assisting at observations... Thomson in other hands could have been made most useful and trained to be valuable...he is now called upon to take command at a disadvantage, but I have great faith he will do well and I hope lives to give us his results.[12]

This is perhaps the most penetrating assessment of the problem between the two men: while acknowledging Keith's qualities, Kirk certainly also attached some culpability to him for not making life easier for his younger assistant or bringing him more fully into the organisation of the expedition, quite apart from the neglect of his essential training in the use of instruments, when there was ample opportunity in their extended period of preparation.

A potential scandal hushed up

Following Keith's death, the RGS – and no doubt the Foreign Office – were most anxious that this difficulty between the two men should not be exposed. It would certainly not have been to the credit of the Society, and could well affect their attempts to raise funds for this and subsequent expeditions. Kirk was instructed to make the point very clearly to Thomson – in other words, Thomson was leant on fairly heavily by officialdom. Kirk wrote to Henry Bates at the RGS on 28 October, 1879:

> I have urged Mr. Thomson to let drop the differences between himself and the late Keith Johnston telling him that he can only injure himself…and in any way re-opening this again. I do not consider that Mr. Thomson will again refer to the subject after getting my letter.[13]

Thomson responded to Kirk on 12 January 1880 first by expressing his relief that the Society approved of the step he had taken in carrying on after his leader's death, despite his incompetence. Kirk had confided in Bates that, because of Thomson's lack of experience in using survey instruments, the results of the expedition would not be so satisfactory. Grace noted the remarks of the President of the RGS, Sir Rutherford Alcock.

> It may safely be said that of all the victims insatiable Africa has claimed in the cause of Science and Civilisation, this is one of the noblest, for Keith Johnston was a young man of exceptionally high attainments…Whether the cause which the Society had at heart will ever be carried out is doubtful. His companion was continuing the journey, but it would be hopeless to expect from this comparatively untrained student the same rich acquisitions which Science awaited at the hands of the late leader, learned in all the learning of Gotha and Berlin and Paris – finished pupil of his still more famous father, and the accomplished author of well-known works on Africa and Paraguay

It is interesting to see the language used above in respect of Africa, likening it to a man-eating predator, which in respect of the numerous early deaths of Europeans at this time was perhaps understandable. (Mrs Kirk told of no fewer than 11 Europeans from a relatively small population of predominantly younger men, dying in six months in 1881.)[14] However, on the question of practical route-finding, Thomson may have been under-rated, even by himself: 'I was vastly surprised and pleased to find that my bearings and estimated distances as laid down on my sketch map actually brought me within one or two miles of Tabora as laid down by Speke and Cameron. I can hardly however call it anything but a curious coincidence.'[15] Other colleagues on later expeditions were to comment on his unusual accuracy in path-finding and that he never got lost.

Writing to John Kirk to the question of his dismissal, Thomson stated:

> I am glad to say that all along my views and intentions agree with the advice you give. I have never hinted to any of my relations anything about the matter and don't intend. All that I have ever thought of doing is to lay my case privately before the committee…as I cannot but think that to take no notice of it, would appear as I had nothing to say in defence of my own character. However I have taken no step in the matter… The worst of it is that someone who had got some knowledge regarding as inserted …is of a very vague character and apparently implying that there would be an equal want of harmony with any other leader – and that it would be therefore dangerous to send one, now that I was for the

time being in possession. If this interpretation is correct I would appear to be a somewhat dangerous character to deal with.[16]

Thomson then confirmed that Bates said the request for recall was a fabrication – 'so much for that matter'. Given the evidence, it is difficult to see how Bates could claim that this was a 'fabrication', but he might well have been attempting to smooth things over and prevent it becoming a controversy. Grace was adamant that, if her brother had lived, there is no doubt that Thomson would have been recalled. One of Thomson's characteristics was apparently a lack of tact, an attribute valued highly by the Victorian middle class, but it did not appear to affect his relations with Africans. He was known to speak his mind in a forthright manner with a guileless openness and he seems both from his own comments and those of others, to be inclined to 'rush in where angels fear to tread', if not to act as the proverbial bull in a china shop.

But if he did not possess the subtlety which his more experienced colleagues expected, he almost certainly knew when to apply tact when it was important and expedient to do so; ironically, it is the one quality which is consistently remarked upon in relation to his leadership of this expedition and subsequent ones, especially in his treatment of Africans. Everything suggests that he had both the necessary authority combined with personal charisma to give his caravan a certain *esprit de corps*, with a singular lack of serious disciplinary problems. It was his ability to sense what was appropriate and sensible, often in potentially hazardous situations, which gained for him the fully justified reputation of not losing a single life on any of his many later expeditions, in marked contrast to other explorers, most notably Stanley, whose brutal methods so outraged liberal opinion. Indeed, Thomson's own motto (from the Italian) 'he who goes softly goes safely, he who goes safely goes far' is often quoted as characterising his diplomatic approach to his travels.

Perhaps 'discretion being the better part of valour' would have best been applied to Thomson, rather than tact as conventionally understood. Tact was not in evidence when, at the inauguration of the Royal Scottish Geographical Society in 1884, Thomson made a public remark about Stanley which could have been construed unfavourably, and for which he felt obliged to apologise in the following morning's Glasgow press. In the same year, Thomson, writing to Henry Bates, expressed his views on Stanley, especially his promotion of Africa for commerce: 'You will see that I have been stirring the waters here and rubbing Stanley's fur the wrong way. He is certainly marvelously thin-skinned and devoid of humour...' Later he was to claim that the Scots were disinclined to 'dance to Stanley's piping... even in Glasgow the merchants are shaking their heads over this windbag that he has been trying to inflate...He has not made a single friend and has succeeded in repelling everyone by his insufferable egotism.'[17] (It is ironic that, in 1890, Stanley was given the Freedom of Edinburgh and that, to honour the occasion, it was the firm of W. & A. K. Johnston which published a new map of Africa.)

By the end of his short life (he died at the age of 37 – only three years older than Keith) Joseph Thomson was regarded as one of the greatest African explorers, having travelled further than anyone, with the exception of Stanley himself, and was given great honour.[18] One authority said that he must stand – even in the least generous estimation – as the peer of Livingstone and Stanley.[19] On his very first journey, at an age when today he might still be completing a first degree, Thomson had covered over 3,000 miles in 14 months, the most successful journey that had ever been undertaken by a European in East Africa.[20] He had achieved many of the objectives set for the expedition, had made important scientific collections, and had kept his expedition in very good order right up to the end of a very demanding African journey, well within a very limited budget. His modern biographer, Robert Rotberg, while acknowledging his romantic restlessness and tendency not to finish off jobs properly in his haste, was still able to state: 'gentle and humane, he was a man whose attitudes and behaviour in Africa gave him a public stature unique among the many successors to Livingstone'. Contrary to Grace's view, he apparently had a disarming charm, making light of the dangers of African exploration, which was unlikely to have been an affectation, even if he did enjoy the plaudits he received.

From two different stables

As for Keith, he had many outstanding qualities which his intimates appreciated: modest to a fault, well-mannered, thoroughly professional in his approach to his work. Bates claimed that his stay in Germany had resulted in him imbibing the German habit of thoroughness and painstaking accuracy in all his work – a characteristic shared strongly with his father.[21] He was kind and thoughtful, sensitive to a high degree, and was a cultured and fastidious representative of his class, with a clear sense of duty and no little bravery, as his Paraguayan exploits had shown. Notwithstanding all of this, he had led a relatively sheltered life largely among his own kind, and his leadership qualities were based mainly on his organising skills rather on obvious personal charisma. Nothing suggests that he was an outgoing extrovert – quite the converse. Many spoke of his extreme reserve and the difficulty of getting to know him as a real person.[22] The initial picture is one of a somewhat remote and aloof personality with refined tastes – and consequently a distaste for anything he considered brash or vulgar. That he could be warm, intimate and sociable among those he felt comfortable with, and had a quiet witty humour, is testified to by Mrs Kirk.[23]

Keith had been raised in a thoroughly middle-class family of high repute and the utmost respectability in a city renowned for its veneration of that attribute. His education at Merchiston Castle School was much along the lines of a nineteenth-century English public school. Apart from the many servants in the household, from an early age, many of his contacts would have been drawn from his father's distinguished scientific and cultural circle. Their home lacked nothing which could reasonably be expected of an affluent well-established professional family, while his opportunities for travel both at home and abroad would have broadened his outlook, and were available to only a very small proportion of the population at that time. However, he had not attended university, which might have obliged him to mix with a wider cross-section of society, including those who were able to attend, not through privilege, but by virtue of their native talents and intellect, and who contributed to the vigour and even boisterousness which was a feature of Scottish university life.

It is not difficult to see how Keith and Thomson might have been less than compatible. The differences in their backgrounds – one from a sophisticated capital city, and the other from what some might consider a rural backwater – would have created a contrast in experience, even if Thomson had tasted the urban delights of Edinburgh during his stay there. Their family circumstances were clearly very different, as were their social circles. But above all, they were quite different in temperament: Thomson was a boisterous and impetuous extrovert, while Keith, 13 years his senior, was a cautious and reticent man who did not make friends easily. While Keith had a number of cultural interests, notably music, there is no evidence of such interests on Thomson's part. Keith would, from his family and other contacts, notably among his brother officers in the Artillery Volunteers and many distinguished fellows of the RGS, have acquired the social graces and manners considered *de rigeur* among his class.

Mrs Kirk's comments suggest that, by contrast, Thomson was intrusive and even boorish, with a lack of understanding of when his presence was not wanted. According to Thomson's brother, the younger explorer tried to develop a warm informal relationship with his leader, but Keith, probably too conscious of his position, his greater social status, and his seniority, refused to reciprocate Thomson's friendly approach.[24] However, if they had differences, the two explorers also shared the Victorian moral values of the time, a sense of high purpose and honourable behaviour. There is no sense of the bitter personal acrimony which so marred the reputations of other explorers, and Thomson was punctilious in eschewing any public criticism of his leader.

Thomson's position in Zanzibar must have been a distinctly uncomfortable one. While both he and Keith (according to Thomson) were warmly welcomed by the Consul-General and his family, and both attended formal receptions, Keith's diary, full of the many dinner parties and tennis games to which he was invited, almost never mentions his colleague. It is not clear whether Thomson was invited to join in this active social life of the expatriate and military class, whether he declined, whether he was simply left out – or whether Keith simply avoided mentioning his presence. The last seems unlikely, since Keith was inclined to enumerate in detail the personalities at these gatherings. If Thomson was cut out of these occasions, which included elaborate dinner parties in the wardroom of HMS *London* and at the Kirks, not to mention beach picnics with them at Mbweni, the question has to be raised – what did Thomson do with his time? Keith appears to have attended to most of the detail of the organisation of the expedition personally, and there was obviously much leisure time. It would have been a very lonely and isolated existence for this young Scot, but nowhere is there any complaint by Thomson about this excluding situation. This was possibly one reason why Thomson so welcomed ('a capital idea!') the proposal of a trial expedition to the Usambaras. However, it may also have crystallised Keith's fears: in close proximity and unable to escape from the company of his colleague, he may have come to realise what future months under similar circumstances would mean for his fastidious soul.

Mrs Kirk clearly attempted, in their more intimate *tête-à-têtes*, to convince the depressed Keith before departure that the problem with Thomson was not one of substance, but of style and manners, and that Keith must 'snap out of it'. That she herself was capable of setting aside her own distaste for Thomson's lack of refinement is shown by the way in which Thomson describes how the Kirks looked after him with great care when he returned to Zanzibar, exhausted and ill, at the end of the expedition. Perhaps however, the situation is best summed up by Grace on the differences between the two men when she says:

> How much he had to endure from the enforced companionship of his subordinate only his own kin and his most intimate friends ever knew, … but it added poignancy to our grief that the last months of his life should have been passed in the society of one who was the very antipodes of himself. For, to his finger-tips, in tradition, in looks, in learning, Keith was a gentleman, while the man picked out on the strength of his promise as a geologist to accompany the expedition, was in every sense the opposite. As the son of a small tradesman in Dumfries, it is no disparagement to him to say that he never had any opportunity of entering refined society, but to one who knows anything of the ways and habits of the Scotch Peasant, it will be readily apparent that there could be no equality of intercourse.

Grace then refers to the 'careless recommendation' by Professor Archibald Geikie on Thomson's application to join the expedition. She bitterly castigates Geikie who, despite being greatly helped in his career by her father and often receiving their hospitality, neglected the family after her father's death. She cannot forbear not to refer to Geikie's own 'humble extraction', although she reluctantly admits that he probably did not '*deliberately* choose T to be daily scourge to our boy, for he would probably in his own case have found nothing amiss in the raw country lad's manners and habits' – the inference being that Geikie was similarly unmannered.

She quotes Mrs Kirk to support her views on Thomson:

> To the hostess of both, the association seemed almost a tragedy, for as she explains in her letters, T. was so entirely lacking in tact, so absolutely certain at all times of his social desirability that even the snub was powerless as a weapon!

It would almost be invidious to comment on this judgement, so neatly does it encapsulate the attitudes of Grace's class at this time. It stands in stark contrast to the acclamation given to the 'lad o' pairts' i.e. the youngster of humble origin but with natural talents, which is so much part of Scottish mythology, but which had its basis in the number of men who rose from lowly social positions to achieve a measure of greatness. Not only were Thomson and his family removed from any so-called 'peasant' class (one of his brothers, who wrote his biography, was a well-educated Scottish church minister) but the eminent geographer J.G. Bartholomew stated that his outstanding characteristic was his 'true spirit of chivalry', which in its literal sense implies a degree of nobility.[25] But the 'Scotch' element may also betray an attitude which was prevalent in some quarters at the time, particularly with those who had taken up residence in the Metropolis, as Grace had done for some years, and came to regard their native country as somehow backward and inferior to the dominant English culture. The irony of this is that the first chapters of Grace's *Recollections* are taken up with delineating the illustrious lineage of the Johnstons of the Scottish Borders, and their high-born ancestors, admitting that they were as lawless as the rest of the feuding Border families in 'The Debateable Lands'. Keith also was not immune from this misplaced pride: after the marriage of one of his sisters to yet another unrelated Johnston, their son was christened Keith after himself, to which he objected partly on the grounds that the son's father was not a Border Johnston.

It is also significant that Grace shared, with many of her kind, a similar estimate of Stanley based on his doubtful parentage and impoverished upbringing as much as anything, no doubt reinforced by Keith's own antipathy to the great explorer:

> Some of his letters to Keith, referring insultingly to 'easy-chair Geographers' – this from the *nameless work-house boy* [my italics] were found among his correspondence and were destroyed. They reflected little credit on the writer and it may be as well for Stanley's reputation – which stands high among the ignorant public – that they no longer exist.

Other writers have in fact ascribed Stanley's bitterness for the rest of his life to his lack of social acceptance by a thoroughly snobbish establishment. Even the much respected Kirk had described Livingstone's wife as 'common and vulgar'. This distinction between on the one hand 'officers and gentlemen' and 'other ranks' on the other may have reached its apogee about this time, but it was to continue among British institutions and social classes to the present day, albeit on a somewhat reduced scale. It was, for instance, a marked feature, with all its petty distinctions, separating the various 'ranks' of the Antarctic explorers at the beginning of the twentieth century.

A grave in the bush

Late in the year in which Keith died William Beardall made an exploratory journey up the Rufiji by boat and made a pilgrimage to Behobeho. He told a somewhat strange story, which appeared with his sketches, in the *Illustrated London News*:

> We passed three villages, and then reached the one in which Mr. Keith Johnston died. Here I stayed all the following day. The grass hut built for Mr. Johnston and in which he died, is still standing. He is buried about twenty-five yards off, under a big 'Inkuyu' tree which stands just inside the belt of jungle surrounding the village. His initials and the date of his death are cut in the bark of the tree. The natives gave me to understand that the grave was some way off away in the bush. They wanted a big present for showing it to me, but just before sunset on the day of my arrival, two green pigeons settled on the 'Inkuyu' tree. I shot them, and going to pick them up, came upon the grave...

Grace records: 'We employed a clever young Scotch artist to make enlarged water coloured pictures of the published black and white sketches and he succeeded well in reproducing the African atmosphere and colouring.[26] This sacred spot is now well protected, thanks to the good offices of Germany.'

In the middle of 1881, Thomson returned to Zanzibar at the request of the Sultan to search for rumoured coal along the Rovuma River, which provided him with an opportunity to present honours to those who had accompanied him on the RGS Expedition. Chuma, who had already received the large RGS medal for his part in the Livingstone journeys, was now presented with a further silver medal and ceremonial sword for his service with the 1878–80 expedition. His next in command, Makatubu, also received a silver medal, and what was described as a 'second class sword' while all of the porters received a bronze medal together with a certificate of conduct bearing the consular seal.[27] (By a singular coincidence, during the writing of this work, one of these bronze medals was offered for sale by a well-known coin auctioneer and described as an unknown medal, i.e. in nusimatic terms 'unpublished'. It seems to have been worn by the unnamed recipient and is apparently the first to have appeared since the presentation of these medals in 1881.) There is no indication of any other pecuniary reward for their 14 months arduous service; himself unpaid, Thomson received an *ex gratia* award of £250 from the residue of the African Exploration Fund which was being wound up – by his own careful stewardship of the RGS funds, he almost certainly saved them considerably more than this.

In 1890, the Imperial German Commissioner, Dr Wilhelm Schmidt, inspecting what was now part of German East Africa, found Keith's grave, and ordered that it be fenced in. Knowing of Keith's strong association with Germany, Schmidt suggested that some permanent memorial should be erected to his memory. The matter was referred to Parliament and the RGS, but the Johnston family decided that this was a matter for them. After taking the advice of (now Sir) John Kirk, in Grace's words 'a large desk-shaped slab of Swedish granite the inscription cut on it and filled in with black, was eventually chosen.[28] The slab, far too heavy otherwise for transport, was cut in sections, and it took 100 native porters just one year to convey it to Beho-beho where it now we hope, permanently marks the spot where a young life was ended.' (Even if only the dry season was used, it seems quite extraordinary that this time and manpower would have been required – the likely expenditure seems quite disproportionate, but is indicative of the family's feelings.) On 20 May 1898, the German cartographer Dr Richard Kiepert reported that one of Germany's foremost explorers, Bergasser Bornhardt, had visited the gravesite, had recorded the inscription on the headstone and, rather touchingly, had plucked two leaves from a plant growing on the grave, which were forwarded to the Royal Scottish Geographical Society, for passing on to the family.[29]

NOTES

1 Thomson (1881a), 119.
2 National Library of Scotland (NLS), Edinburgh: Bartholomew Archive V, 40. Mrs Kirk to Mrs Johnston, 20 July 1879.
3 Ibid., 20 July 1879.
4 Ibid., Mrs Kirk to Grace Johnston, 21 July 1879.
5 NLS: Bartholomew Archive V, 40. Mrs Kirk to Mrs Johnston, 1 June 1881.
6 RGS Committee, 30 April 1879; RGS Copy Letter Book, Bates to Kirk, 2 May 1879; Bates to Johnston, 2 May 1879.
7 NLS: Bartholomew Archive V, 40. Mrs Kirk to Mrs Johnston, 11 November 1879.
8 Today, personnel of even modest expeditions or outdoor activities would be expected to have basic health and first aid training, which Thomson almost certainly did not receive.
9 NLS: Bartholomew Archive V, 40. Mrs Kirk to Mrs Johnston, 2 March 1880.
10 Ibid., Mrs Kirk to Grace Johnston, 10 December 1879.
11 Ibid.
12 Kirk to Bates, 23 July 1879, RGS Archives.
13 The letter referred to is not available, but interestingly all of Kirk's letter quoted above is heavily scored through in red crayon in such a way as to make it entirely readable – by whom and for what purpose?
14 NLS: Bartholomew Archive V, 40. Mrs Kirk to Mrs Johnston, 1 June 1880.
15 Thomson to Kirk, 26 May 1880. RGS Archives.
16 Whatever the insertion was as enclosed by Kirk is missing from the RGS file.
17 Thomson to Bates, 13 December 1884, RGS Archives.
18 McLynn (1992), 126.
19 Miller (1972), 90.
20 Rotberg (1970), 298.
21 Bates, in Thomson (1881a), v.
22 Ibid., xviii.
23 NLS: Bartholomew Archive V, 40. Mrs Kirk to Grace Johnston, 10 December 1879.
24 Rotberg (1971), 33.
25 *Scottish Geographical Magazine* (1895), 524–8.
26 I interpreted this as a fig tree and used this in attempts to relocate Keith's grave in 2001.The original of the tree sketch still exists in the safekeeping of a relative.
27 Simpson (1975), 153.
28 One of Keith's sisters, Belle, was resident in Sweden, where her husband had business there. This may account for the origin of this stone, which was shipped from Gothenburg – this sister was the only one of the family to see it.
29 The pressed specimens, now in the W. and A. K. Johnston archive in the National Library of Scotland, have been identified as from the Rubiaceae family (which includes coffee), possibly *Chassalia* or *Psychotria* known to grow in the area (identification and information provided by Brian Harris, Edinburgh).

11

Epilogue

On the banks of the Rufiji, with its grey-brown waters swirling round the almost fluorescent cream-coloured sandbanks, hippos were constantly grunting and blowing nearby, while some of the largest crocodiles I had ever seen were still basking in the low evening light. I felt that I had come full circle: we – that is Mike Shand, Senior Cartographer at Glasgow University, and myself – were attempting in July 2001 to retrace the steps of Keith and Thomson from Zanzibar to Behobeho, with the hope that we might even find Keith's gravestone. We had seen where Keith had stayed for much of his time in Zanzibar at the old consulate, had admired the Arabian architecture of John Kirk's town house overlooking the harbour, and had watched the old dhows being patched up in the traditional way, using adze and local timber. Being roused by the amplified call to prayer each morning at around 4.00am by the *muezzin* had reminded us that this was very definitely a Muslim town. The shell of Livingstone's house had become Zanzibar's tourist office, while at Mbweni we had walked along the beach where Keith had often picnicked with the Kirks. Near the ruins of the girls' school that Caroline Thackery administered for so many years, we admired the pair of ancient cycads, which may well have been the two that Keith described Kirk bringing back from a visit to the mainland.

I had been advised by a Johnston relative who had been in Zanzibar in the immediate post-war period that there was much material in the Zanzibar Museum relating to the 1878 expedition. In the event, this poorly organised museum proved a disappointment in that respect. By contrast, the Zanzibar Archives, with substantial foreign funding, had been greatly improved and provided a number of manuscript items of relevance, including correspondence between Bates and Kirk referring to the sending out of two small books on the use of mathematical instruments and *The Stars and How to Find Them* for Thomson, following his plea for instruction in these subjects,[1] and another from Kirk to Lord Salisbury reporting the departure of the expedition and describing the route it proposed to take, among other official correspondence. Also, poignantly, was the letter from Thomson to John Kirk informing him of Keith's death at Behobeho.[2]

Most moving was the view of the tall three-sectioned coloured glass window in Zanzibar Cathedral, with its interlaced floral motif, dedicated to Keith's memory by his widowed mother and sisters, surprisingly omitted in the otherwise detailed description of the Cathedral in the *Zanzibar Guide*, and which as a result we almost overlooked. Beside the window, a brass plaque read 'In remembrance of Keith Johnston who died at Behobeho 25 June 1879. This window was placed here by his mother and sisters.' Near the altar was a small wooden cross reputedly made from the tree under which Livingstone's organs were buried. But the link with the past was personified by Peter, the African church officer, at St John's Church at Mbweni. We found him in a hut attached to the church, dressed in a tattered army shirt and an old pair of Wellingtons, boiling up his lunch of fish and meal on a Primus stove. Very courteously, he told us how his grandfather had been captured as a slave in Nyasaland, and showed us the grave where his own father, the first African Bishop of Zanzibar Cathedral, was buried. His grandfather might well have been one of the many slaves freed by the British Navy from their supply ship HMS *London*, where Keith had been a frequent visitor. It was difficult not to feel the hairs prickling on my neck at this history coming alive in the presence of Peter and indeed the whole story of Mbweni so closely associated in time with Keith's story.

Since I last saw it nearly 40 years ago, Dar-es-Salaam has expanded to a city of 3.5 million, i.e. two-thirds of the total population of Scotland. Wealth and extreme poverty sit side by side – my introduction to it, from a late-night flight, was a taxi journey over seriously pot-holed dirt roads, through unlit streets to my hotel in the Upanga district, aware of the guttering oil lamps of street vendors still plying their wares at midnight. On the following day, we were enthusiastically welcomed by Dr Rolf Baldus and Dr Ludwig Siege of the German Technical Aid Programme, when we exchanged notes on the Selous. While we were very grateful for their practical help, they in turn became very excited when we provided the older maps and the animal census results of the Reserve in the 1960s which we had been able to obtain from contacts in the United Kingdom, especially the evidence of the changes in species numbers such as giraffe.

The low-level flight in the tiny Cessna 206 from Dar-es-Salaam to Kiba Airstrip Sand Rivers, accompanied by our expedition guide, John Corse of Nomad Safaris, more or less following the route of the RGS expedition, demonstrated vividly the terrain through which Keith and Thomson passed in the late spring of 1879. Leaving the sprawl of the city behind quite quickly, we flew over cultivated land for only a short distance before the great extent of wooded grassland and scrub took over, with the smoke from large fires billowing upwards at intervals. The great *mbugas* or grass swamps, interrupted only here and there by small tree-covered knolls, seemed to stretch verdantly to the horizon, an apparently endless sweep of undifferentiated green. It was easy to imagine the caravan floundering through waist-high water or the donkeys panicking at the edges of the many streams which meandered through this wilderness. Over the site of the former Behobeho village, on a very distinctive series of sharp curves in the Behobeho River, we banked sharply and were able to get a good view of the wooded bush we would be searching in and the dry river bed which would be our base camp for several days.

At this time of year, just as Johnston described his problems in obtaining sextant readings on the sun due to overcast skies, we encountered similar lowering clouds, the hangover from the long spring rains. Everywhere, game tracks formed a dense network of trails, and it was not difficult to identify on the ground below elephant, buffalo, hippopotamus, giraffe and crocodile, here forming the largest concentrations of some of these species in the whole of Africa. But it was the great meandering Rufiji and its many tributaries rising in the mountains to the west, glinting like polished steel, which dominated the landscape – a scene which, from the description of Keith and others, had not significantly changed since the time of the expedition. Instead of his claustrophobic tents, we slept in the open under mosquito nets on a dry sand river, able to view the amazingly starlit southern sky from our paliasses: clearly visible were the stars Arcturus and Crux (Southern Cross) used by Keith for the astronomical observations to fix latitude and longitude. As dawn broke, the dying embers of the flickering night fire still wafted the aromatic smell of the *mpingo* or African blackwood across the camp.

Around Behobeho Thomson was delighted with the luxuriant forest

> of the densest nature, formed of colossal trees, with deep, green, shady foliage… there are feathery acacias and mimosas, branching hyphene palms, and fan palms with their abnormally bulged trunks…fill up the intervening spaces between the trees with ivy-green shrubbery, until not a clear bit of ground is seen, and passage through the forest is rendered impossible. From tree to tree hang creepers of every description; slender leafy kinds swaying gracefully in the breeze; giant forms thick as a man's thigh, gnarled and twisted, binding the tree trunks as with bands of iron. The whole forms an impenetrable mass of vegetation through which it is impossible even to see.[3]

What was missing from this description was any reference to the vast congregations of wildlife which have enabled the Selous Game Reserve, one of the largest protected areas of the globe, to be given the accolade of a World Heritage Site, some twenty years after my own first forays into its north-west corner. Thomson records:

> I was forcibly struck during these jungle marches with the very marked absence of animal life of whatever class. This indeed had been observable over the entire country we had traversed…few mammals were seen, and the existence of birds was chiefly noted by the hoarse caw of the hornbill, or the exasperating squeak of a small parroquet. The dreariness of these marches can hardly be conceived, and the distant glimpse of a herd of antelope was quite sufficient to excite the whole caravan.[4]

(However, near the Rufiji, and around Lake Tagalala, he also commented on the way that the ground had been ploughed up by the feet of numerous game animals which he thought must be abundant in other seasons.)

We speculated on why this might be so. Keith recorded passing through and staying in the vicinity of a number of villages on which his caravan depended for food – now with the clearance of all local habitation within the reserve, ostensibly because of tsetse fly and associated sleeping sickness, the population is largely confined to the relatively few visitors using safari lodges north of the Rufiji and the anti-poaching patrols of the Wildlife Service: although hunting is allowed, it is now strictly controlled. (The village of Behobeho itself no longer exists, as William Beardall in his 1880 expedition recorded that it had been burnt down by the neighbouring Wamahengi a few months previously.[5]) Undoubtedly the establishment of the reserve with its legal authority and the increased enforcement of its provisions in recent years, assisted by the Selous Conservation Programme, has greatly contributed to the protection of this vast sanctuary. Even before the nineteenth-century expedition, the area was known for its rich resource of ivory which, carried by slaves, the Arab traders had exploited without compunction.

Since the time of the 1878–80 RGS expedition – with the winding up of the African Exploration Fund, this was the last mounted in Africa by the Society – important changes had occurred in Tanganyika and in this region in particular. The German Government had officially taken control over the country from the German East Africa Company in 1891, leaving Britain with a protectorate over the Zanzibar archipelago. Local resistance to the German occupation and enforced plantations culminated in the Maji Maji rebellion of 1905, which started near Liwale south of the Rufiji and extended north as far as Kilosa on the first railway from Dar-es-Salaam to Tabora. Following this uprising, the ruthless 'scorched earth' policy of the German administration, combined with drought, resulted in widespread famine and deaths among the African population, not least in the Southern Province around the Rufiji; together with the direct casualties of the rebellion, this may have resulted in as many as 300,000 deaths. Much previously cultivated land was abandoned and reverted to bush, with incursions of wild animals, which further discouraged agriculture from the 1890s onwards. There was a spread of tsetse fly, and the resulting *trypanosomiasis* killed large numbers of cattle and debilitated the human population. Together with famine and natural disasters, the execution of many of the indigenous leaders who had supported the uprising resulted in a breakdown in traditional tribal authority, and disruption.[6] It is hardly surprising that, even today, much of the area that Keith traversed (with the exception of the coast and its immediate hinterland) has remained undeveloped and relatively unpopulated, with a dearth of modern communications. By contrast, the cool moist highlands that Thomson travelled through before reaching Lake Malawi have become important areas of economic agricultural crops such as tea, coffee, pyrethrum and wattle.

Mike Shand had carried out a very painstaking comparison of all the available maps of the area and following a German map of 1900, and assisted by the modern Global Positioning System (GPS) equipment, he was able to identify the approximate

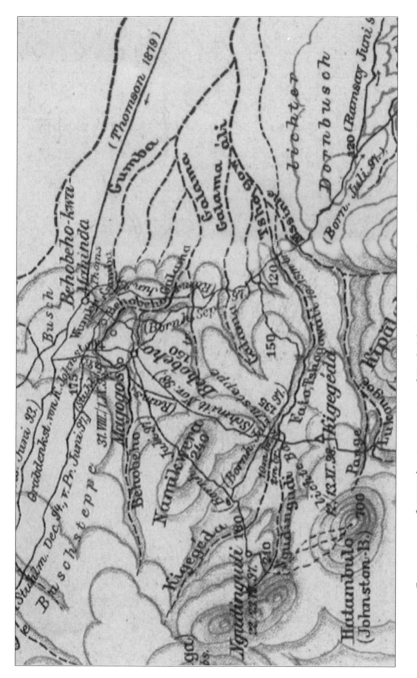

German map of 1900 showing gravesite of Keith Johnston (Source: Library of Congress/Mike Shand)

location of the gravesite on the Behobeho River. We used the now dry bed of that river, liberally decorated with the droppings of elephant, hippo and buffalo, as a base camp (*Campi ya Fisi* or Camp of the Hyenas) to search for Keith's grave. Despite several days of systematic searching on parallel compass bearings, often through dense riverine bush, interspersed with large fig trees and anthills, and making a number of local enquiries, we were unsuccessful in finding any sign of either the grave or the headstone. Comparison of maps of different dates showed that much of the Rufiji river system has changed course over time, while the shifting 'sand rivers' might very well have obscured any last vestiges of the grave. The area of Behobeho had also seen some of the fiercest fighting of the East Africa campaign during the First World War, and the remains of trenches and fortifications can still be discerned, so that the grave might also have become a casualty of war. However, it may still be waiting at Behobeho to be rediscovered. Here the famous hunter and conservationist Frederick Courteney Selous, whose boyhood hero had been Livingstone, and whose name was given to the reserve, was killed by a German sniper's bullet in 1917.[7] It seems ironic that this remote area round Johnston's recorded gravesite, at one time carefully protected by order of the German administration, should be so fiercely contested by the two warring nations as far as could be imagined from the main theatre of war in Europe.

From Behobeho, Thomson attempted the ascent of Hatambulo, the highest point in the Selous, renaming it Mount Johnston, in honour of his deceased leader. Thomson was defeated in his aim of reaching the summit – a mere 700 metres high, apparently because he was suffering from fever. Even without this excuse, we found it a very challenging climb over boulder scree disguised by grass and at times almost impenetrable thorn scrub up to 3 metres high. After walking and scrambling, frequently on hands and knees over steep slopes for 7 hours, with an enlivening near-encounter with a solitary buffalo, we reached the summit with a distinct sense of achievement. From here the wilderness of the Selous stretched on every side for as far as the eye could see, much of it largely unexplored in any detail – as late as the 1980s it had been described as 'that vast wild place that scarcely anyone knew'.[8]

The ethos behind the RGS expedition, encapsulated in the aim of bringing the triple 'C's, i.e. Christianity, Civilisation and Commerce, to this part of Africa, had only been very partially achieved: at the present time, only a third of Tanzanians are Christian. (There are at least as many Muslims.) Whatever else might be meant by 'civilisation', the communications which the expedition was charged to establish have certainly improved – we were able to travel by air in an hour a distance which had taken the original expedition 10 weeks. And what of the anticipated trade road from the coast to the interior and the Central Lakes? The great irony is that the road to Behobeho and beyond never was constructed, as it proved easier to ship goods from these lakes south-westwards to the Indian Ocean at Beira in Portuguese East Africa. However, almost a century after Keith's death, a railway was built from Dar-es-Salaam to Zambia which for considerable stretches now follows approximately the route of the RGS expedition. To compound the coincidences in this story, the section where the two routes are closest is precisely the area where my forest survey of the early 1960s was concentrated. (This work was only interrupted for a short period to allow me to assist in the local organisation of the first national elections, which resulted in the establishment of the independent Republic of Tanzania under the presidency of Julius Nyerere, who subsequently persuaded the Chinese to construct the railway.)

However, Tanzania has not proved to be the commercial Eldorado that some nineteenth-century entrepreneurs thought it might be; they could not have conceived that its most important hard currency earners would be its wildlife reserves and national parks, nor that the wildernesses which the explorers regarded with apprehension would prove to be one of its main attractions and economic assets. There is therefore a certain symbolism that Keith died and was buried in the largest game reserve in Africa, whose purpose is to protect it from those forms of twenty-first century 'commerce' and 'civilisation' which might endanger it. As far as 'Christianity' is concerned, that purpose transcends both individual religions and personal beliefs in its ethical basis, which Keith Johnston may well have approved of.

Against the background of nineteenth-century Scotland and the expanding Empire, what is the significance of Keith's relatively short life? In the first instance, he represents an important tradition of scholarship, amply demonstrated by his father, which was a feature of Scottish publishing and cartography in the post-Enlightenment period. Both father and son were genuine enquirers over a broad field, not simply in the techniques of map-making, but also in many aspects of modern geography and natural science, unconstrained by the narrow confines of traditional cartography. They were truly pioneers in attempting to integrate basic elements of the natural world – climatology, meteorology, geology, hydrography and natural history – into their view of the world, and to go beyond this in a practical way, i.e. to develop methods of representing this visually in a systematic way which had not been done before. They brought their assiduously honed technical cartographic and printing skills to bear on the interpretation of the scientific and geographical information coming in at this time from all quarters of the globe. Their scholarship was marked by a degree of accuracy and painstaking attention to detail which became the hallmark of the firm of W. and A. K. Johnston, at least during their own lifetimes.

While Alexander made his own important contribution, in both cartography and research, to 'the science of Empire' through maps which would be used by immigrants, soldiers, administrators, missionaries and traders, Keith took this one step further. Not content with simply converting the results of the explorations of others into maps, he joined that legion of Scots who distinguished themselves as field surveyors in the period which Bridges has described in East Africa as the 'unofficial empire'. He was in many ways characteristic of that time before overt – and some would say, crude – imperialism, formally underwritten by the British Government. He came just within the time when individual explorers could still claim to be fulfilling the original ethos of societies such as the RGS. Despite the political and often commercial undertones which were beginning to influence so-called 'exploration' at this time, Keith maintained the tradition exemplified by Livingstone of geographical discovery for its own sake. Paradoxically, in this respect he would have been in close company with Joseph Thomson, who with the authority of a seasoned and popular explorer, became a fierce critic of the imperialistic Stanley, and was later to decry the decline in disinterested exploration.

NOTES

1 Zanzibar Archives, General Correspondence Out Fo. 367.
2 Ibid., Kirk to Lord Salisbury, 30 May 1879, Fo. 81/209, file AA1/23.
3 Thomson (1881a), 144–5.
4 Ibid., 172.
5 Beardall (1881), 645.
6 Iliffe (1979).
7 Taylor (1989), 7–8.
8 Matthiessen (1981), 5.

Appendix 1

―――

May 23 Mzugu to Mkuranga

*Left Mzugu at 7 – fine morning cloudy and fresh. Go on SW 7.05 past a small village in
the woods and at 7.10 enter a dense thicket. At 7.15 going SW going over grass with
thickets and small trees. At 7.20 a shallow marsh in which fortunately only one donkey
fell. Go on SSW. At 7.30 descended to small valley. (going SSW) and five miles passing the
marsh knee deep in the hollow. At 7.45 we were going SW through grass and small trees
nearly on a level. At 7.50 past a small stream running to right. At 8 going through the
same sort of grassy and small tree country S by W. Halt at another hollow with larger
stream running SW [?Mzinga] waist deep.(1) At 8.20 across and the donkeys reloaded.
Go on SW. At 8.30 going S past clearings and we enter the grass and thicket country. At
8.35 halt at a small village and on a hill called Hoyoyo commanding view over undulating
wooded country east of us. At 8.45 go on S and SW passing muhogo (cassava or manioc)
cultivation and coconut trees. At 9 SW and 9.10 maintain SSW undulating country grass
and trees. At 9.25 SW by S. At 9.30 halt in going S by W passing a stream running to
the left (or E to NE). At 9.50 go on S. At 10 the guide having taken a dead path notice
several chiefs' graves along the route today straw roofs and six small posts with short post
driven into the ground some of which are carved. Sometimes small strips of cloth are
pegged into the ground beside these. Copal digging (2) seen all along the path, copal digging
pits each about 10 inches in diameter. At 10.15 halt passing a small stream till 10.35
when we go on up the slope – 10.40 going S among trees and grass. Muhogo cultivation
small valley on left, turn WSW reach village of Mkuranga at 11 o'clock having passed
Madagwe. Their names seem to apply to village groups and districts the houses being
scattered two by two or so. This however is a large village with coconut trees in its square.
Gave out cloth to value of 9 rupees from bale number 17 and 10 rupees to different
villages a choice of money. Standard bearing reads 29.740 at 3pm. Aneroid 29.720.
Evening clouded over no obvs [= astronomical observations] possible.*

Appendix 2

1878–80 RGS East African Expedition Instruments

	£	s	d
1 watch	35	0	0
1 1.6 in sextant	10	0	0
1 artificial horizon	5	0	0
1 George's barometer (complete)	12	12	0
1 trygonometrical apparatus	5	0	0
2 boiling point thermometers	4	10	0
1 aneroid	5	0	0
1 set maximum and minimum thermometers	1	17	0
1 prismatic compass	4	10	0
1 pocket compass	1	10	0
1 ordinary thermometer	0	10	0
1 pocket case and drawing instruments	2	10	0
1 measuring tape	0	14	0
1 wood box sealed	0	15	0
1 brass circular protractor	0	16	6

Source: RGS Archives

Appendix 3

JOSEPH THOMSON'S FIRST AFRICAN OUTFIT AND EXPENSES

	£	s	d
3 sleeping pyjamas	0	15	0
3 sleeping jackets	0	15	0
6 flannel shirts	3	9	0
6 merino vests	1	13	0
2 sweaters	0	13	0
2 tropical tweed suits	6	0	0
3 linen tweed suits	4	10	0
4 pairs white drill trousers	2	0	0
12 handkerchiefs	0	4	6
6 towels	0	10	6
6 undervests	1	3	0
1 camp bedstead	0	14	0
1 cork mattress	1	3	0
2 blankets	1	7	0
1 mosquito curtain	0	10	6
1 pair shoes	0	7	6
4 pairs short boots	6	10	0
1 pair gaiters	0	7	6
1 waterproof coat	2	0	0
2 waterproof sheets	2	0	0
1 tent	2	12	6
1 pair long boots	3	8	6
1 basin	0	1	6
geological hammers, axe, chisel, and sheath knife	2	19	6
diary and notebooks	0	16	0
lantern, flint, and steel	0	19	0
2 felt hats	0	15	0
1 inkbottle	0	2	6
1 set of blowpipe apparatus	1	12	6
12 pairs socks	1	4	0
2 galvanised iron boxes	2	0	0
quinine	2	0	0
1 double-barrelled gun	10	0	0
1 double-barrelled rifle	22	0	0
ammunition	4	10	0
1 colts revolver with ammunition	4	0	0
Total	96	3	6

Source: Robert I. Rotberg (1971), *Joseph Thomson and the Exploration of Africa*, London.

Bibliography

Unpublished sources

The Bartholomew Archive (curently being indexed) contains the letters from Lady Kirk to Mrs Margaret Johnston, which have been quoted extensively in this work

Bridges, R.C. *'The British Exploration of East Africa, 1788–1885, with Special Reference to the Activities of the Royal Geographical Society'*. PhD thesis (University of London 1963b)

Edinburgh University Library Special Collections. Archives on Sir Alexander Geikie and Frederick and John Moir

Gavine, D. M. (1982), *'Astronomy in Scotland 1745–1900'*. PhD thesis (Open University, 1982)

Johnston, G. (n.d.) *Recollections of the Keith Johnstons*, 2 vols. Private family papers

Koninklijk Museum voor Midden Afrika, Tervuren, Belgium. Archive of H.M. Stanley – Correspondence with Keith Johnston

McCarthy, J. (ed.) (2000) *The 1878–80 Royal Geographical Society Expedition to East Africa: The Diary of Keith Johnston. Transcribed with Explanatory Notes*. National Library of Scotland, Edinburgh

National Library of New Zealand Manuscript and Archives Section, Wellington Papers of Sir Julius Haast

National Library of Scotland, Edinburgh. Substantial mss. collections on Scots associated with Africa, including archives on David Livingstone and Sir John Kirk. It also contains the archive of W. & A. K. Johnston (Acc. No 5811), which although it includes much material on the family apart from this company, has virtually nothing on Keith Johnston Jnr

Royal Geographical Society Archives London. Specifically folio 25 relating to the 1878–80 RGS East African Expedition

Royal Scottish Geographical Society, Glasgow. The 1883 diary of William McEwan and associated letters and notes

University of Edinburgh, New College Library (Special Collections). Correspondence relating to Alexander Keith Johnston Snr, including letters exchanged with Thomas Chalmers

University of St Andrews Library Mss. Collection. Papers relating to James David Forbes in Letterbooks III–V1

Published sources

The Academy, 2 Jan 1875 (London)

Anon. (1848), 'The Physical Atlas: A Series of Maps and Notes, illustrating the Geographical Distribution of Natural Phenomena by Alexander Keith Johnston' *North British Review*, 9: 359–69 (Edinburgh)

Anon. (1863), 'On Recent Geographical Discovery and Research', *North British Review* 39

Anon. (1872), Alexander Keith Johnston, LL.D. Late Geographer to the Queen for Scotland, *Sunday at Home*

Anon. (1873), *In Memoriam of the Late A. Keith Johnston, LL.D.* (Edinburgh)

Anon. (1875), *Geographical Magazine* (London)

Anon. (1922), 'The House of W. & A. K. Johnston: A Record of Enterprise', *Bookseller and the Stationery Trades Journal* (London, June)

The Atheneaum 11 July, 18 July, 25 July 1874; 11 December 1875 (London)

Barrie, J.M. (1926), *An Edinburgh Eleven* (London)

Beardall, W. (1881), 'Exploration of the Rufiji River under the Orders of the Sultan of Zanzibar', *Proc. RGS* **11**

Bennet, N.R. (ed.) (1969), *From Zanzibar to Ujiji: The Journal of Arthur W. Dodgshun* (African Studies Center, Boston University)

Boud, R.C. (1986), 'The Highland and Agricultural Society of Scotland and the Ordnance Survey of Scotland, 1837–1875', *Cartographic Journal*, **23**, 3

Bradnum, F. (1970), *The Long Walks: Journeys to the Sources of the Nile* (London)

Bridges, R.C. (1963a), 'The RGS and the African Exploration Fund, 1876–80', *Geographical Journal*, **129** (i)

Bridges, R.C. (1973), 'Europeans and East Africans in the Age of Exploration', *Geographical Journal*, **139**, 220–32

Bridges, R.C. (1987a), 'Nineteenth Century Exploration and Mapping: the Role of the Royal Geographical Society', in *Maps and Mapping of Africa*, ed. Patricia M. Larmby, SCOLMA & BRIMICS (London)

Bridges, R.C. (1987b), 'Nineteenth Century East African Travel Records', *Paideuma*, **33**

Bridges, R.C. (1994), 'Maps of East Africa in the 19th Century', in J. C. Stone (ed.), *Maps and Africa: Proceedings of a Colloquium at the University of Aberdeen, 1993*

Bridges, R.C. (ed.) (2000), 'Towards the Prelude and Partition of Africa', in *Imperialism, Decolonisation and Africa* (London)

Browne, J. (1983), *The Second Ark: Studies in the History of Biogeography* (Boston)

Calder, A. (1996), 'Livingstone, Self-Help and Scotland', in *David Livingstone and the Vicrtorian Encounter with Africa* (London)

Cameron, I. (1980), *To the Farthest Ends of the Earth: The History of the Royal Geographical Society* (London)

Cameron, L. (1876), 'On his Journey across Africa, from Bagamoyo to Benguela', *Proc. RGS* **20**

Carpenter, W.B. (1874), 'Further enquiries on oceanic circulation', *Proc. RGS* **28**

Christison, Sir R. (1871), Presidential Address, *Proc. R. Soc. Edin.* **7** (Edinburgh)

Clowes, Sir W.L. (1903), *The Royal Navy: A History from the Earliest Times to the Present* (London)

Cockburn, H. (1874), *Journal of Lord Cockburn 1831–54 II, in Memorials of his Time* (Edinburgh)

Coupland, Sir R. (1939), *The Exploitation of East Africa 1856–1890* (London)

Crone, G.R. (1950), 'The Men behind Modern Geography: vii Mackinder and the Revival of Geography in Britain', *Geographical Magazine* **23**

Crone, G.R. (1964), *Reproductions of Early Maps VIII – The Sources of the Nile Explorers' Maps 1856–1891*, RGS (London)

Crone, G.R. (1978), *Maps and their Makers* (Folkestone)

Cunningham-Graham, R.B. (1901), *A Vanished Arcadia: Being some Account of the Jesuits in Paraguay 1607–1767* (London)

Daiches, D. (1980), *Edinburgh* (London)

Delano-Smith, C. and Kain, R.J.P. (1999), *English Maps: A History* (London)

Dreyer-Eimbecke, O. (1997), 'Two Cartographers who made Mapping History in Gotha: Heinrich Berghaus and Augustus Petermann', *J. Map Collectors Society*, **7**

Driver, F. (2001), *Geography Militant: Cultures of Exploration and Empire* (Oxford)

Drummond, H. (1889), *Tropical Africa* (London)

Dugmore, A.R. (1900), *Camera Adventures in the African Wilds* (London)

Edinburgh City Council Minutes (1850–51), **255**, 29 October 1850–8, April 1851

Edinburgh Evening Courant (1824), 'The Late Dreadful Conflagrations' 29 Nov. 1824

Edinburgh Evening Dispatch (1904) 'The Industries of Edinburgh: The Making of Maps: A Visit to W. & A. K. Johnston's Works, Edinburgh', 3 March 1904

Englemann, G. (1977), 'Heinrich Berhaus: Der Kartograph von Potsdam', *Acta Historica Leopoldina* **10**

Fleming, F. (1998), *Barrow's Boys* (London)

Freeman, T. W. (1980), *A History of Modern British Geography* (London)

Fry, M. (2001), *The Scottish Empire* (Edinburgh)

Galton, F., (ed.) (1878), *Hints to Travellers,* 4th edn (London)

Geikie, Sir A. (1875), *Life of Sir Roderick I Murchison* (London)

Gierson, Sir J.M. (1909), *Records of the Scottish Volunteer Force 1859–1903* (Edinburgh)

Gilbert, E.W. (1958), 'Pioneer Maps of Health and Disease in England', *Geog. Journal* **24**

Gilbert, W. M., (ed.) (1901), *Edinburgh in the Nineteenth Century* (Edinburgh)

Haldane, J. M. (1824), *The Importance of Hearing the Voice of God: A Sermon Preached after the Late Fire in the City of Edinburgh* (Edinburgh)

Herbert, F. (1983), 'The Royal Geographical Society Membership, the Map Trade, and Geographical Publishing in Britain 1830 to 1930: An introductory Essay with Listing of some 250 Fellows in Related Professions' *Imago Mundi* **35**

Hutton, J. (1875), *A Theory of the Earth*, Trans. R. Soc. Edin.

Hyam, R. (1993), *Britain's Imperial Century 1815–1914: A Study of Empire and Expansion* (London), original edition 1976

Iliffe, J. (1979), *A Modern History of Tanganyika* (Cambridge)

Jeal T., *Livingstone* (London, 1973)

Johnston, A. K., Snr (1848), *Atlas to Alison's 'History of Europe'* (Edinburgh)

Johnston, A. K., Snr (1850), *Dictionary of Geography, Descriptive, Physical, Statistical and Historical forming a complete general Gazeteer of the World* (London)

Johnston, A. K., Snr (1851), 'Historical Notice of the Progress of Ordnance Survey in Scotland', *Proc. R. Soc. Edin.* **3**

Johnston, A. K., Snr (1853), *A School Atlas of Classical Geography: With a Complete Index of Places* (Edinburgh)

Johnston, A. K., Snr (1862a), *The Geographical Distribution of Material Wealth: Historical Notes regarding the Merchant Company of Edinburgh and the Widows Scheme and Hospitals* (Edinburgh)

Johnston, A. K., Snr (1862b), 'Recent Observations on the Florida Gulf Stream', *J. Scot. Met. Soc.* Jan.

Johnston, A. K., Snr (1870), 'The Temperature of the Gulf Stream in the North Atlantic Ocean', *Nature* **1**

Johnston, A. K., Jnr (1869), 'The Annual Range of Temperature over the Globe', *Proc. R. Soc. Edin.* **6**

Johnston, A. K., Jnr (1870a), 'On the Lake Basins of Eastern Africa', *Proc. R. Soc. Edin.* **7**

Johnston, A. K. Jnr (1870b), 'Dr. Livingstone's Discoveries', *Nature* **1**

Johnston, A. K. Jnr (1870c), 'The Sources of the Nile', *Nature* **1**

Johnston, A. K. Jnr (1875), *Geographic Magazine* **2**

Johnston, A. K. Jnr (1876), 'Notes on the Physical Geography of Paraguay', *Proc. RGS* **20**

Johnston, A. K. Jnr (1879a), 'Native Routes in East Africa, from Dar-es-Salaam towards Lake Nyassa', *Proc. RGS* **1**

Johnston, A. K. Jnr (1879b), 'Notes of a Trip from Zanzibar to Usambara in February and March 1879', *Proc. RGS* **1**

Johnston, A. K. Jnr (1909), *A Sketch of Historical Geography* (London)

Johnston, T.R. (n.d.), *Recriminations of the Johnston Family* (Edinburgh)

Johnston W. & A. K. (1875), *The Law of Literary Criticism as Illustrated by the Atheneaum Libel Case* (Edinburgh)

Kelner, W. (1963), *Alexander von Humboldt* (Oxford)

Klein, M. (1975), *Love, Guilt and Reparation* (London)

Lawman, T. (1960), *From the Hands of the Wicked* (London)

Lee, S. (ed.) (1908), *Dictionary of National Biography* (London)

Levi, L. (1875), 'On the Geography and Resources of Paraguay', *Proc. RGS* **18**

Liebowitz, D. (1999), *The Physician and the Slave Trade* (New York)

Linke, M., Hoffman, M. and Hellen, J.A. (1986), 'Two Hundred Years of the Geographical-Cartographical Institute of Gotha', *Geographical Journal* **152**

Livingstone, W.P. (1923), *Laws of Livingstonia* (London)

London Missionary Society *Report of the Rev. R. Price of his visit to Zanzibar and the Coast of Eastern Africa*, in Bennet 1969

Lynch, M. (1991), *Scotland: A New History* (London)

MacLagan, D. (1876), *A History of St. George's Church, Edinburgh 1814–1843 and of St. George's Free Church 1843–1873* (London)

Marsh, Z. and Kingsworth, G.W. (1972), *A History of East Africa: An Introductory Survey* (Cambridge)

Marshall, B. (1998), 'New Zealand Maps published in Nineteenth Century Periodicals' (University of Auckland Occasional Paper)

Matthiessen, P. (1981), *Sand Rivers* (New York)

McLynn, F.J. (1992), *Hearts of Darkness: The European Exploration of Africa* (London)

Merchiston Castle School Register 1833–1962 (Edinburgh, n.d.)

Miller, C. (1972), *The Lunatic Express: An Entertainment in Imperialism* (London)

Moir, D.G. (1973), *The Early Maps of Scotland with a History of Scottish Maps*, 3rd edn (Edinburgh)

Moir, F.L.M. (1923), *After Livingstone* (London)

Morrell, J.B. (1973), 'The patronage of Mid-Victorian Science in the University of Edinburgh', *Science Studies* **3**

Munro, J. F. (2003), *Maritime Enterprise and Empire: Sir William Mackinnon and his Business Network, 1823–93* (Boydell & Brewer)

Murray, D. (1915), *Merchiston Castle School* (Glasgow)

Packenham, T. (1991), *The Scramble for Africa, 1876–1912* (London)

Pillans, J. (1852), *Rationale of Discipline as Attempted in the Rector's Class of the High School of Edinburgh* (Edinburgh)

Raban, J. (1999), *Passage to Juneau* (London)

Robinson, A.H. (1982), *Early thematic Mapping in the History of Geography* (Chicago)

Rotberg, R.I., (ed.) (1970), *Africa and its Explorers: Motives, Methods and Impacts.* (Cambridge, Mass.)

Rotberg, R.I., (1971), *Joseph Thomson and the Exploration of Africa* (London)

Saunders, L.J. (1950), *Scottish Democracy, 1815–1840: The Social and Intellectual Background* (Edinburgh)

Schenck, D.H.J. (1999), *Directory of the Lithographic Printers of Scotland 1820–1870* (Edinburgh)

Scott-Moncrieff, L. (1966), *Third Statistical Account of Scotland: Edinburgh* (Glasgow)

The Scotsman, 'Disastrous and Extensive Fire', 17 Nov., 1824

The Scotsman, 28 May 1881

The Scotsman, 'An Edinburgh Centenary – A Hundred Years of Map-making', 25 March 1925

Scottish Meteorological Society, Council Minutes, 10 January 1862

Shapin, S. (1983), 'Nibbling at the Teats of Science: Edinburgh and the Diffusion of Science in the 1830s' in Inkster, I. and Morrell, J. (eds.) *Metropolis and Province: Science in British Culture 1780–1850* (London)

Shepperson, G. (1982), *Scotland and Africa Exhibition Catalogue* (Edinburgh)

Shirley, R. (2000), 'Berghaus and Johnston: Pioneers of the Thematic Atlas', *J. International Map Collectors' Society* **83**

Simpson, D. (1975), *Dark Companions: the African Contribution to the European Exploration of East Africa* (London)

Simpson, J. (1836), *The Philosophy of Education with its Practical Application to a System and Plan of Popular Education* (Edinburgh)

Smith, D. (1985), *Victorian Maps of the British Isles* (London)

Smith, D. (1998), 'The Business of the Bartholomew Family 1826–1919', *J. International Map Collectors' Society* **75**

Smith, D. (2000), 'The Business of W. & A. K. Johnston 1826–1901', *J. International Map Collectors' Society* **82**

Smout, T.C. (1969), *A History of the Scottish People, 1560–1830* (London)

Smout, T.C. (1986), *A Century of the Scottish People, 1830–1950* (London)

Stafford, R. (1989), *Scientist of Empire: Sir Roderick Murchison, Scientific Exploration and Victorian Imperialism* (Cambridge)

Stanley, H.M. (1890), *In Darkest Africa* (London)

Stevens, W. (1849), *History of the High School of Edinburgh* (Edinburgh)

Stevenson, R. L. (1878), *Edinburgh: Picturesque Notes* (Edinburgh)

Stevenson, S. (1981), *David Octavius Hill and Robert Adamson: Catalogue of their Calotypes taken between 1843 and 1847 in the Collection of the National Portrait Gallery* (Edinburgh)

Sulivan, G.l. (1873), *Dhow Chasing in Zanzibar Waters* (London)

Sunday at Home, 'Alexander Keith Johnston, LL.D. Late Geographer to the Queen in Scotland' 647–50 (Edinburgh, 1872)

Taylor, S. (1989), *The Mighty Nimrod: A Life of Frederick Courteney Selous* (London)

Thomson, J. (1881a), *To the Central African Lakes and Back: The Narrative of the Royal Geographical Society's East Central Africa Expedition, 1878–1880*, vol. 1 (London)

Thomson, J. (1881b), 'To Usambara and Back', *Good Words* **22**

Thomson, J. (1883), *Through Masailand: A Journey of Exploration among the Snowclad Volcanic Mountains and Strange tribes of Eastern Equatorial Africa* (London)

Thomson, J.B. (1896), *Joseph Thomson, African Explorer: A Biography* (London)

Wakefield, T. (1872), 'Map of Eastern Africa', *Proc. RGS* **16**

Waugh, J. L. (1905), *Thornhill and its Worthies* (Dumfries)

Whitson, Sir T.B. (1932), *The Lord Provosts of Edinburgh* (Edinburgh)

Withers, C.W.J. (2001), *Geography, Science and National Identity: Scotland since 1520* (Cambridge)

Woodcock, G. (1969), *Henry Walter Bates: Naturalist of the Amazon* (London)

Young, J.R.S. (ed.) (1933), *Edinburgh Institution 1832–1932* (Edinburgh)

Index

Montevideo 94, 98–9
Morning Post 82
Morocco 128
Mozambique 166
Msangapwani 192–3, 195
Munich 30
Murchison Falls 137
Murchison, Sir Roderick
  Impey 31, 35, 37, 41, 43–5,
  48–50
Muscat 152
Muslim 161
Mzugu 235
Napier, John 60
Napoleon III 62
Napoleonic Wars 23, 34
Nares Expedition 102
Nasibu 170
National Gallery 114
National Library of New
  Zealand 43
Nature 46
New Zealand 43–4, 51
Niger, River 71
Nile, River 41
North America 156
North Atlantic 46
North British Review 30, 41, 51
Nyamwezi/Unyamwezi 134,
  155, 170
Nyasaland 226
Nyassa, Lake 104, 106–7,
  116, 118, 127, 156–7, 169,
  172, 176–7, 183
O'Neill, Lieut. Henry 165
Observer 82
Ocean Highways 82
oceanography 45
Oman 152
Ordnance Survey 23, 34, 35
Osborn, Capt. Sherard 102
Otago 20
oxen 133
Oxford 70
ox wagons 13, 133, 184
Paisley 13
Palestine Exploration Scheme
  40

Panadero 91
Paraguay 92–5, 97–8
Paraguayan 91, 93–5, 97, 99
Paraguayan Boundary
  Commission 96, 99
Parana 92, 94, 98
Paris 35, 36, 41
Park, Mungo 103, 132, 199
Peebles 62
Pemba 165
Penpont 119
Pentland Hills 56
Pentland, Joseph Barclay 38,
  45, 58
Petermann, Augustus Henry
  36–9, 43, 51
Pillans, James 24, 26, 33, 50
Pitlochry 63
Playfair, Baron Lyon 43–4
population 23, 37, 38
Portobello 47
Portuguese 73, 151–2, 173
Portuguese East Africa 230
Potsdam 36–7, 51
Presbyterian Church 15
Price, Rev. Roger 133
Prince Albert 34
Prince Consort 34
Prince of Wales 34
Princes Street 41
Pringle, Thomas 104
Queensland 19
Raban, Jonathan 132, 148
Raleigh Travellers' Club 77
Ramsay, Alan 59
Rawlinson, Sir Henry C. 71,
  76, 80, 107, 118
Rawson, Sir William 108
Reid, Tony x
Ribe 113
Rigby, General Christopher
  Palmer 108
Rio de Janeiro 94
Ritter, Carl 36, 41, 50
Robb, Dr. 37, 163
Rocky Mountains 43
Rome 45
Rosario 98

Rovuma, River 222
Royal Academy of Sciences,
  Turin 33
Royal College of Physicians in
  Scotland 61
Royal Geographical
  Society/RGS x, 3–9, 30, 34,
  37, 39, 41, 43, 48–9, 51,
  68–71, 75–85, 87–9, 91,
  96, 98, 100–3, 106–13,
  115–18, 120, 122–3,
  127–8, 130–1, 133, 141,
  142, 145, 148–9, 156–7,
  159, 167, 172–3, 176–8,
  181, 185–6, 197, 199–201,
  211–12, 214–16, 219, 222,
  224, 226, 228, 230–2
Royal Scottish Academy 14
Royal Scottish Geographical
  Society/RSGS x, 2, 5, 217,
  223
Royal Scottish Society of Arts
  30
Royal Society of Edinburgh
  30, 34, 44–5, 46, 51
Ruaha, River 161, 188
rubber 156, 159, 163, 168
Rufiji, River 187, 192, 195,
  200, 222
Russian 68
Russo-Turkish War 65
Sabine, Colonel J. 31, 50
St. Andrews, University of 28,
  40, 43–4, 46, 51
St. John's Church, Mbweni
  226
St. Petersburg 75
St.Vincent 93
Sand Rivers Safari Camp x,
  226
Sang, Edward 59
Saunders, Trelawney 65–6, 74
Schmidt, Dr. Wilhelm 222
science 29, 33–9, 44, 45
Scoresby, Dr. William 103
Scotland 24, 28, 34–5, 38,
  40–1, 43, 45, 49
Scots 29